D1168786

BEYOND *the* WALL

A MEMOIR

DOLORES E. CROSS

WestBow
P R E S S

Copyright © 2010 Dolores E. Cross.

All rights reserved. No part of this book may be used or reproduced by any means, graphic, electronic, or mechanical, including photocopying, recording, taping or by any information storage retrieval system without the written permission of the publisher except in the case of brief quotations embodied in critical articles and reviews.

WestBow Press books may be ordered through booksellers or by contacting:

WestBow Press
A Division of Thomas Nelson
1663 Liberty Drive
Bloomington, IN 47403
www.westbowpress.com
1-(866) 928-1240

Because of the dynamic nature of the Internet, any Web addresses or links contained in this book may have changed since publication and may no longer be valid. The views expressed in this work are solely those of the author and do not necessarily reflect the views of the publisher, and the publisher hereby disclaims any responsibility for them.

ISBN: 978-1-4497-0094-2 (sc)
ISBN: 978-1-4497-0096-6 (dj)
ISBN: 978-1-4497-0095-9 (e)

Library of Congress Control Number: 2010923391

Printed in the United States of America

WestBow Press rev. date: 9/9/2010

For my children Jane Ellen Cross, Thomas Edwin Cross Jr.
and grandson Jackson Tucker Cross.

No Ordinary Life

My mother told me that
If people said
What she was doing
Or was about was
Ordinary
Usual
Common,
That they were
LYYYYYYING
They just had no imagination
And hadn't heard of courage.

My life has been
An extradition from
Tradition,
Leaving behind the well-worn
Contours of lives already explored
In the terrains on the silent fray
Of human potential.
I have been everything, but ordinary.
I have no memoirs to recite, no
Moment etched in stone by repetition, or
Highlighted by its distinction from monotony.
My life is as undefined as the spray of the sea
Leaping beyond the bounds of wetness
And freefalling back into the froth of society.
I fall into the heave of wet cohesion
Looking ordinary, very ordinary,
Until I curve up the next swell
And fly for my one moment
Of detached eternity.

Anyone can fly, anyone can,
But few, too few survive

The fall from the light back into
The wet depth of darkness,
Where memories of flight taunts
The undertow so mercilessly
That they drag you deeper into the
Obscurities of ordinary life.
But, honey, this ain't no ordinary life.

Each time the earth
Pulls me back in her fold,
She laughs ever so loudly
At my unearthly notions!
Of life, of freedom.

You know this ain't no conventional life,
Because my mom
Refused to teach me any better
And I still haven't learned
How to be ordinary.

Jane Ellen Cross
1992

Foreword

At the age of 50, I ran my first marathon and have run 20 since then. Preparing to run the Boston Marathon in April 1992, I traveled back home to Newark, New Jersey, for a 13-mile training run that would take me through the streets of Newark to the housing project which had been my home until age13. As President of Chicago State University, I was in Newark to give a keynote address to college and university administrators from all over the country. As I planned my run, I thought of other black women, like me, who returned to their roots, to see how far they had come and how far they still had to go to help others achieve a personal best.

In this memoir, *BEYOND THE WALL*, I draw a connection between the life experiences that motivated me to accept the presidency of a struggling and financially-strapped historically black college and my arduous climb from the depths of the abyss that followed my resignation.

Over the past decade a small number of experienced educators were nominated for presidencies at financially-strapped and struggling Historically Black Colleges and Universities (HBCUs). After serving 7 years at a predominantly black university in Chicago, Illinois, I accepted a second presidency at an HBCU in Atlanta, Georgia precisely because of the challenges it posed, which I knew would not allow a quick solution. I came to assume the position of leadership at Morris Brown College not knowing that my journey there, after being a professor, department head, administrator, and a university president was leading me to what would become my crucible. *BEYOND THE WALL* offers a distinctive view of how far we can climb.

In December 2004, I was indicted by the Department of Justice on charges pertaining to financial irregularities at Morris Brown. In the aftermath of the indictment I never had an opportunity to tell my story. After a three-year ordeal the government, while acknowledging that I did not personally benefit one penny, sentenced me to a year of house arrest, with the first six months wearing an electronic bracelet, 500 hours of community service and five years probation.

The fundamental intention, in pushing forward with my memoir, is to speak to the truth of my being innocent of charges of embezzlement of student financial aid funds and of conspiracy to commit fraud in my capacity as president of Morris Brown College.

For my children, my generation and subsequent generations I describe what it took for me, in the face of unfounded allegations and distortions to move beyond my darkest moments. I want *BEYOND THE WALL* to appear alongside the disembodied rumors, media misinformation, and unsubstantiated talk that would suggest I lost my way and dishonored my roots.

When the electronic 'monitoring' bracelet was fitted on my ankle, I plunged into a depth of despair that shackled my mind, body and spirit. I came to a halt. Despite my passions I didn't have the energy to go any further. Writing my memoir became a way for me to emerge on my feet again. As a marathoner, I had to persist with reflections and move from one place to another to uncover my strengths, as well as, my flaws and to gain from the lessons of my life and those of my family and friends. Achieving distance helped me forgive and above all to love.

Whether you are Black, Asian, White or Hispanic, male, female, young, middle-aged or accomplished in years; Ph.D.-educated or venturing forth with a GED; whether you have never run for more than a bus, or are an Olympic marathon champion, I feel you will appreciate what it means to hit the wall and persist. I hope you will stay with me as I traverse through the marathon of my life. See me as the runner beside you.

So travel these laps of time with me, for if you, too, are in your own marathon, I hope that reading about mine will help you to hold your head high, triumph, and honor your marathon.

With grace,
Dolores E. Cross

Part I

Chapter 1

It's 2 a.m., February 18, 2007.

The phone rings. As directed, I wait three rings then answer:
The male caller asks, "Are you Dolores Cross?"
I respond in the affirmative.
"Ms. Cross, where were you 15 minutes ago?"
"I was in my bedroom."
"Ms. Cross, we're calling from House-Arrest and we want you to
press the button on your electronic monitoring bracelet."
I raise my ankle to the phone and press the button until it rings.
"Ms. Cross, where is your watch-patrol device?"
"In my dining room."
"Ms. Cross, where are you?"
"I told you, in my bedroom."
"Goodnight."

Getting up, I walk into the living room and sit down at my desk, gazing out the window at Lake Michigan in the distance. The surface is as barren as a strip of onyx that goes on and on without relief of light.

Then I notice her, a black woman, staring at me from the reflection in the window.

The face in the reflection is kind, evincing the wrinkles that age has bestowed. My gray hair shapes my head like a cap pulled down over it.

Shifting my leg, I feel something snug against my ankle. Glancing down, I stare at that strange instrument that has become part of my life.

3

In the darkness under the table, the smooth object could be a piece of exotic jewelry. But it isn't. I lean down and run my hand around the circle that now encloses my life.

How did it happen?

How have I found myself, a Ph.D., former university and college president, a prisoner in my own home, restricted in my movements and having to respond to this stranger's voice?

A car passes in the street below, its headlights moving through the night like two small candles. I look back down, staring at the electronic bracelet strapped to my ankle, and I can't help telling myself, "Dolores, look at you. Your great grandfather was a slave and he wore a shackle around his ankle. Now here you are, 160 years later, sitting in the darkness in the middle of the night, wearing something that strips you of your dignity and freedom as much as the shackle did your ancestor."

I let everyone down. Me, the empowered black woman, the marathon runner, and educator.

"Well, Dolores, you met your wall, didn't you? Didn't see it coming, did you? So busy running ahead, picking up one award after another, and all the time the wall was waiting."

The impulse to put my head down and cry ripples through me. No, not now. Save the tears, I tell myself.

She doesn't answer. I guess I had better try. I look back at the woman in the glass. "How did you ever end up here?"

To sustain myself during dark days and nights I knew I would have to call on all my strength, not only physical but emotional. I would have to draw forth the lessons of memories, taught by my roots, the ancestors, my family, and heroes as well as others who embraced the realities of the human condition with dignity in every possible way. Could I do the same?

I needed to call on forces I had never needed before. I sensed the best way to weather the approaching storm that threatened to overtake my life was to seek out unbreakable moments in my past.

I took time to allow my mind to drift back through my life until settling upon New Jersey roots that had brought so much meaning to my life – and could sustain me again. I sought to draw a connection between the experiences that motivated me to break through the imprisoning walls of Newark's Baxter Housing Projects to attain the heights of college presidencies. I searched for ways to life myself from the crisis and despair that threatened to change my life forever.

Chapter 2

I grew up in a Newark, New Jersey, divided into ethnic and racial enclaves. Baxter Terrace was a racially-divided housing project. Blacks lived in an area bounded on the east by Orange Street and on the west by James Street, and the whites lived west of James Street. The small but significant distance was as defining as the Mason-Dixon Line. While similar in class, the two groups were divided by race. As children we knew not to venture into the white area of Baxter Terrace. The violence perpetuated by the white gangs was not unlike what we heard about racial conflict in the South.

The opportunity to move to the projects in 1941 was a step up from the tenement where I was born. The advent of World War II provided employment in munitions plants for Ma, Ozie Olean Tucker and service in the Merchant Marines for Daddy, Charles Timothy Tucker. By the time we moved to Baxter Terrace, my parents were divorced.

In highlighting the achievements of others for my sister, Jean and me, Ma put her dreams for us in motion. Our eyes would grow sleepy as Ma read the social page of the Afro American Newspaper and we heard of the courage of Marion Anderson and compassion of Eleanor Roosevelt. I took to swishing my hair up and belting out "don't know why there's no sun up in the sky" like Lena Horne in the movie "Stormy Weather," and pursing my mouth in a serious pose as I had seen in photos of Marian Anderson.

Ready or not, Ma was intent on taking giant steps to achievement. This we saw when she purchased a brand new piano with nothing in the coffers for instruction. Yet Ma arranged for a photo of Jean and me to be captured in the social page of the local Negro newspaper. There we stood hands clasped together with the caption: Jean and Dolores Tucker, daughters of Ozie Tucker, celebrate their 9th and 8th birthdays.

Ma was overjoyed and had copies of the photograph made for her sisters and friends. I was horrified at the suggestion in the article that we could play the piano. What would happen if they asked me to perform on the instrument? I took the couple of dollars I had saved, ran to the 5 & 10 cent store after school and purchased a book to teach myself how to play the piano.

We danced in the courtyard when the end of World War II was announced. And we saw the dancing stop when relatives and neighbors returned from fighting in segregated armies and found no jobs and broken homes. Ma's mood turned dark when the war plant closed and we were forced to go on welfare. We would join other families in line for food as Ma raged about the government providing so much cheese to folks with health problems. Her moments of public outrage embarrassed my sister and me. Yet we saw her face relax after she had her say.

My father came in and out of our lives. His sense of humor and adventure contrasted with Ma's serious focus. Daddy would appear at the schoolyard and scoot us off to the circus or visit us at his mother's house in Newark or take us to his favorite place, Harlem, and its jazz clubs. Ma would be furious. "Your father is into fooling, I want you into schooling."

While discouraging our hanging out with Daddy, Ma encouraged our closeness with Daddy's parents, Mary Winston Tucker (Grandma) and Rev. Dr. Thomas Timothy Tucker (Pa). Jean and I boarded the bus every Friday to spend weekends with them. From Grandma I learned that Pa was born on a former slave plantation at the end the Civil War. At age 19, Pa had traveled by foot and established churches as he made his way North to Newark, New Jersey. I knew from his sermons at Union Baptist Church, Newark and visits from Rev. Boaz Harris of St. Marc, Haiti that he was educated in the history of the Black Republic of Haiti. I was introduced to the country's rich history, pride and strength. When I was nine years old, Pa suggested that I might seek a career as a missionary in Haiti. Grandma's body shook with laughter when I blurted: "Pa is not happy with our spending so much time here and he is trying to ship me off somewhere." On seeing me close to tears, she sat me at table with a small pan of warm rolls and a cup of tea with milk and explained: "Child, Pa's wanting you to be a missionary in his beloved Haiti is as much of an expression of his truly caring about you that you are ever going to get from him." I thought of pleasing Pa and becoming a missionary in Haiti.

Ma made sure we were in touch with and knew of her side of the family, the Johnsons. Photos of her parents and siblings were displayed throughout our apartment. My grandparents, Melissa Johnson and Haywood Johnson were from North Carolina. Grandpa Haywood died when my mother was three. He had worked as a stone mason constructing building foundations and chimneys. Haywood traveled from North Carolina to Virginia for work to support his large family. With children to care for, Grandma Melissa worked as a laborer in tobacco fields outside of Raleigh, North Carolina. Ma's siblings were hard working, independent and one by one migrated beyond the segregated South to factory jobs in the North. While they had memories of whites lynching blacks and the fury of Southern racism, North Carolina was still their home. My mother saw it that way too. At the age of 8 and 7, Jean and I spent summers with her sister, Lucy and husband Noah in Raleigh where we were farmed out to work on a cousin's tobacco farm. When I returned to school in Newark, the adventure of killing tobacco worms, sleeping on pallets on the floor, and using an outhouse proved to be a great "how I spent my summer" story.

I didn't see that much difference in the Tuckers and the Johnsons. They seemed to want slavery behind them and believed that learning to read and write would take you a long way. They approached me with the same question: "How are you doing in school?" Never mind I had cardboard inserts in my shoes, no socks, oversized dresses and a host of fashion mistakes. All this was overlooked as I earned good grades and took it on myself to get to school every day.

While Ma encouraged close ties with family, she would 'out of the blue' make it clear: she wouldn't have any of them taking credit for what she had to do on her own in raising her girls. She would do what was needed to make us mind. Her feelings for Jean and me came through with the mean strap when we fought each other or were lax in household chores. We kept a heavy blanket tucked in the corner of our bedroom and knew how to run and huddle to muffle blows. Ma's frustration would turn to laughter as we peeked out to get the status of our whipping. Ma wasn't into hugging. Reaching out for an embrace was like grasping in air. Embracing didn't seem to be a family thing. This I saw when her sisters would visit. There would be a "Hi, Ozie," and what sounded like a clearing of the throat as their eyes swept the front room to see walls painted different colors and a bright green bookcase crammed with books.

While on welfare, Ma took evening classes at the YWCA (Young Women's Christian Association) to train to be a telephone operator and stenographer. For her homework, she would read from her textbooks and show us how she could race her fingers in the language of 'Putnam Shorthand'. I watched and visualized the day when I'd have my hair in an upsweep, wearing bright red lipstick, round pearl earrings, starched white blouse, and a knee length black skirt and with legs crossed holding a stenographer's book taking notes from a white male boss.

As our life changed, so did Baxter Terrace. With each year we witnessed management neglect and erosion of services. Working families who had the means moved to the outskirts of Newark to East Orange and Montclair. They were replaced with unemployed and recent black migrants from the South. Over time, these new tenants were greeted by a place where wall to wall concrete had replaced grass, jungle gyms and young children's play lots. They would not find programs in the vacant recreation room or basketball hoops and benches in the playground.

Despite the changes, Ma was committed to urban life. I seldom heard her speak of moving out. She held meetings in our living room in which she tried to rally tenants when housing management became lax in the upkeep of the courtyards and did not require residents to submit to apartment inspections. I heard her encourage others to join her at the YWCA for classes. At home she would urge Jean and me not to read or listen to the bad things said about Negroes in Newark. In rapid fire, Ma would list our neighbors who were doing odd jobs, taking care of their children, and keeping nice homes. And she would add, "Nobody sees them."

By 1950, Ma was off welfare and had secured a civil service position as a telephone operator. She beamed with pride in learning that she was the first black woman to pass the test for telephone operator in the State of New Jersey. Her assignment was in Hoboken, New Jersey, an area regarded as a hostile white territory. It wasn't long before Ma would return from work to tell of being insulted with racial slurs and once even finding a dead mouse in her desk drawer. The stressful situation took its toll. In the fall of 1951, she stopped going to work, purchased cloth to sew winter coats for my sister and me, and spent hours at the sewing machine. I felt her drifting away into a well of silence. Jean and I danced, sang, and told funny stories to rouse her. We couldn't reach her and prayed to God for help. In the past Ma had been firm in telling us "not to tell our business" and we didn't talk about the changes we saw in our mother. We went to school as usual and knew what to expect when we got home: There was Ma slouched, head down, moving cloth across the sewing machine.

On December 15, 1951, I raced home with news of the honor of being asked to write the eighth grade graduation play. Coat opened, feet taking two steps at a time I stood in front of our apartment door and stared at a shiny new lock. We had been evicted. We were homeless and would spend weeks living at the Salvation Army. I don't know how he found us, but there was Uncle Roger at the shelter to take us to live with my father's parents. We learned the same day that Mom recognized her breakdown and had made plans to commit herself to a mental institution.

I had read fairy tales and myths and believed in magic. I blamed my mother. At age 13, I faulted her for not having embraced the world enough to change it.

STILL STANDING

Forty-one years after our eviction from Baxter Terrace, I was returning to Newark as the President of Chicago State University to give a keynote address before higher education administrators at the downtown Hilton Hotel. My life had changed greatly since I had last been back, and so had Newark. I had peppered my speeches by drawing the analogy between running figurative and literal marathons. In each case you had to establish a base through training, strengthening and enduring. "My roots had enabled me to go the distance."

Within two weeks, I would be racing in the Boston Marathon. I packed my speech and my running shoes and gear. I was pumped with the idea of running what I measured as a 12 to 14 mile round trip course between the Hilton Hotel and Baxter Terrace. Running at an eight-minute pace, I could leave the hotel by 6:30 a.m. to be back to shower and change before my 10 a.m. keynote address. I was up before 6:30 with thoughts of "Why am I doing this?" "Why look back?" While taking deep breaths, I felt myself relax. I laughed. I didn't have to have a reason to "just do it."

I quickly dressed for the run and set out for 200 Orange Street, Baxter Terrace. I ran north from the Hilton to Broad Street then east to Orange Street and then north. At Broad and Market Streets, I paused to look at the corner where, at age 14, I spent summers bussing tables in a large cafeteria. I continued east passing the site of my old job at Abelson's Jewelry Store where I worked after school sweeping, as well as tagging and polishing jewelry. I quickened my pace, smiled and recalled my mother's pride in my having saved $116 toward the unpaid rent due to Baxter Terrace.

Now running at a good pace on Broad Street, I noticed that the large department stores had been replaced with discount and dollar stores. And unlike what I had seen here years ago, there were clusters of homeless men, women and children huddled in spaces where they had spent the night.

In the opposite direction of my run was the Newark Board of Education. I had been among the first group of blacks employed as a senior clerk stenographer there. My supervisor, Mrs. Malone had seen the anger and tension that preceded our arrival. She confided to me that she had seen similar emotions directed at her as an Irish-American immigrant. The Department of Research and Testing where we worked reviewed and reported standardized test results of students in the Newark Public Schools. I caught on quickly and Mrs. Malone inquired about my college plans. She was visibly upset when I told her I had not been counseled in high school to take college preparatory courses. With her encouragement I studied and took State Examinations for the academic units I lacked and matriculated at Seton Hall University. I had worked at the Newark Board of Education for seven years while attending night school as a wife and mother of two children.

I had lost track of Mrs. Malone. There was not enough time to cover all the ground I would like to have revisited. I felt myself shifting down to a nine-minute mile pace as I looked around.

I picked up my pace, feeling energized as I ran past Newark's Public Library. It had been my favorite place to go after school. I recalled searching through the card catalogues in search of a book, wandering into the stacks to find the book I wanted, and dashing home to do my chores. Now years later, Dolores was running home again.

I was breathless, not from running, but by the shock of what I had seen as I approached Baxter Terrace. The corner store where I had been sent to buy food was now a liquor store, with bars across the door and windows. Baxter Terrace now stood in stark isolation to what had been a project bordered by factories, food markets and shops. Baxter Terrace seemed to have shrunk in size. Or had my world simply gotten so much larger?

My mind was racing to keep pace with my feet: As a child, living in Baxter Terrace Housing Projects didn't define residents as poor. Yet if you continued to reside in the housing projects through the '60's, as my mother had, then, according to some you had slid into the underclass.

In checking my watch, I realized I had run slower than an 8-minute pace. It was close to 8 a.m. and I was now standing in the courtyard of my former residence. Stillness replaced the vibrancy I had known then. Shades were drawn, while broken bottles and debris met the broom of an elderly man sweeping off a stoop. There were no children running about, yet I heard the faint cries of a baby calling out from an apartment window. There was no evidence of the courtyard as I had known it -- only a concrete space and a barren tree not far from my former home.

I recalled a young sapling of a tree appearing beyond my window when I was a child. In what had been its place was now a fully grown tree, its roots breaking through the concrete. With abandon, I ran up to the tree and hugged it, not caring if anyone was watching. I had not expected to find it still standing.

Tears flowed. I'm 55 years old, I thought, and here I was crying at finding an old friend in this tree, standing like me in the courtyard of Baxter Terrace.

The tree had been defiant in persisting even though there had been no room for it to endure in the space it occupied. The concrete around the tree's roots was cracked, and even though there were broken branches, tiny green buds appeared on the ones that were left, evidence of the approaching spring. The tree was a living monument to everything it had seen in Baxter Terrace.

The bench where my mother had sat after our eviction was no longer there. Like the tree standing before me, Ma, had through sheer will and guts, emerged strong. Two years after our eviction, we were together as a family and living in Newark's Seth Boyden Housing Project miles away from Baxter Terrace. By then, Ma was working in the tailoring department of Bamberger's department store in the heart of Newark's downtown, attending night school, taking and passing State Civil Service Examinations. She was number one in the exam for supervisor of telephone operators and passed over for a white woman with a lower score. Ma kept on working and spent evenings collecting documents and going through law journals. She'd made the decision to take her case to court. While fighting to win her case, she accepted a position of telephone operator without the rank of supervisor at Ivy Haven Nursing Home. She carried files from her case against the State everywhere and engaged anyone who'd listen about her case. "Ozie is crazy" was what I overheard from her sister. The weight of the case reversed the role Jean and I had with Ma. We traveled with her to her attorney's office, managed all the household chores and entertained her. It would be years before the State of New Jersey settled with my mother and awarded her $10,000.

As I surveyed the courtyard at Baxter Terrace, I knew among the residents of Baxter Terrace there were parents like my mother who wanted a better life for their children. I realized as well the constraints to breaking out stronger and achieving all they were capable of achieving.

Standing there reliving the past, I received a few glances, nods and some smiles from a few occupants sitting on the stoop in front of the building that had been my home. As a few young residents started to appear and observed me clad in a blue sport outfit, I took a mental snapshot of my starting point. I knew not to linger or engage in conversation. The stories of gang activity, crime, and the violence of Baxter Terrace had not escaped me. As I began moving out of the courtyard, I realized that the successes of those who had moved on to make a difference for their family and the community should also have meant improvements for those who followed. But glancing back, I sensed this wasn't the case.

I retraced my steps back downtown at a faster pace. I stayed on course back to the Hilton Hotel. I focused on moving ahead. I had absorbed as much as I could bear. As the hotel came into view, I realized I would not be giving the speech I had written weeks earlier.

I had been nourished by seeing the tree in the courtyard. It had given me a sense of how grounded I was in my roots. As an African-American woman, I had entered history at a time far different from that of the family now residing in apartment 3A, 200 Baxter Terrace. The safety nets of adequate housing, jobs, social service programs and a decent living wage were just not available. The present residents of the housing projects were presented with examples of African-Americans, like me, who had made it in the face of racism, sexism and poverty. Reports ignored the fact that while there are more blacks with advanced academic degrees, and more who are college presidents, executive officers, doctors, lawyers, judges, movie and sport stars, there were also more blacks in poverty and in prison than at any time in American history. The numbers at the bottom of the social success roster had increased and no one seemed to be noticing.

During my speech in Newark, I used the opportunity to raise these concerns and more questions. Was there a commitment by government to address the needs of underserved students and their families? What was the impact of government regulations and procedures on promoting access to improved housing, health and educational services? All the time I spoke, I mentally kept the image of the tree and Baxter Terrace courtyard before me; I knew I had to stay in touch with my roots and always remember who I am.

I glanced at the faces before me, searching for the tell-tale yawn or empty seats, but found neither. I found every seat taken by an attentive listener. My audience could feel the emotion in my words, and I was encouraged to go on.

My listeners had come to hear about Chicago State University (CSU) and I felt my voice rise with pride as I talked about our having instituted a three-point model, a pipeline program that had helped us move forward. The first stage helped students prepare for college through precollege enrichment programs in the summer and academic year. The second stage provided academic support services to help students persist and graduate. These services included writing classes, remedial and tutorial, as well as counseling support. At CSU, grants were provided for faculty to develop strategies to improve the success of students in academic areas. And in the third stage, we provided opportunities for advancement in careers through the established Career Development Center and the development of articulation programs for graduate and professional studies. That three-tiered vision guided my leadership in higher education and became the focal point of all my strivings as an educator.

Two years earlier, after 20 years in higher education, I had become the first woman to head a four-year public university in the State of Illinois. As a commuter university, the CSU students were largely graduates of the Chicago Public School System and many were the first in their family to attend college. They attended college full and part-time, often while working. Some of the students were parents and even grandparents. By and large, the students viewed education as a means to improve their lives and contribute to their community.

I provided examples of our outstanding students, such as Mary Murphy, who had completed her undergraduate degree at Chicago State University and through the pipeline program with the University of Minnesota had been accepted for their doctoral program. There was also help from our community. Ida Bohannon, a community volunteer, worked with faculty to develop a women's resource center. And if individual successes weren't enough, I proudly revealed how the office of fiscal affairs at CSU had been praised by the Illinois Board of Higher Education for their work in our becoming the most cost-effective university in the State of Illinois.

CSU had made major strides in responding to its number one goal: improving the recruitment, retention and graduation rate of students. By 1997, Chicago State University graduated one-third of all the African Americans who received undergraduate degrees in the Midwest, had increased the first year retention and seen our enrollment grow from under 7,000 to close to 10,000 students.

In Newark that day, I concluded with words from a speech I had delivered to a group of professional women in Chicago weeks earlier:

"Much of what we do involved taking risks and confronting stereotypes. Those risks include a commitment to women's connectedness with other women, not only those in the same social and economic groups, but also in terms of raising the right questions about women in poverty. That means raising questions that may not be popular. Confronting stereotypes means dealing with the preconceived notion that a woman, and in my case, an African-American woman, will not take charge. We learned a lot about taking risks and confronting stereotypes from the women we met and got to know at Chicago State University. It's always been my view that if we are to become the leaders we want to be and need to be, then we must look at our connectedness with one another. We must continue to ask ourselves how much we understand about the lives of other women, not just our colleagues and neighbors, but also our urban sisters and brothers."

Nods, smiles and "amens" coming from the diverse audience said that in speaking from my heart I had made a connection. The sustained applause wasn't for me, Dolores E. Cross, but for those on whose shoulders I stood— ancestors striving for freedom all the way down to the first slave who yearned for a place in the sun.

On April 16, 1992, two weeks after my trip home to Newark, I completed the Boston Marathon in four hours and one minute. It was my eighth marathon. My finishing time came as no surprise to the Chicago State University community. Students had joined me in early morning training runs around our 167-acre campus. Upon my return to campus, I was greeted with a surprise gathering in which I passed around the finisher's medal. One student was quick to exclaim, "This is our medal."

SHOULDERS THAT I STAND ON

I had gone the distance from Newark's housing projects to Chicago State University's 14-room president's mansion. Its seven bedrooms, six baths, two formal dining rooms, huge living room, sun room, wide elegant staircase, pink, marble ornate master bedroom, were palace-like. How many years before had I spent homeless nights in the Salvation Army facility with Ma and Jean? What would my service as president of Chicago State University mean to students with dreams of a better place?

My mother was convinced that despite frequent receptions, meetings and designated space for community volunteers that the 'mansion' was an extension of the president's office. "It is your home, Dolores." I would remind her that the residence was an extension of the campus. It is a place of expectations, a place where dreams could be realized and attained, a place where people who were academically underprepared could prepare themselves to pursue meaningful and satisfying careers and be productive members of their communities. Ma would just give a sly smile and say, "Mr. Amberg should see you now." I laughed and recalled Mr. Amberg's beefy face as I ran into his office protesting our hasty eviction from Baxter Terrace.

Ma lived with Jean and my brother-in-law, Clinton, in Plainfield, New Jersey. Jean had her hands full in working full time and keeping up with Ma. We talked often on the phone. Ma was not the shrinking violet she appeared to others outside the family. She gave Jean a hard time in everything: from her playing cards, to laughing too hard or from failing to engage her in an argument. Ma could always manage to make you back off by stretching her five foot five, full bodied presence in front of you as she had the last word. We knew not to get her started on how much of a part she had played in our lives growing up or mentioning time we spent with our father. She had done the best she could and our success was a testimony to her having been a good mother.

Jean would confess, "I can't please Ma." "She gets along with you better." "I need a break." "Let her spend time with you in Chicago." Ma would be with me within a week. I figured her shenanigans with Jean had a getaway purpose. Ma would arrive with a present for Ms. Paul, the housekeeper, and her favorite gift of underwear for me.

Ma was more affable with me than I had seen her with Jean. Like Ma, I had taken the risk of going it alone. She was in the process of earning her Associate's Degree, working as a volunteer delivering food to seniors and documenting her success with a huge album containing articles she had written, as well as photos and reports on awards that her children and grandchildren had received. She maintained images of herself dressed in the style of the day.

Having a conversation with her was like switching channels on a remote TV. The topic kept shifting and was not always connected. She would go on about obituaries that drew you first to the age of the deceased. "Are they saying the person has lived long enough?" "Do you know they listed slaves by their age?" "Slaves didn't know how old they were." "Have you ever noticed how white people will ask you your age before black people will?" "Just a lot of 'ism', racism, sexism and now ageism, I'm not telling anyone my age." She was true to her word -- we didn't know her age.

No matter how physically fit I was from running, my mother seemed to be waiting for me to collapse. "Dolores, you're working too hard" or "Let's take the Greyhound Bus to Nevada. You need to slow down." To Ma's thinking, being "president" meant having less, not more to do. At the same time, she was aware of the political dimensions of my position and the struggle of leading a predominantly black institution. She collected articles from *USA Today, The Chicago Tribune* and *Chicago Sun Times* that referred to the connection between my urban roots and leadership at Chicago State University.

Ma treasured the photos of me shaking hands with President Bill Clinton and Vice President Al Gore as well as other prominent public figures. She would question me at length on how being invited to participate on the Boards of the American Council of Education (ACE), American Association of State Colleges and Universities (AASCU), as well as President Clinton's America Reads Commission helped the university. I responded that these forums became a means for me to communicate successes at Chicago State University and the challenges we faced, given declining student financial aid support for low-income students, insufficient funding to provide remedial, tutoring and counseling, as well as inadequate technology support for minority students with potential who were disadvantaged academically. She knew as well that, like her, I would make my presence known. From her questions, I knew she worried about me being out there alone with my point of view. She learned more when I invited the Presidents of ACE and AASCU to CSU's graduation to receive honorary degrees. They spoke of my being a champion of students having access to higher education and having the support they needed to succeed. It was a shared commitment to greater diversity and improved resources for underserved and low-income students in higher education.

Ma had danced at my inauguration for President of Chicago State University, planted flowers at the residence in the spring and attended pre-Thanksgiving Dinners where we served seniors in the community. She videotaped an interview in which she spoke of expecting her children to achieve and be successful. When asked what she thought of my leadership, Ma responded: "She can lead, if they follow."

My mother's mobility was hampered when she suffered a fall in early 1995. She also suffered from angina. Her visits grew more infrequent. Ma had made it clear that she didn't want to be with "old" people in a senior's residence or nursing home. Her visits with friends in similar facilities had been too depressing. She was growing frailer and rather than have her go to a nursing home, my sister equipped her room with everything she needed for home care. Jean held Thanksgiving at her house and the family came to Ma. Visits from her grandchildren perked her up. From the looks of things, she wouldn't give a caregiver any grief. Jean and I knew better. Ma was not going to go quietly into the night.

In the spring of 1997, Ma died. Her death plunged me into deep remorse and grief. I kept hearing her suggestion for me to slow down as her way of saying, "Dolores, we haven't spent any quality time together." She had wanted us to travel the country together and I hadn't found the time. There was always an excuse to attend one more conference, or run in one more marathon. "Then we would do it", I promised. Now there would be no more moments together, forever.

When I was 13, Ma had passed the baton to me. I had run hard and fast to bring her to her feet and see her move from strength to strength. She achieved beyond women of her generation and, in telling me to slow down, sought to persuade me to enjoy life more.

Now the light was gone.

I recalled entering her hospital room shortly before her passing.

"Hi gorgeous," she said.

"Gorgeous yourself," I replied, searching her face for clues on how she was doing and immediately hearing she was having difficulty breathing.

"Dolores, you've done enough to make me proud," she whispered, before I told her to save her strength. I began doing what I had done as a child, singing her favorite song: "Dancing in the dark, till the thrill ends we're dancing in the dark…dancing in the wonder of why we're here…"

As children, my sister and I had seen Ma return from work weary and be renewed by our entertaining her with song and dance. I felt her moving back in time as she closed her eyes and began singing her throaty version of 'Stormy Weather.' "Don't know why there's no sun up in the sky stormy weather since my man and I ain't together. It's been raining all the time, the time." She was quiet as we spent the next day together. With her assurances that she was improving, I returned to Chicago.

I was at my desk at Chicago University when I received a call from Jean saying that our mother had passed. A few days later I found a letter in my home office that Ma had handwritten during one of her visits and tucked among my papers:

"I was born February 11, 1916 in Wake County, North Carolina. I am the daughter of Haywood and Melissa Holmes Johnson. Haywood supported his family of ten children by

contracting jobs in stone masonry building inside water wells and chimneys from Creedmore to Durham. I was the second youngest of ten children."

"When I was three we moved to Mecklenburg County, Virginia. My parents made a poor living on farming. Most of the older sons worked part-time farming and part-time at a nearby sawmill. The oldest daughters married men from Virginia. They were well liked, upright and working men."

"Three sons who were close to me in age who had helped Haywood at his try at farming left for jobs in northern New Jersey and Philadelphia. Another sister worked away from home in nearby Chase City. The youngest boy, Roy remained at home. Lottie the youngest also remained at home. I also stayed at home until I was ready for high school. My mother then sent me to stay at the home of my second oldest sister, Lucy. Lucy was married and lived in Raleigh, North Carolina. There was an opportunity for me to go to a government-funded high school. It was a time that there were few schools opened to Negroes or Blacks as all schools for the public were segregated in Mecklenburg County and elsewhere in North Carolina and Virginia."

"At age 14 or thereabouts I began school in Raleigh at Washington High School and attended there until I was in the third year of high school. Then I enrolled in the church-supported Presbyterian School in Chase City, Virginia near my home and graduated in the fourth year."

"My mother and the remainder of the family had followed our oldest brothers and sisters to Newark, New Jersey. It was there that I met and married Charles Tucker who was also a member of a large family of eight. His father was a Baptist Minister and his brothers were businessmen."

"I served as secretary at neighborhood organizations such as tenant leagues, clubs for women and church clubs throughout Newark. I had with my husband Charles become the proud mother of two daughters, Jean and Dolores. World War II had been declared. I was a war worker living in Baxter Terrace Housing Projects. We moved there to pay adequately for decent affordable living quarters with inside running water and play space without broken glass. My children's father and my only husband went to work in Connecticut to make munitions for

the war. I worked for ten hours each night leaving my young children from six p.m. to eight a.m. with prayer, and sometimes I would leave them with my mother who could leave her two full-time grandchildren at night. My mother had been left to care for grandchildren because of the illness and death of her sons' wives."

"During my husband's employment three states away from New Jersey, we divorced. While a war worker, I enrolled in the YWCA in Newark for telephone operator training and later at Girls Vocational High in office work, secretarial and accounting skills. I had accepted work in a dry cleaning store using sewing skills I had learned as my sister Lucy's helper in Raleigh. Lucy was a very good dressmaker who made most of the fashion clothes of her neighbors."

"I began employment as a Civil Service telephone operator in 1947. I was employed in this capacity at the New Jersey, Employment Services, Hoboken Office, Newark City Hospital and Ivy Haven Nursing Home."

"After fifteen years as a telephone operator and supervisor at Ivy Haven, I went to work at Newark's Municipal Court as well as the financial department in Newark's City Hall. It was there I began my life of uncertainty about where my life would lead me and began seasonal work at several retail stores in Newark, mainly Macy's, then known as Bamberger's; Canadian Fur; and Franklin and Simon. My children were now grown and I lived alone in Seth Boyden Housing Project."

"I became the proud grandmother of five grandchildren, Thomas Cross Jr., Karen McRae, Jane Cross, Steven McRae and Tina McRae. These children have now reached adulthood and together with their parents are the sources of my strength. I face health problems and am attempting to finish college or reach a higher level to become able to have some measure of independence as needed in today's world. I am now at Union County College trying to get an Associate Degree in Liberal Arts Communication and Liberal Arts Business. I have accumulated 144 credits."

"My story as written here has been done in Chicago at the home of my daughter, Dolores, where I have been able to get away from familiar surroundings which have both good and bad memories."

> *"My life is now being lived with the aid of my daughter Jean and her husband, Jake. Members of my family have dwindled. Most are older and living in other towns. I shall try to live with the reality of life as others do; however, it all seems so unreal."*
>
> *"My husband, Charles died in Bronx, New York in December 1980."*
>
> *signed, Ozzie Olean Johnson Tucker*

My mother had spent long hours writing in longhand at my desk and telling her story. I had sat in the same chair at a computer composing material for my autobiography that would provide my children a view of how our lives have been intertwined, the impact of choices and the road to a university presidency.

No Ordinary Life

"Now they pay the slaves," was my eight year old daughter's response to the question I'd raised on her understanding of Black History and the progress her father and I were making in striving to become middle class. I hoped she would see how far we had come and was stunned and saddened by her view. As parents, we were passionate in our efforts to protect our children from being denied opportunity because of the color of their skin. In Jane's response I felt that discrimination haunted us as it did our ancestors.

While Jane and, her brother, Tommy, had been uplifted and inspired, they had been tested by the course their parents had taken to achieve equality and recognition. They had seen barriers appear and learned to endure during their parents' struggles; finally, they looked to us for evidence of new freedoms. My children had entered history during the Civil Rights movement and the Vietnam War, a time of change and tremendous social transformation. They often found themselves coming second to the cause; even if the struggle was being waged in the name of the future they would inherit. I had entered history during the last years of the Depression and grew up during World War II. My parents believed that achievements would make things better for all Negroes. In their minds the worst was over. They visualized the obliteration of discrimination and encouraged me to achieve. Success meant I would complete high school, find a good job, and marry a respectable, responsible husband.

Chance brought Tom Cross and me together. Shortly after I completed high school, a friend took me to a party in Montclair, New Jersey, a suburb of Newark where more of the black middle class families lived. It was there that I met him. Tom was seated on a couch and stood up in his six-foot-ten-inch frame to take my hand in introduction for a dance. I learned he was from Hagerstown, Maryland, and was on basketball scholarship at Seton Hall University. Within a few minutes he advised me that he'd been cautioned about city girls. I read that to mean girls from Newark were seen as less prosperous, less refined, and less likely to be college-bound. I smiled as I thought of what hard-working folks in my family might say in response and that I better wait a while before introducing Tom Cross to my fiery mother. I anticipated that she would waste no time in telling him how lucky he was to find an upstanding, city-wise family to look out for his country butt before going on to tell me I had hit the jackpot in finding a college man.

Tom and I spent the evening talking and discovering common ground in our shyness and a sense of humor, which extended to poking fun at the stereotypes we'd confronted. He was a French major. But there were expectations that he'd be majoring in physical education.

He laughed when I told him that some people thought only poor people lived in the housing projects. I went on to say, "Those folks don't know that where I lived, Baxter Terrace Housing Projects, was known as 'Sugar Hill' and lots of folks from the projects had Civil Service jobs like me and some were looking to attend college part-time." We danced to 'Blue Moon' and by the time he arranged to escort me home, we had made plans for our first date.

No matter how good a basketball player Tom was, he continued to encounter discrimination. When playing in basketball tournaments in the South, he and other black players on the team were denied opportunities to swim in hotel and public pools. They also faced racial slurs from crowds supporting opposing teams. Such barriers had been part of our growing experience. In turn, we were buoyed by the defiance of sit-ins in the South and joined freedom demonstrations in the North. We were together in the promise of the end of segregation and improved opportunities for blacks. We also recognized our love for each other and viewed it as a means to an end. We knew as well that we were a source of pride for our families.

In 1956, Tom Cross and I were married in his hometown, Hagerstown, Maryland. In the fall of the same year, I matriculated at Seton Hall University, majoring in elementary school education, all the while continuing to work full time while attending night-college. Tom continued as a full time student and ultimately became co-captain of the Seton Hall

University basketball team. Unfortunately, even with my good grades, and being on the Dean's list, I couldn't find financial support for undergraduate study at Seton Hall.

A year later, Tommy Jr. was born. I had worked until shortly before his birth and returned to work full-time when he was seven weeks old. I didn't believe our having a child would be an obstacle to Tom's success as a student and basketball player. I had heard how fellow students, his advisor, and coach had warned him that marriage would hold him back in doing his best as a player and student. I fought feelings that our marriage had put him at peril. I added two part-time jobs to my full-time job at the Newark Board of Education: working nights at a physician's answering service and on weekends as a temporary typist, and doing what I could to make sure his papers were typed, edited and presented on time. In turn, Tom did what was necessary to keep the household running by cooking, doing the laundry and shopping, as well as baby-sitting. He used his skills with machinery to keep our '49 Pontiac running and took the lead in interior decorating.

It was difficult financially and we made ends meet by scrimping to get the bare essentials. "We Shall Overcome" was our mantra. We were young married: dancing, studying and expecting freedom to ring. News of the sit in demonstrations in the South, progress of the Civil Rights movement and encouragement of our families made dreams look possible. I was caught up in the notion of change, involved in and excited about the role I would take in the Black Power Movement. My clothing, wide afro hairdo and choice of reading matter reflected a greater consciousness of the strength imbued in our slave ancestors. They had endured and transcended the brutality of slavery and we could end the humiliation of segregation.

In 1961, Jane was born. A second child didn't slow my pace. I was hitting my stride: mother, career, and wife could be handled without stumbling. Jane seemed to know she had entered a busy household. She was easy to care for, quick to learn and full of questions.

Her growing years were anything but ordinary. How could they be? Her Dad and I were first-generation, college-educated African Americans who grew up with extremely limited financial resources, who endured discrimination, and were challenged to balance studying, working, and being parents – all the while holding our life together. Our apartment in East Orange, New Jersey, became a meeting center as we provided living space for other college students and a place for friends and family to party, relax and share concerns about inequities we saw in our lives and hopes for the future.

In 1963, while our friends and family were gathering in Washington, D.C. for the March on Washington, we were listening to Martin Luther King's speech on the car radio as we traveled to a new home and teaching jobs in Long Island, New York. We were uplifted by his inspirational message and from what we knew of demonstrations in the South and of opportunities demanding equality for blacks in the North as well.

In no time, we joined Jewish friends in confronting racial discrimination in housing within cities in Long Island. For example: a house would be posted for sale and taken off the market when, as a potential buyer, I made an appointment and met with the seller. This type of racial discrimination happened in places like Baldwin, West Hempstead, and other cities on Long Island during the 1960s.

We were caught up in the promise of change. Our revolutionary rhetoric to end racist practices in housing and education characterized emotionally charged gatherings we held in our living room. The Long Island News ran a story that featured Tom Jr., his father and me as we discussed resistance to plans to integrate the predominantly white Malverne School District with the predominantly black Lakeview School District. The reporters were interested in my leadership in organizing the community to provide its own bussing of K-4 students to Malverne. Our passion for moving ahead had good and bad consequences for our children. We would have Jane and Tommy with us in demonstrations against the war and marches for school integration, and miss or be late for their engagements.

As she entered a previously all white elementary school in Malverne, Jane's first day at kindergarten was covered by the press. I had dressed her in a yellow pinafore, prepared her hair with bows and instructed her to look forward and not be afraid. I was there and holding her hand as we entered the school. We faced angry faces and jeers. How could Jane's life ever be ordinary?

Tommy was having a difficult time in adjusting at newly integrated Woodfield Road School. He was 10 and his teacher had, without hesitation, suggested 'special education.' In prior conversations with teachers, I'd experienced firsthand concerns that many black educators were having about the tendency to recommend special education for young black boys. I politely confronted his teacher and described what I had observed in teaching in the New York Public Schools. As a special education teacher, I saw a preponderance of young boys at seven and eight being referred to classes for emotionally disturbed students, when better intervention, counseling and instruction might have gone a long way. Young black boys were being written off early and I didn't want to see this happen to my son. I urged my son's teacher to focus on his strengths in mathematics and reading comprehension. I was saddened when I thought what would have occurred if I had not intervened. I was also saddened to think that other parents who, without question, most probably would have accepted the school's authority and the teacher's whim in removing students from the mainstream.

I knew we couldn't offer to ourselves or others the excuse of working, parenting and being activists to let up on keeping our family on track. I held images and stories of black trailblazers who preceded me. Yet, there were few role models for breaking educational barriers, holding the family together and raising hell in the Black is Beautiful Black Power Movement of the '60s and '70s.

Our Lakeview neighbors invited our children to join the black middle class social group Jack and Jill. They traveled as a group on the Long Island Railroad to midtown Manhattan to see movies and attend the ballet. They would have chances to see a world that for reasons of class, segregation and inadequate financial resources were out of reach for their parents when they were children. Jane and Tommy got a chance to see Oliver, The King and I, and Mary Poppins on Broadway. I began to fashion Jane's hair in the style of the young women in the King and I, and dressed her in a Mary Poppins' life cape and hat. The children learned the lyrics of all the musicals and, as was the custom in black families, were encouraged to perform them for their elders. Jack and Jill meetings focused on social skills, involvement of children in cultural, educational, and community service experiences. Our Lakeview neighbors lived a life that wasn't captured in the news of the day. We were a self-help community of activists who related to our community and urban communities throughout New York. We saw ourselves as black families not separated by class distinction. Most of us had not moved from cities to get away but rather to show the way. We were troubled by the fact that blacks were too often portrayed as uninspired, barely making it and not interested in expanding their horizon. We questioned the motives of those who saw us as the "exception" in our race. The focus was on black 'stars', black gangs, absent fathers and drug filled ghettos. We were invisible people.

In 1969, we sold our home on Three Colonial Road, Lakeview, New York, and relocated to Michigan. Tom and I had decided to pursue advanced degrees. As Head Advisor at Brown Hall, Eastern Michigan

University in Ypsilanti, Michigan, my children saw me become a surrogate mother to young women who, divided by color, didn't get along with each other, were vocal about their dissatisfaction with less than home cooking and generally felt in the shadows of the University of Michigan at Ann Arbor. Close friendships for Tommy and Jane were limited to children of the Head Advisor's family in the adjoining residence hall for men. We enrolled Jane in dance lessons and the Girl Scouts. Tommy was given clarinet instructions and membership in Ypsilanti, Michigan's Junior Deputy organization. We experienced a surge of pride and a broad smile out of seeing Tommy, the only black youngster Junior Deputy, carrying the American flag and leading the troop down the street during the city's Fourth of July Parade. We were trying to fill the void we had created by uprooting our children. At the same time we realized our steps didn't make up for our family and collie, Sam, being crammed in a small apartment at Brown Hall at Eastern Michigan University.

I took graduate courses toward a second Master's at Eastern Michigan University, scored well on the Graduate Records Examination, applied and was accepted to the Ph.D. program in Education at the University of Michigan. I was riding on the tide of affirmative action and I would have to dig in and ride that sucker out. I added more to every assignment, read the publications of my professors and changed my doctoral advisor three times. Had it not been for a black female research professor, Dr. Betty M. Morrison, I might be ABD (all but dissertation). She cut to the chase: "You can float out of here on the waves of white guilt with a crappy study or take my courses in research and statistics and be on track for a career in higher education." Betty would add without a blink of the eye that being black didn't give you an advantage with her. She had you work on tough assignments in and out of class and made herself available as a tutor and mentor. She could make you cry when you struggled to do well in her class and jump for joy when you succeeded.

In making the choice to relocate to Michigan to continue our education and manage our responsibilities as working students and parents, we had impacted our children's lives in ways that we could never have anticipated. There was much I didn't see at the time.

I felt the truth of no gain without pain when we received a call from Jane's fourth grade teacher requesting a conference with me. I was surprised by the call. Jane had not been a problem in school and my visits had been semester parent-teacher conferences. I left my class at the university early to meet with Jane's young white teacher, Ms. Smith. I read the concern in her face. She began by assuring me that Jane was a good student, top in the class. Papers were shuffled on her desk as she remarked, "We don't usually share our students' innermost thoughts as expressed in their journals, but Jane has written things you should know," she said. The teacher then picked up the notebook which I recognized as my daughter's journal and read, "I am nine years old. I have a mean mother. I hate her. She doesn't pay attention to me. My mother always has something important for her. If she is upset she takes it out on me. She gets mad, looks ugly and she punishes me. She studies and I have no friends. I am miserable at home."

Ms. Smith stopped there. My eyes clouded and she could tell that I was shaken. I was surprised by the depth of my daughter's frustration and ashamed at how I had behaved toward her. I was hurt that my daughter had chosen to express such emotions in her journal, and that it had been shared with this young white teacher.

When I returned home, I scolded Jane. I felt my face tense and heard my mother's voice as I cautioned her not to tell family business. In a gentler tone, I spoke as my family had with me of the importance of good grades and 'a good education' to assist in resolving problems and achieving what she wanted in life. I expected her to appreciate what we were doing for the family. With tear filled eyes she stood tall and said, "It was my assignment and my private journal." I could not imagine confronting my mother with the words and tone Jane had used with me. In the silence that followed, I pondered what lay behind my admonition, Jane's hurt and the boundaries she had set up. Though she experienced my caring, Jane viewed me as being self absorbed and neglecting her. There was no defense and no turning back. Fast tracking my educational plans to achieve greater opportunities and open new doors and joys for our family was the option I chose.

With a Master Degree earned at Hofstra University, additional graduate hours taken at Queens College, CUNY, as well as at Eastern Michigan University, I pressed forward and fast-tracked my doctoral coursework, a teaching fellowship and graduate research at the University of Michigan. In August 1971, I completed my Ph.D. in education and was ready to move on. We made a visit back to Lakeview, New York, to celebrate. Our road trip was full of anticipation at seeing our extended family. We sang, stopped frequently for picnics and listened to tapes of favorite musicals. After a day's travel we had gathered with former neighbors for a reunion. Chairs were spread on the lawn, barbecues were lit, and we danced to the music of the Supremes. Everybody was on their feet dancing and hugging.

None of our friends in Lakeview seemed surprised when Tom and I announced our advanced degrees. They were on the same track with new job and educational options. Gates to new opportunities were open to blacks in the 70s. We had concerns about maintaining the momentum as white women became more vocal in calling attention to the inequities and discrimination they also faced. The 60s Civil Rights movement focus on blacks appeared to be fizzling out. And integration had been answered by 'white flight' to neighborhoods free of blacks next door and in their schools. Our pensive mood was broken when someone yelled "Party! Party, folks! It's the time to party." With gusto, we returned to the moment and started line-dancing, moving step to the right and step to the left to the music.

But the music and dancing didn't last. Our family was moving on. Our frequent relocations would continue to be unsettling for our children, as well as a strain for Tom and me. As parents we viewed our decisions as paving the way for them and future generations. Tom would become the first black principal in Evanston Township High School, North; and I had been accepted as Assistant Professor and first black female Director of Tutorial Clinical Programs and Masters of Arts in Teaching Program in Northwestern University's School of Education.

Disagreements between Tom and me deepened as we moved on to new positions in Evanston. I became increasingly involved in the professional challenges I was facing and did not agree with what I saw as his passive attitude to the politics he faced as an outsider who had been selected over a prominent black educator in the community. I tended to make fewer excuses for him as he experienced the alienation of his faculty at Evanston Township High School. In the spirit of the early-seventies I wanted him to get fired up and confront blatant racism as white faculty aggressively questioned his decisions. I saw established blacks in the community join whites in opposition to him. I saw in his gentle demeanor an easy target for a community who felt Tom was the superintendent's choice and not theirs.

The position of Assistant Professor and Director of The Master of Arts and Undergraduate Tutorial Clinical Programs in Northwestern University's School of Education provided a harsh introduction to the discrimination faced by women and minorities in higher education and the affirmative action hoax. The white male faculty fraternity showed scant interest in my success or that of the three white women who joined the faculty in the fall of 1971. In comparing notes we saw the pattern of giving lip service to diversity by making sure that numbers were met by maintaining a revolving door. All too often our white male colleagues would express their view of the scholarship of women and minority students as "lacking rigor." The women who joined me in 1971 knew that this view extended to us as we were weighed down with heavy advising and committee loads, while being subject to the "publish or perish" whip. I was given the burden of wearing multiple hats: administrator of two programs, teaching, advising undergraduate and graduate students, committee leadership, as well as that of researcher. Some white male faculty would claim we women were treated like everybody else and would assuage their conscience by giving a passing grade to women and minority doctoral students who they cajoled without the intention of recommending or supporting for advancement to research and faculty careers in higher education, that is, given a status where they might be become their colleagues. I felt the double whammy of racism and sexism. Our group of four women continued to meet and support each other. We were not optimistic about our staying power. Yet we pressed on. I expanded the number of internships for students in the Chicago Public Schools, secured a grant to develop the publication, Teaching in a Multicultural Society and maintained an open door for students. There were days I imagined myself as a "black nanny" with a bandana. I'd get a laugh from students when I referred to the black servant's words in Gone with the Wind: "Ms Scarlett, I don't know nuttin' about birthin' babies."

No Pain, No Gain

I didn't think either Tom or I would survive in our positions in Evanston. In the fall of 1974, I welcomed the invitation to join Claremont Graduate School, Claremont, California, as Associate Professor and Director of Teacher Education. Tommy was devastated with a decision that meant he would have to forfeit the honor of being selected business manager for YAMO, Youth of America March On, for the upcoming school year. The opportunity was an honor and would mean leadership in music, an area he loved. Jane wasn't eager to move either. She had found a place in an Evanston Theatre group and looked forward to launching relationships with peers interested in the arts. Our children were not aware of how the challenges of our positions factored into our decision to move. To them, it was capricious and done without regard for them. Years later, I would learn that the move from Evanston was the most disrupting move of their young lives. I saw us as an airplane carrying precious cargo, stalled and trying to find a runway to land on before taking off again.

I would be the first black person appointed to a tenure-track position at Claremont Graduate School (CGS). I focused on multicultural education and facilitated the development of culturally diverse perspectives in the development of the doctoral thesis. The challenge was facilitated by steps I took to develop a joint doctoral program with San Diego State University. This provided students access to non-white faculty with similar interests. I had seen at CGS a pattern I had observed at Northwestern University, specifically the discouragement of minorities and women students by failing to foster dissertations emanating from their gender and cultural backgrounds. In turn, I seized the privilege of learning from and working with a talented and enlightened core of doctoral students with different linguistic, ethnic and cultural backgrounds. Their enthusiasm led to our coming together to contribute to publications and to develop papers on "Perspectives in Multi-Cultural Education". I came to recognize teaching as my true love. I knew, as well, that having to enter academe as faculty with extensive administrative and advising responsibilities would make it difficult to attain tenure as faculty in Education at CGS. Given the politics of indifference, the rhetoric of "working to foster faculty diversity in higher education", was a cruel joke.

Tom had secured a job as Assistant Principal at Ontario Junior High School, Ontario, California, and was developing a niche in sales. I described our family of four as roommates. We shopped separately, didn't eat together as a family, and owned four cars. Tommy and Jane were in high school and increasingly self-reliant. Tommy was chosen co-captain of the Claremont High School Marching Band and Jane was a straight A student with achievements in all areas of high school sports.

I made the last payment on my undergraduate school debt shortly before Tommy graduated from high school. As our children approached the end of their high school years, Tom and I felt the pressure of not having funds to see them through college and couldn't come together in figuring out our financial problems. Tom had left his position at Ontario Jr. High and branched out into sales. He expected the family to support his venture in a new field. He found instead a circle of friends committed to Amway sales.

Life as we knew it was falling apart. Participation in a National Institute of Education Postdoctoral Seminar for Women and Minorities in the summer of 1976 changed my course. The experience provided the nudge I needed to explore leadership positions and redefine my role in our family.

Tom and I had been instrumental to each other's success. We had paid our own way, moved ahead and lost sight of what we would need to help meet the cost of our children's education. I viewed my decision to seek an administrative position in higher education as a way to assist them in realizing their dreams and another means for me to attempt, test and implement strategies to help students with potential succeed.

I felt the contradiction in my talking about the 'plight of black men and their losing ground to black women' and my moving ahead to assume a leadership role in my family and in my profession. "Would Tom be there to carry my coat?" "What would be the cost to our marriage of 20 years?"

Tom and I struggled to keep our marriage on track. As a family, we had lived in five different states, participated in the Civil Rights Movement, protested against the War in Vietnam, witnessed changes brought about by affirmative action legislation, and had seen a negligible impact of the nation's 'trickle down theory' on poor people.

Arguments between Tom and me became more frequent as we railed against injustices and experienced realities threatening our relationship and our role as parents. The differences in how each of us dealt with stress led to our drifting apart and developing separate interests. Tom started repairing cars and finding new friends who shared his interests in sales, while I began running daily and taking cues from Angela Davis, a political activist's message, posture and the feminist movement. We had as a couple become casual and careless in attending to our vows to each other.

By 1978, our nest was empty and the marriage was crumbling. Tommy was in his second year as a music student at Sonoma State University. And Jane had begun her first year as a student in international relations at the University of California, Davis. Tom Sr. had decided to remain in California and I was leaving for a new position in New York City.

My mother was waiting to meet me at the airport in the summer of 1978, when I arrived from California. I could see by the frown on her face that she was not happy at seeing me arrive alone. She knew as well that I'd be stepping into a highly sought-after position. I would be Vice Chancellor of the City University of New York – but she must have been wondering at what cost. Still, she said nothing about Tom not accompanying me. Instead, she simply shook her head, saying, "If this fancy new job works out, send me the press clippings."

She became more vocal and said in no uncertain terms that in leaving Tom behind, I had abandoned a trophy. My mother exclaimed, "You'll never be happy." I heard her saying that my marriage was by far my biggest achievement: "Tom was a good catch for you, Dolores." Was she saying that I was less attractive without my handsome husband at my side?

What I seemed to be hearing most often was, "We can understand when a strong man leaves a woman. He's outgrown her; she fails to keep pace or simply was not good enough." I felt this when a friend described my separation from Tom, as my "having let a good man go."

I would be on my own and if I failed, I anticipated hearing, "See, she gave up that good man and see what it got her." I would remember my grandmother's words: "Your friends will understand whatever you do and your enemies won't believe you anyway."

In accepting the position of Vice Chancellor for Student Affairs and Special Programs of the City University of New York, I would be living in Manhattan and working under a champion of disadvantaged students, Chancellor Robert (Bob) Kibbee. My job was to work with presidents and staffs of the system's 18 colleges to develop and implement guidelines to promote the success of academically disadvantaged students, monitor student affairs and to supervise staff in setting in place a centralized system of admissions and student financial aid. Bob Kibbee's approach to helping all students fueled the eagerness of a talented and student- focused executive team in the Office of Student Affairs and Special Programs. He worked in sync with me to present achievements of disadvantaged students to local and State Legislators. I learned from him as he reviewed technical aspects of the admissions and financial aid operation, attended my meetings with college presidents and counseled me as I interacted with the CUNY Board of Trustees. The Chancellor appreciated my inviting my parents to CUNY receptions. He enjoyed a cigar smoking pause with my father and a feisty political discussion with my mother.

My father, Charlie Tucker lived in the Bronx, New York City, and stepped into the role as my escort. He was dapper, well-dressed and knew how to keep me laughing. On Saturdays he'd come to my apartment, fuss around the place and smoke cigars he was not permitted to enjoy at his home. He was glad I'd returned East and we started seeing each other to 'dance the light fantastic' at receptions and formal events. My mother had described my father as a 'ladies man and jitterbug.' He enjoyed peering into my empty refrigerator, shaking his head and commenting, "Baby, you have the only refrigerator in New York where roaches come to die." He could make me laugh by just looking at me. He was a charmer.

Dad was a flirt. He checked my calendar for events where he might appear as my date. He reminded me of the actor Keenan Wynn and I told him so. He was quick to respond, "Not to worry, baby, I can dress like him too." A smile filled my face when Dad showed up for our next date in a bright plaid jacket.

I found time to take a break. In the fall of 1980, I left for Spain to spend vacation time with Jane. We traveled throughout Spain, visiting places familiar to her from her studies in Madrid. Toward the end of our stay, I felt restless and for reasons unknown wanted to return home early. Jane was disappointed, and felt and communicated I was just not permitting her more time with me. "Mom, you're getting back to your job."

I couldn't explain the tug, changed my return ticket and soon was moving. I couldn't sleep on the long flight back. As I passed through the terminal to baggage claim at Kennedy Airport, New York, I received a page. It was a call from my sister, Jean. She told me that our father had died of a heart attack a day before.

When I returned to my apartment, I found a handwritten note from my father.

Baby, I did the best I could.

Suddenly the person who understood me and was there for me was gone.

True, he had been absent during most of my growing up years and moved to his treasured Harlem. He was pleased to have so much of my attention now. He seemed to be trying to make up for what we had missed.

I thought of having left Jane in Spain. In a sense my father's words to me were mine to my children ..."I did the best I could." As with my father, I knew I could not make up to my children the company they had missed with me. And that last time he must have known something, for he had never written about the past before.

Baby, I did the best I could.

That same fall Chancellor Kibbee died after surgery for a brain tumor. He had stood with me and my family at my father's funeral and now he was gone. A dream for disadvantaged students at CUNY ended with his death.

Tom and I vacillated before settling on divorce. By the fall of 1980, we were living separately in New York City. We met in my apartment toasted with a cup of coffee and without any acrimony signed divorce papers. As in a dance, we spoke of finding each other as partners when our song played again.

Within a few months, I accepted Governor Carey's offer to become President of the New York State Higher Education Services Corporation (NYSHESC). I would be the first black woman to head a statewide agency that provided over two billion dollars in student financial aid to students in 700 postsecondary institutions in the State of New York. With an Executive Vice President, team of four Vice Presidents and a staff of close to 1,000 employees we were legislatively mandated "to promote access to a postsecondary education to all eligible students in the State of New York".

The agency, located in Albany, coordinated the centralized management of State and Federal Student Aid, mobilized college and university presidents to oppose Federal cutbacks in student financial aid, and conducted the nation's first state-wide survey on how recipients and non-recipients of student financial aid meet the cost of education. We uncovered areas of unmet student financial aid need and worked with legislative staffs to propose new legislation to improve the State's Tuition Assistance Program (TAP) and establish TAP for part-time students.

I became a member of the Boards of the Association of Black Women in Higher Education and the National Association for Equal Opportunities in Higher Education, the College Board, and was elected Chair of the Governor's School and Business Alliance Task Force. There I found colleagues to join me in challenging the prevailing myth that federal and state student financial aid adequately addressed the needs of poor and low-income students. In 1984, I joined other women leaders in the country as a founding member of Women Executives in State Government (WESG). I was honored to be presented--along with Christine Todd Whitman, Governor of New Jersey--with the Breaking the Glass Ceiling Award in Washington, D.C. My mother loved New Jersey and was thrilled to see me standing with her Governor.

I traveled throughout the state encouraging young people to stay in school and to stay informed of opportunities to assist their completing college. My hosting an interview show on an independent TV station, as well as co-chairing the Martin Luther King, Jr. Task Force with Harry Belafonte, enhanced the agency's exposure. In introducing Harry Belafonte to an audience gathered to celebrate Dr. King's birthday, I told of having traveled to see him perform at Lewinson Stadium at the City University of New York's City College shortly after giving birth to my daughter, Jane. Harry laughed and responded: "I remember seeing you there."

My children made themselves available as I moved in new circles. Tommy enjoyed being enlisted to be my escort to social events in Albany.

He was living in California and would, on a few days' notice, be at my side. Tommy's charm, twinkling eyes and engaging demeanor was a reminder of my father. With a broad smile, he would view meeting the Governor of New York or a State Senator as routine and know how to involve them in his passion for jazz as well as current events. He would insist on photo opportunities to send to his 'keeper of the clippings,' his grandmother.

Jane was living in New York, practicing law at the firm of Phillips and Nitzer. She lived in an apartment close by and was available on short notice for dinner or a movie. Jane was willing to join me for receptions hosted in New York, where she made connections with legislators and colleagues. On one occasion as we worked the room at a corporate reception, she noticed me break out in a sweat as I conversed with a colleague.

"Mom, you're getting sick," she whispered to me.

As heads turned, I motioned her aside. "It's normal," I replied. "I'm having a hot flash."

Jane folded with laughter as we continued our tour of the room; I had introduced her to what menopause looked like.

There had been other changes as well. Tom had remarried and gone into business with his new wife. He called occasionally to check on how I was doing and would at times add, "Dee, you were responsible for the divorce" to which I would laugh, yet feel a little sad.

In 1986, I decided that I would enter my first 26.1mile marathon, a challenge I had dreamed of doing. After I broke my ankle ice-skating a year before, I committed to healing and doing what it took to prepare for and run the 26.1 marathon. I had been happy jogging for many years; the marathon was the ultimate physical challenge for a runner. After all, I told myself, wasn't the act of literally going the distance simply a manifestation of what I had been doing all my life? I purchased books on nutrition, handling injuries and strategies to stay focused, subscribed to Runner's World, and joined the New York City Running Club. I planned summer vacations to spend time at Craftsbury Running Camp in Vermont to train with runners in the 45-plus age group.

I laughed at my mistakes. I never had a thought that I couldn't complete a marathon. Over the course of a year, I trained by incrementally increasing my mileage, running a long run every other week until I could run 21 miles in a stretch. I traveled with my New Balance running shoes and would often find short distance races to compete in. I began to see my signature as that of a marathoner.

There was an outpouring of applause when, as President of HESC, I succeeded in coming in first among the executives in a 10K Corporate Challenge in Albany, New York.

Months later I ran and completed the New York City Marathon in 4 hours and 42 minutes. In collecting the Finisher's rose and having the Finisher's medallion placed around my neck, I was feeling invincible.

My family was at the finish line, and I felt their obvious pride. I couldn't recall a time when their presence had meant more to me.

After eight years in state government I was eager to return to a university campus and work in the academic community. In August, 1988, I accepted the position of Associate Provost and Associate Vice President of the University of Minnesota in Minneapolis, Minnesota. The appointment was a match for my research interest in multicultural education. I would have the job of working with Deans and Presidents on the four campuses to develop plans to improve the recruitment and retention of students of color. As I had in New York City and Albany, I enlisted the support of a former doctoral student, Dennis Cabral to join the team there. We set in place a blueprint for action and instituted a statewide pre-college fair that hosted Native American, Hispanic, black and Asian students. When asked what my favorite place to live was, I would respond Minneapolis. The house there was the first place I had bought on my own. I loved the proximity to Lake Calhoun, the uptown district and the ease at which you could join others running on trails throughout the city. Had the right offer not come, I would have stayed on at the University of Minnesota.

A PERSONAL BEST

In 1990, Dr.Peter Drucker, Professor in Management at Claremont Graduate School, nominated me for the presidency of Chicago State University. Peter warned me how intensely political Chicago would be. He knew as well that it wouldn't stop me from taking the job. The challenge of relating to and helping students with a background similar to my own was priceless.

I saw life change for my children, as well. Jane traded a lucrative position as a corporate attorney at Bank of America and moved to Florida. She quickly moved to the position of Associate Professor and Director of Nova Southeastern Law School Caribbean Law Program. Tommy moved from California to Minnesota where he continued his career as a music teacher in the Minneapolis Public Schools. A year after moving to Minnesota he fell in love and married a fellow music teacher, Patricia Kelly.

My children were moving forward, always keeping each other and me in their sight as we assumed our respective marathons.

During my first year as president, I taught Freshman Seminar at Chicago State University. In telling students of my journey to the position of university president, they opened up as they had not done before. They appreciated my keeping it real and the ease with which I related my experience to the concerns they held. They were eager to develop and read from their journals. I expected to see them use their personal stories of how they handled challenges to inspire others.

One student's presentation before the class shattered the stereotype of teenage mothers. In her words: "If your boyfriend is not supportive, let him go. It is one thing to have one baby....but two or three? No, that is not the way. Holding onto something or someone that brings you down gets you nowhere but down. Revise your plans, make the adjustment you need to make – but do not – I repeat, do not give up on your dreams and the attainment of your goals." Winnie's story was one of courage, her own saga and that of other women students in the Chicago State Community.

The university established a Women's Advisory Committee and invited women from the corporate, civic and educational sector to work with us to establish the Women's Resource Center at Chicago State University. Many of the women on the Women's Advisory Committee knew little of the 167- acre CSU and the city's Southside. The exchange with CSU students gave them a sense of the challenges faced by students with potential who were challenged in paying their bills, caring for their children, and in some cases being caregivers for elderly parents. The university was surrounded by a community of long-time black Chicagoans who lived in well-cared-for middle-class homes as well as low-income and public housing. En route to campus you would see boarded up homes, stores and unkempt houses. Blocks further, you would pass through areas of middle-class neighborhoods with signs of Neighborhood Watch, well-kept lawns, neat houses, and small busy shopping centers. In traveling to CSU, you experienced the diversity of the Southside of Chicago and were reminded that Chicago continues to be one of the most segregated cities in this country.

In 1996, as a member of the Chicago Board of Foreign Relations, I traveled with Chief Executive Officers and community leaders to South Africa. Through the American Council on Education, I had been assigned as Senior Advisor to my counterpart Vice Chancellor Ndebele of the University of the North in South Africa. Members of the Chicago Board of Foreign Relations were made aware of the partnership developed between

University of the North and Chicago State University. Their interest contributed to additional support for CSU. In traveling with the board, we had access to white and black leaders in South Africa. We met Winnie Mandela in Soweto and through her we gained an audience with President Nelson Mandela. Our conversation with him concluded with his making arrangements for us to be present for his message to the South African Parliament. From the balcony, we listened as President Mandela spoke from the floor of Parliament. More than a few tears were evident on our faces.

I looked at additional appointments to the Boards of the Chicago Urban League, Chicago United Way, and Institute for International Education, Field Museum and College Board, Campus Compact, as well as Northern Trust as a way to learn of the mutual concerns of improving educational opportunities. I was aware of a growing support for pipeline programs that linked elementary, secondary and postsecondary instititutions with other entities, as well as the expansion of internships and opportunities for community and international service. The involvement was part of my continuing education. I envisioned an 'educational summit' where the leadership of colleges and universities, the corporate, civic and community sector would develop a shared vision and strategy for its implementation.

When I arrived at CSU in August, 1990, it was no secret that Chicago State University had a terrible record in the retention of students. There were rumors of merging the university with another four-year institution. CSU had the potential for being a model for urban education. I had seen how the City University of New York, under Chancellor Kibbee, provided remedial, tutoring and writing support to help underrepresented groups of students succeed. The results had been documented. I knew as well that I could enlist my former colleagues in bringing their knowledge to Chicago State. We convened college retreats to develop a 'shared vision'. What emerged was a pre-college, in-college and after college, a Three Point Model to improve the retention and success of students. From my experience on diverse Boards, I felt it was an approach that leadership in every sector could embrace. The MacArthur Foundation provided a grant of 4 million dollars for CSU to partner with the University of Minnesota for a program that linked the two universities to facilitate the development of scholars who might be selected for admission at the University of Minnesota with full scholarship support. We had a strategic plan and community support. I made the case to the State of Illinois for additional resources based on improvements in the retention and graduation rates of students and established an office of internal audit to keep us on track. Our mantra became: Students Matter.

I had been president of Chicago State University for over seven years when the Governor of the State of Illinois changed the university's governance structure and named political appointees to form a local CSU Board of Trustees. The university had made major strides in improving the retention and graduate rate of its students. Yet the questions raised by some outspoken members of the new Board of Trustees suggested we had nothing to build on. They didn't seem to appreciate the sense of ownership expressed by staff, faculty and students as they articulated the college's strengths. Students had been involved in designing the campus' new student center. Faculty from other universities had joined CSU to establish our newly-constructed residence hall as a living learning center to extend community service activities. Staff at CSU was continuing graduate work in order to advance their profession. CSU's progress in increasing the retention and graduate rate of underserved students was becoming the envy of other campuses in the State of Illinois. The City of Chicago Commission on Human Rights, Chicago Metropolitan YWCA, Cabrini-Green Tutoring Program, Jackson Park Hospital Women's Board, Muhammed Ali Economic Development Corp, Operation Push, and The Anti- Defamation League were the entities that saluted our service to students. There was much to build upon.

On a call to a sister president, Dr. Johnnetta Cole, she advised: "Leave while they love you." I smiled, knowing full well that not everybody loved me. I had uncovered administrative problems and dismissed a popular administrator, engaged a consultant who was felt by some to have too much influence, had gone toe to toe with the union on faculty issues, and had not backed down when a few faculty argued that I was lowering standards. The glass was more than half full and I had been true to our mantra: Students Matter. While I knew I had a great deal of support at CSU, I was open to new possibilities.

My mother had not lived to see my decision to step down after serving seven years as president of Chicago State University. In leaving CSU, I would miss the comfortable interactions with students, faculty and staff. Underneath it all, I knew that I would continue to make my mother proud of me. For the May 1997 graduation ceremony, I invited Congressman Donald Payne from Newark, New Jersey, whom my mother admired, and remembered him growing up and visiting friends in Baxter Terrace. Donald had told me how he had been encouraged to participate in politics by my uncles Frank and Samuel Tucker. He had worked diligently to make a difference for residents of Newark and had led legislative efforts to secure relief for AIDS victims in Africa. I would confer a Chicago State University Honorary Doctorate of Law on him.

Katherine Dunham was present to receive an Honorary Doctorate in Humanities. She was brought on stage in a wheelchair. She had been a role model to many for creative dancing and remained a fierce champion for young people through mentoring and making speeches on behalf of human rights. A smile filled her face as I shared how my mother had admired her and written of her successes as a reporter for Newark's local Negro newspaper.

Somewhere my mother was watching. She had always known that in relating to my roots, family and the ancestors I had established a base to finish my marathons – a marathon with thousands of others striving to achieve a personal best. I would be running alone toward a finish line only I could see, if at all.

Shortly before leaving Chicago State University, I received a call from a vice president at General Electric (GE) in Fairfield, Connecticut, requesting that I interview for the position as president of the GE Fund. I didn't hesitate. At GE I was given an opportunity to participate in the company's Six Sigma training for managers and executives. The intense workout provided a view of a different work ethic to produce results. Even more, I had an opportunity to implement an interactive approach to community service that linked GE volunteers (Elfuns) with faculty at Cleveland State University and students in the Cleveland, Ohio, public schools and roll out new pre-college programs in other states. While the job at GE expanded my universe, it was not the best fit. I was able to negotiate support to fund a professorship at Manhattan's Graduate Center of the City University of New York.

Within a few months, I received a call from a search firm to interview for the Presidency of Morris Brown College, a Historically Black College. It was an irresistible call.

Grandfather, Haywood Johnson, North Carolina early 1900s

Grandmother, Melissa Johnson in front of storefront in Newark, New Jersey 1942

Grandfather, Rev. Dr. Thomas T. Tucker in the pulpit of his church, Union Baptist Church, Neward, N.J. 1949

Portrait of my mother, Ozie Tucker,
age 28

Thomas Cross Sr. and Dolores Cross,
Lakeview, N.Y

Jean and Dolores, ages 9 and 8 at the piano

Jane and Tom Jr. ages 4 and 8,
Lakeview, N.Y

Jane in front of the UN age 16

Tommy Jr. in class age 16

Tom Jr. and his grandfather, Charles Tucker

Receiving honorary degree with Senator Ted Kennedy at Marymount College, N.Y.C., NY

As President of the New York State Higher Education Services Corporation attending meeting with New York State Governor Hugh Carey

New York State Governor Mario Cuomo, Dolores Cross and Tom Cross Jr. after
signing the Liberty Scholarship bill

Jane and Dolores in Albany 1987

Arriving in Chicago in 1990

Chicago State Inauguration with Governor
James Edgar

Dolores, Ted Jackson & sister Jean
at inauguration celebration

My mother and I at Chicago State University

BOSTON ATHLETIC ASSOCIATION

This is to certify that

Dr. Dolores E. Cross

Finished 6837 in 4:01:46
Women Overall: 1127
Women 50-59 : 36

GUY L. MORSE III
Race Director

THOMAS W. WHELTON
President

96th BOSTON MARATHON.
April 20, 1992

Certification of Completion for 1992 Boston Marthon.

CSU Black Writers' Conference
w/ Ossie Davis

Dolores and Jesse Jackson Sr

Attending graduation ceremony at CSU with Senator Paul Simon

At CSU, presenting honorary degree to Vice Chancellor Ndeble, University of the North, South Africa

Attending meeting with students and Vice Chancellor Ndeble at University of the North, South Africa

Receiving Award of Merit, City of Chicago Commission on Human
Rights from Clarence Woods and Mayor Richard Daley

As a Board Member of the American Council on Education, being greeted
by President Bill Clinton during our meeting in Washington, D.C.

Receiving the First Muhammed Ali Award, 1996

Morrina Williams, Renee Williams Jefferson and my mother at CSU Pre-Thanksgiving Dinner for seniors

Completing New York City Marathon with
Gail Vanderheide in 1994

Being greeted by Hilliary Rodham Clinton at
American Council on Education Reception in Washington, D.C.

Meeting with Winnie Mandela in South Africa as a member of the Chicago Council on Foreign Relations in mid 90s

Meeting at the home of President Nelson Mandela as a member of the Chicago Council on Foreign Relations

CSU graduation in 1997: planned as a tribute to my mother. left to right: Gwendolyn Brooks, Katherine Dunham, Dolores Cross, Congressman Donald Payne, Senator Carol Mosely Braun, Ed Garner and Wilma Sutton

Part II

Chapter 3

Budd Blakey had been clear in telling me, "Dolores, you're crazy to consider a presidency of a college that has had four changes in presidencies in a ten-year period." Budd, an attorney and currently consultant for the United Negro College Fund (UNCF), had known me since 1981. As legislative assistant to Senator Paul Simon, he had arranged for me and college presidents in the State of New York to testify before the Senator's Education and Labor Committee on Reagan's proposals to drastically cut student financial aid. He had worked with me at CSU in handling communication with the Department of Education (DOE). Budd knew of problems faced by fragile Historically Black Colleges and Universities (HBCUs). He also expected me to throw his caution to the wind and accept the position. Budd was accustomed to my sense of purpose and sense of humor. He let out a hearty laugh when I said: "Budd, not to worry, the Morris Brown College Board of Trustees, governed largely by men with roots in the South and the African Methodist Episcopal (AME) Church, were considering me, a Baptist with roots in the North, as their first female president." Whatever my decision, I knew Budd had my back.

A tour of the campus with students followed my meeting with the Trustees in October 1998. I surveyed the approximately 37 acres of Morris Brown College in Atlanta, Georgia. The campus bordered both sides of Martin Luther King Boulevard in the southeast section of the city. The administration and science buildings, Fountain Hall, the Gym, and the Tower residence halls bordered one side of the Boulevard. On the other side was Gaines Hall, Sara Allen Quad, Furber Cottage, and further down the hill were Cunningham and Herndon Athletic Stadium. It was home for approximately 2,000 students.

I saw in the student leaders who accompanied my tours of the campus a sense of purpose. Student Government representatives were quite impressive in rallying other students to press on—and have hope.

"Why urge them to have hope?" I wondered, thinking that hope constituted the very air of a college campus, or should. The answer came as the president of student government shared with pride, the legacy of the college, how students had competed and succeeded in Model UN debates, and how the college's music program and marching band was the envy of other colleges in the Atlanta University Center. He pointed with pride to a newly-paved parking area and explained how students had been the driving force to get the college to complete it.

In November 1998, I was announced as the first woman to become President in the 113-year history of Morris Brown College. I accepted a compensation package less than I received as Professor at CUNY's Graduate Center. I received an anonymous grant of $250,000 that paid my salary, benefits and supported special projects through June 30, 2000. The Trustees had plans to commit close to a million dollars from construction funds to build a President's residence on campus. Shortly after touring the campus, I made the decision to use the equity from the sale of my house in Minnesota and personal savings to purchase and renovate property in midtown Atlanta to serve as the President's residence. Funds from the construction fund were used to address deferred maintenance projects on the campus.

I felt that we were in this together. I would lead a college founded by blacks for blacks that had a commitment to endure. The following month, I made the decision to also spend time living in the Sara Allen residence hall. On those occasions, the students would join me for morning jogs and gather in my room for evening chats. The conversations had no boundaries. The students were intrigued with me being the first woman to be appointed president and my having attended a Catholic University in the North as a commuter student. They wanted to know if I always knew I would become a college president. I shared with them my 28-year journey, beginning with my career as a kindergarten teacher in Newark, New Jersey, continuing as a special education teacher in Brooklyn, New York and Brentwood, L.I., New York, and teaching and administering programs at various Universities. I also told them about the encouragement I received from my mentor and friend, Peter Drucker that helped me set my sights on a presidency. I wanted them to stay encouraged and I treaded lightly on the depth of the racism, discrimination and sexism I had experienced along the way. The message for them, as it had been for me was: "Yes, we can overcome."

Conversations with students gave me an opportunity to learn firsthand why it had been important for them to attend a Historically Black College. The students spoke of having options and of having observed the success and confidence reflected in graduates of HBCUs. I heard how they had seen friends disillusioned by predominantly white colleges that failed to perceive them as having potential. The Morris Brown students loved the history and its traditions as well as the pride and success of its alums. They knew, as well, that while I had inherited the college's rich legacy, I would also have to deal with long-standing and immediate problems faced by the college.

Into The Fray

In 1992, Morris Brown had weathered a fiscal crisis that threatened to close its doors. The serious concerns raised by the Southern Association of Colleges and Schools (SACS) regarding long-standing issues on financial viability led to the galvanizing of the Atlanta community to strengthen the college's financial base for its outstanding obligations and to initiate responses to unaddressed audit findings in the management of fiscal affairs and student financial aid. While the college did not close, it would have to answer questions on its fiscal viability and overall stability for the 1999 reaccreditation. In joining the college in the fall of 1998, I had arrived at a critical juncture. The college was not "in the black" and continued to be plagued by long-standing fiscal and audit problems and was now being reviewed by the Southern Association of Colleges and Schools (SACS) for its reaccreditation. The process required the college to assess progress it had made in meeting objectives outlined in its 1988 reaccreditation, rectify pre-existing academic and operational issues, and achieve an unqualified audit in its student financial aid management.

Prior to my joining the college, the Department of Education (DOE) had agreed that the college be placed in manual reimbursement status in lieu of an audit of student financial aid for the 1997-98 academic year. Manual reimbursement status created a cash-flow problem for the college. To meet the cash flow shortfall the Trustees had entered into a four million dollar line of credit that had to be repaid in mid-1999. There were more steps and new procedures to be undertaken before federal student financial aid funds reached the college. The DOE would review what had been student files that had transmitted for payment and, if satisfactory, transfer student financial aid funds to the Office of Fiscal Affairs.

Morris Brown College was also under pressure to address years of fiscal mismanagement findings by external auditors. The college was hampered by having an outdated accounting technology system and having to enter transactions manually. We also had to develop our technology infrastructure to respond to a DOE government mandate that required colleges to be able to transmit data electronically by the year 2000 and be Y2K compliant.

A Marathon Team

Realizing the size of the task before me, with the approval of the Trustees, I engaged a consultant to assist me in interviewing candidates for my executive team. She and I had been colleagues at Northwestern University. I had assisted her during her tenure as an administrator at the University of Illinois-Chicago and had become familiar with her dedication and progress in creating opportunities for minority and poor students in Chicago. In assisting me in identifying candidates, I knew she would be forthright in articulating my vision for the college and candid in sharing my expectation that members of the team own their respective responsibilities.

I selected an administrator I had worked with at Chicago State University to become Dean of Faculty and later Vice President and Provost. He had been successful in working in pre-college programs and the pipeline program for students going on to graduate school. His credentials included being one of 14 Blacks to graduate from the University of Chicago with a Ph.D. in Physics. I viewed him as someone who could document the college's response to re-accreditation criteria and assist in developing grants. The college had to demonstrate it had a viable strategic plan which would sustain it for the next ten years and beyond. He understood that the college's approach to improving the recruitment, retention and graduation rate of students meant that the Office of Academic Affairs had to take the lead in developing a strategic plan which would set the direction of all operational areas of the college.

I invited Chicago State University's Director of Student Financial Aid to consult with the college and meet with representatives of the DOE Atlanta Regional office. Following his interview with the Trustees, we announced his continued support as consultant until he could join us as a full-time employee. He would have to take over an office that had experienced numerous changes in the position of Director of Student Financial Aid. He would be the college's liaison with the DOE in addressing recurring concerns in the college's mismanagement of student financial aid.

I called on my former Director of Public Affairs from Chicago State University to serve as Vice President for College Relations. She was familiar with my administrative style and had since leaving CSU taught at a historically black college in Florida. She would have to take the lead in promoting strategies to move the college forward, getting buy-in from faculty, staff and students as well as the civic, corporate and church communities in the state; plus managing steps to spread the word about the campus community's response to our challenges, undertaking a survey to determine directions for success, and celebrating the traditions unique to the college..

I was fortunate to enlist a former member of Governor Cuomo's cabinet as the college's Executive Vice President of the college. He was respected for his administrative leadership in various government positions. I saw in him someone who understood the importance of uncovering issues to improve the college's fiscal operation. He would quickly gain the support of staff in implementing procedures to improve accountability.

I hired an experienced university fundraiser to join the team. She presented a written plan for success in raising private funds for scholarships, grant writing and tracking donors, as well as a list of critical local, state and national networking opportunities. I welcomed the pace she would set. She was undaunted by concerns about the acceptance of a white woman in the job. It was her Southern roots and track record in fund raising and grant writing that should matter. I agreed and welcomed her to the position of Vice President of Institutional Advancement. I also identified experienced individuals within Morris Brown College to assume leadership positions in alumni affairs, admissions, academic affairs, facilities, student affairs, as well as office of college counsel.

My weekly executive staff meetings would bring together the Executive Vice President, Vice President for College Relations, Vice President for Institutional Advancement, Dean of Faculty, Director of Facilities, Director of Admissions, Director of Student Financial Aid, College Counsel, Secretary to the Board, Dean of Students, Executive Assistant, Student Government President and the Transition Team Consultant. Program managers would attend for reports in specific areas. As president, I would have to rely on their professional judgment as well as reports on our progress that we would receive from the Southern Association of Colleges and Schools, the Atlanta Office of the Department of Education and the college's external auditor. I looked around the table and felt that with the right team in place the situation we faced was manageable and despite our problems we would make progress. On the table was the fact that the clock was running out on the college's presentation of its report for reaccreditation. We were on the SACS agenda for a visit and review of all areas of Morris Brown's operations in February 1999. The DOE was present to monitor operations in the Office of Student Financial Aid and the Board of Trustees expected progress reports in academic and operational areas. We were operating in a fishbowl and beginning the task before us with a mere $40,000 reserve for addressing SACS criteria.

Within a few weeks of our getting started, the Atlanta Regional Office of the Department of Education (DOE) brought to my attention that the college faced a potential 8 million dollar audit disallowance for findings identified in its 1992-93 review. I contacted Budd Blakey to join me in meetings with DOE officials from the Atlanta Regional Office and Washington, D.C. At the end of our deliberations, the findings of the DOE concluded that while some of the documentation was missing, the students were likely eligible to receive student financial aid and reduced the 8 million disallowance to less than half a million dollars.

I welcomed the opportunity to collaborate with the DOE. They provided staff to train employees in the office and were given full access to Morris Brown College staff involved in adhering to regulations of their office. We agreed that the Office of Student Financial Aid would be responsible for verifying and documenting student eligibility and a separate office, the Office of Fiscal Affairs would be responsible for ensuring that students had enrolled prior to disbursing funds to students or any other operating expenses of the college. This would provide checks and balances that had not been in place in prior years.

Prior to the SACS visit, I reached out to the Association of Governing Boards (AGB) to engage the Trustees in a retreat. I appreciated questions raised by the Board of Trustees on my appointments. They would have to answer questions about their choice of me as president and wanted me to understand the relationship with them as the governing Board of the College. I was their agent and should expect that Trustee meetings might include face-to-face reports from those to whom I had delegated responsibility. The Chair of the Trustees took time to reaffirm their commitment to setting the administrative side of the house in order. Other trustees provided information on the Board's involvement to keep things on track during difficult times for the college. Their comments suggested they'd been under siege in the past and would assert at will their role as stewards of the college. They had been down this road of working with new presidents before, and to my thinking, they were not inclined to air "the dirty laundry" with their new president. Without coming right out with it, I felt I was there to save the college.

I turned to the United Negro College Fund to get funds to support the development of the college's technology infrastructure to facilitate meeting year 2000 technology mandates of the Department of Education. Without an adequate infrastructure the college did not have a platform to respond to the requirements of Y2K or improve its internal management. Dr. William (Bill) Gray, President of UNCF (United Negro College Fund) had made major strides in securing technology to assist colleges in responding to the new environment. I wasted no time in reaching out to him on the possibilities for Morris Brown College and directed staff to secure what we needed to accelerate the process. In the end, we would secure over three million dollars worth of hardware and equipment from the UNCF program. In subsequent months, Bill Gray came to the Atlanta University Center and announced that Morris Brown had exceeded other colleges in using the resources made available to them from UNCF.

The Executive Vice President identified budget discrepancies caused by the lack of adequate systems. He turned to an outside firm to review accounting for expenditures. The process uncovered a 3.2 million dollar budget deficit and the problem of the college's having approved budgets that were not based on actual expenditures. Subsequent budgets would reflect an increase caused by our having to make this adjustment.

Our meetings with the campus community communicated our progress. We were taking steps in improving the appearance of the campus with new benches, lighting, and greenery. Renovations were underway in the residence halls, the student computer lab was being expanded, the enrollment process was being streamlined and the Office of Admissions would be relocated from the Administration Building to a building we were renovating on campus.

The transition team undertook a faculty review that resulted in the dismissal of 13 faculty members and also the threat of sanctions by the American Association of University Presidents (AAUP). The faculty leadership contacted the press and the Atlanta Journal Constitution ran the story and highlighted the change that had come to Morris Brown

College. I was addressing yet another long-standing problem. There were fewer than 10 tenured faculty at the college and some had served more than a dozen years without a promotion or tenure review. The process also led to faculty promotions and an increase in the number of tenured positions at the college. I had made changes, not only in administration, but also in the heart of the institution, academic affairs. We had to focus on how the accreditation criteria would be the incentive to make strategic changes to secure our future for the long haul. I knew as well that at the end of the day, this approach might not win friends in the faculty, staff and some members of the Board. I risked being perceived as using the presidency and my team as the criteria for accreditation spelled out by the Southern Association of Colleges and Schools (SACS) as a means for imposing my grand plans and having my way. I heard this from a faculty member who declared he "was tired of hearing me refer to what was called for by SACS." I was reminded by an alumnus that "things had looked bad many times before and the college always survived."

The executive team joined faculty, staff and students working round the clock to prepare the campus for review by visiting teams evaluating us for reaccreditation. Neglect had taken a toll at Morris Brown. Lettering had faded on buildings, paint in public spaces was chipped, and the grounds needed extensive maintenance. Having made a personal investment to purchase and renovate a house for the president's residence, I was able to use the college's construction fund that the Trustees had designated as funds to build a new president's residence on campus to address extensive deferred maintenance needs at the college. We spent weekends working with the building and grounds team painting the halls of the Towers Residence Hall, planting flowers and participating in sessions to get the college ready. The mood of optimism was motivated by resilience and creativity. We had to get our house in order to demonstrate that we were ready to handle what would be uncovered in the initial review visit.

The results of the visiting team's report were not surprising. The college would have to respond to 68 findings that impacted every area of the college. In the spring of 1999, we were presented with a lot of terrain to cover in a compressed time period of two years. The college would have to apply assessment processes to document progress it had made in responding to objectives laid out 10 years earlier. Faculty and staff would have to spend long hours and weekends in workshops developing action steps to respond to findings with the SACS criteria. The overriding question of accreditation was whether or not the college had a financial base and a vision to sustain itself financially for the long run.

We would have to be guided by a plan that would improve the recruitment, retention and success of our students. In response, I presented the vision of "The Learning Tree" to trustees, alums, faculty, staff and students. The vision had deep roots. My grandfather had shown me how to help young people in the church community by teaching weekend and summer classes. It was a vision shared in Chicago State University's three-point program for student success. The three points were represented by branches of a tree, signifying pre-college programs, in-college programs, and after-college programs, all rooted in the African-American tradition of reaching back to move ahead.

At Morris Brown, we would bring in elementary school classes from the Atlanta Public Schools each summer and hold periodic meetings with the students and their parents during the academic year. The young students, their teachers and parents, gathered with MBC administrators, faculty, staff and students as a tree was planted on the grounds in front of the Administration Building. As we shoveled dirt over the roots I envisioned these youngsters returning as freshmen and being greeted by a tall tree, reminding them how they too could grow at Morris Brown.

Each year we would invite a new group of students to share in the vision of "The Learning Tree." The objective was to have potential students enter Morris Brown College better prepared, to encourage them to view the college as their first choice and to improve the recruitment, enrollment, retention, graduation rates and success of students.

The vision was meant to make a difference for students and to help us in gaining financial support from foundations, corporations, alums and the AME Church. The staff from college relations and institutional advancement met on promoting our strategic vision and to plan for speaking engagements to outline the college's intentions and actions taken to realize the vision. In addition to the pre-college program in the summer we were negotiating a grant to host an after school program to develop the technology skills of students in an adjacent elementary school. We were identifying internships for our students and I had begun discussions with a graduate program in Atlanta for a path for our students. Results matter and we were walking our talk. Our efforts led to the college obtaining in 1999 a $300,000 grant from Coca-Cola to implement the precollege program. The financial contributions from alums exceeded what we had raised in previous years. Faculty matched my $10,000 gift to the college.

We received corporate and civic donations of $25,000 each for four trees planted in the Sara Allen Quad, as well as funding to conduct a statewide survey of parents on their expectations of an HBCU. I appealed to CEO's of Boards that I had participated on and received sponsors to support our plans to raise scholarship funds through a new "Going the Distance Gala." to be held at Atlanta's downtown Marriott Hotel. It would be an annual event.

HITTING OUR STRIDE

On Founders' Day, March 25, 1999 and five months into the job as president, I joined the jubilant community to sing along with them. The spirit was infectious and strangers new to Morris Brown were swept away by the profusion of colors and joyous song as we prepared to celebrate our proud heritage. "I'm so glad I'm at Morris Brown' I'm so glad I'm at Morris Brown, singing glory hallelujah, I'm so glad."

The college band played and the audience of students, faculty, staff and alums joined as the procession led by the trustees, distinguished guests, and executive team marched into the college gym. The stage was set with flowers and draped with the school colors of black and purple. As president I was the last to enter the room. Dressed in purple regalia I approached the lectern before taking my seat and joining in another round of a rousing version of the rhythmic song, "I'm so glad I'm at Morris Brown, I'm so glad, I'm at Morris Brown, singing Gloria hallelujah, I'm so glad."

The college had stayed the course as implied in its mission statement that it "becomes a haven for all hungry souls." The college had created a system that functioned to channel its energy to serve the needs of students from low socio-economic backgrounds and its founding in 1885 was linked to the African Methodist Episcopal Church (AME). The college was named to honor the memory of the second consecrated Bishop of the AME church.

I felt in the singing, and the inspiring tone in the gymnasium setting for this Founders' Day, a pride in being at an institution that mattered. It provided access to an undergraduate education, cultural traditions and a community of alums, faculty and staff who valued what the college sought to achieve.

I observed the quiet anticipation as the chair of the Board of Trustees, the Bishop, was introduced to preside over the occasion. I sensed a need for the reassurance he would provide in the board's choice of a new president. In the ten years prior there had been four changes in the leadership of the college. He had withstood criticism on the impact of these frequent changes and the view that the Board of Trustees was micromanaging the college.

The Bishop's voice was filled with passion and he hardly required a microphone as he announced, "Founders' Day brings the whole Morris Brown family together to celebrate with fellow churches, the Atlanta community, schools, donors, students, faculty and administrators to remind us how we've come to be."

His love and passion for Morris Brown College was evident in his serious demeanor and attentiveness to the festivities that honored the former slaves who had founded the College. In closing the Founders' Day Ceremony, the Bishop stepped to the lectern in the midst of applause, spoke of the college's rich legacy and expressed confidence in my presidency. The Bishop ended his message by proclaiming in a loud voice 'there will always be a Morris Brown,' to which he received a thunderous applause.

Given the historical struggle that blacks had to endure to gain access to a postsecondary degree, there was much to be proud of on this wonderful day. Morris Brown College was one of the pillars of the Atlanta University (AU) Center, along with Clark Atlanta University, Morehouse and Spelman Colleges, Interdenominational Theological Seminary and Morehouse School of Medicine. The AU Center occupies hallowed ground in African American educational and church history, having been the home of significant leaders and scholars, from W.E.B. Du Bois to John Hope Franklin, Howard Thurman, Benjamin Mays and Martin Luther King, Jr.

By the summer of 1999 we implemented our first pre-college program and satisfied 34 of 68 findings. The college had also opened a Center for Academic Excellence and Leadership (CAEL). The purpose of the CAEL was to assist students in developing analytical and critical thinking skills for leadership. Things were definitely looking up.

The president's residence provided a meeting place for staff, faculty, students and the community to dialogue with each other and with me. Housekeeping, and buildings and grounds employees were among the first to be invited for an early morning breakfast. They shared years of dedicated service to the college that included the use of personal resources and spending hours beyond the work day to keep up appearances. The college housekeeper assigned to provide support at the residence proudly gave her co-workers a tour of the house. I had transformed it with space expanded for formal dining, double ovens, new floors, an additional bath, laundry, a restored fireplace, guest room and a rebuilt front and back porch, as well as new landscaping.

From discussions with the Dean of Faculty, I knew that some faculty felt that as president I had been over promoted in press reports, while the depth of their contribution received little attention. The focus was on 'maintenance' through administrative means and not on the academic center as the engine of the college. With her help, we reached out to every faculty member and invited them to small dinner meetings at the residence. The intimate setting of the residence lent itself to openness in our communication. A faculty member pointed out that I had used the term "I" rather than "we" when referring to the college's achievements. I took note of his observation and thereafter refrained from using "I" when presenting the college's accomplishments. I also had an opportunity to hear what the Offices of College Relations and Institutional Advancement could do to promote their scholarship and improve an awareness of their contributions to Morris Brown College. The Vice President of Institutional Advancement and I traveled to New York City to meet with foundation leaders and were successful in negotiating a faculty development grant, as well as securing grants to provide student stipends for community service.

We enlisted students to join me in presentations to the corporate community. They were delighted to meet Ted Turner of CNN and he was intrigued with the students and the vision for the college. He responded by agreeing to speak at our commencement and receive an honorary doctorate degree. He went on to enlist Morris Brown College students as interns at CNN.

Through monthly meetings with the college community of staff, faculty, and student leadership, we provided periodic updates on our progress in responding to government mandates and accreditation findings, as well as information on the extent of our networking with AME churches in Georgia and HBCUs throughout the country. We traveled extensively with leadership of the alumni association to participate in meetings in Washington, D.C, Newark, New York City, Miami, Chicago, Detroit, Oakland and Los Angeles. As was my style in these forums, I presented the proverbial glass as half-full and infused my presentations with references drawn from the history of the South, "Slaves had taught themselves to read and write. The richness of our past must infuse our will to go the distance." We communicated excitement about the successes of staff and faculty and the impact on students. It was one thing to have a vision and quite another to fully implement a direction to sustain and build the college. Achievements mattered to alums. They increased their giving and participation in alumni affairs and supported a pre-alumni group led by student leaders. There was much to be proud of. The college had problems but it was making progress.

Through weekly meetings with the college's administrative team, I received periodic updates on administrative issues referred to them for a response. My Executive Assistant maintained a correspondence control log to help us keep pace with concerns and kudos. The practice of delegating responsibility was intended to promote ownership of duties of their respective offices. I knew as well that should I lend my views on aspects of operations, I would be viewed as micromanaging. What I heard most often was "the president doesn't know anything about fiscal affairs and should focus on academic and fundraising areas."

There were those in the campus community who felt that I hadn't used the president's pulpit to offer an adequate dose of doom and gloom – instead, I was seen as creating a false sense of hope and progress in the midst of a dire situation. There seemed to be not enough thought to the impact of my being negative on fundraising efforts, recruitment of students and faculty, or keeping the faith, as we worked with government regulators and accrediting agencies. I relied on what I had learned from my parents and mentors at various stages of my life: "stay strong, stay positive, and organize what you do around a purpose that makes a difference, and keeps you in touch with who you are."

I had never run a marathon thinking I couldn't make it to the finish line and I couldn't imagine a coach worth her salt telling a team "it is all against the odds, we should not have gotten this far and woe is we."

We experienced a setback when my Executive Vice President resigned in November 1999. We were equally strong-willed. He and I had disagreed on administrative styles, the handling of the strategic planning process and my having a say in operations. He was not happy that the Director of Student Financial Aid had delayed joining the college full-time, and about what he viewed as serious glitches in the communication between them. The EVP's attention to system needs of the college, retiring the college's four million dollar line of credit and improving processes in fiscal affairs had given us much to build upon. I turned to a consultant he had hired to assist him. She was a Certified Public Accountant and had worked closely with staff in the office as well as the college's external auditors. She began as Director of Budget and within a few months was named Vice President of Fiscal Affairs. She took steps to improve procedural processes and addressed findings from the college's external auditors that were years in arrears. Resources were reallocated for her to implement a technology system to interface with other offices and to train the staff in fiscal affairs.

The Dean of Faculty was promoted to the position of Provost and Vice President of Academic Affairs. He would be second in line to me, while working with leadership in academic and operations areas to monitor the development and transmission of documentation required for reaccreditation, as well as dealing with faculty, admissions, registrar, as well as student affairs' issues.

In the fall of 1999, The Director of Admissions left for another position. For a period of three months the Director of Student Financial Aid was requested to expand his responsibilities to include oversight of the Office of Admissions as Dean of Enrollment Management. At the end of three months, the Provost had identified a Vice President of Student Affairs to whom the Director of Admissions, the Dean of Students, the Director of Residence Life and other sundry student services would report. The Vice President of Student Affairs was recruited from California. Her extensive experience prepared her to tackle student legislative issues and uncover and solve problems. She quickly established herself as no-nonsense, firm, yet kind. She recognized the need to establish a connection with the college's rich traditions and supported a highly capable and respected alum of the college as our Dean of Students. The Dean of Students involved students in the traditions of Morris Brown College. As in the past, freshmen students were required to wear beanies, conform to a dress code and participate in established college rituals. I viewed him as someone who might someday be at the helm of Morris Brown College.

In addressing the SACS findings in the areas of administration and operation, faculty was, on occasion, enlisted to assume administrative positions. The college's Professor in Architecture was named Executive Director of Facilities. His talent led to major changes in the physical appearance of the campus. With the leverage of construction funds, he engaged students in the building plans for a kiosk for student information, restored historic aspects of the campus, renovated spaces and addressed deferred maintenance concerns raised by SACS. His love of the college was reflected in the presence of new plants, flowers and trees.

Dr. Johnnetta Cole, former president of Spelman was instrumental in my being sponsored to become a member of the Rotary Club. I was given an opportunity to address this largely male group and tell them about the legacy, hope and promise of Morris Brown College, and explain what motivated me to accept the position as president. The women of the Rotary Club reached out and provided support. The president of Rotary was a woman, and with her help the corporate leadership of Atlanta came to the campus of Morris Brown College. For many of them this was their first visit to the college.

I was delighted to be named by the Mayor of Atlanta as Chair of the Commission on Women. The women on the commission easily became my friends. I was included in social functions sponsored by the women on the commission and they were guests in the president's residence. The committee researched salary equity issues for women as well as policies being promulgated at the local and state level to promote opportunities for women.

For some folks at the college, I was traveling too much, for others not traveling enough and for another group my presence on campus was totally irrelevant. Presidents expect these reactions. Fundraising and college relations were enhanced by travel associated with my participation on professional and corporate boards. The college was fully reimbursed for expenses associated with my involvement on the external boards. I also reimbursed the college for personal travel arranged by staff at the college and provided access to travel records. The bottom line for colleagues on campus was how much money I was bringing back to campus. The return was good for the College. During the first two years, the college dramatically exceeded records in fundraising, attracted more students as their first choice, improved first to second year retention rates and extended its internships. The Woodruff Foundation provided a 2 million dollar grant to be matched with other funds for the creation of a technology center on campus.

In the summer of 2000, I received an invitation from the American Jewish Committee to be part of a delegation of college presidents to participate in seminars in Israel. As with other personal travel, I paid my own way and was ready to have a welcome break. It would also be an opportunity to learn what my colleagues were experiencing on their campuses. We spent ten days in Israel and had the opportunity to meet with Jewish, Palestinian and Christian leaders, students, and citizens. As college presidents we found time to discuss issues on our respective campuses. They were alarmed to learn of the intention of Morris Brown's Trustees to move to Division One Athletics and shared their views on the cost impact. I heard more than once that "boards and alums will go to the mat on maintaining a strong presence in athletics and should things get tight say it was the president's grand idea."

My time in Israel also was when I learned of the blessed birth of my first grandchild. During my visit to the Church of the Nativity in Bethlehem, my colleagues joined me as I lit candles in the crossroads of three great religions. Then I called Tommy on his cell-phone to congratulate him and Patricia on the birth of their child. Hurrahs shouted down the telephone line as his name and date of birth was announced: Jackson Tucker Cross, born June 29, 2000.

Jackson was Patricia's family name and he'd been given the middle name of Tucker, my family name. I made a special trip to an artisan's shop in Jerusalem to have a unique tile wall plate made with his full name inscribed. I envisioned it placed over his crib and found myself filled with thoughts of introducing myself to Jackson as his "Nana."

Shortly after my return from Israel, I appeared on the NBC Today Show to promote Morris Brown College and the publication of my book, *Breaking Through the Wall: A Marathoner's Story.* In approaching daunting challenges in my life and in my leadership at the college, I spoke of the "analogies I had made as a long-distance runner." In talking with the moderator and the other guests, I imagined I was also speaking to students when I said that all proceeds from the sale of my book would go to support scholarships for students at Morris Brown College and Chicago State University. Sadly, I found the moderator on the program asking more questions about my personal life than ones pertaining to my role as college president. After one question was directed to my being a divorced woman, I felt slighted and wondered if the interviewer would have asked the same questions of a male president.

RACE CREDENTIALS

"President Cross, why would someone with your background come to Morris Brown College?"

The question was raised by a young coed. It was September 2000; the fall semester had just begun. I had left my office to lead a student seminar. The sun was streaming through the stained glass windows of the meeting hall. The question followed a reading I had given from my book, *Breaking Through the Wall: A Marathoner's Story.* I realized that in my comments, I didn't communicate my sense of going the distance in having assumed positions that had been closed to black women in previous decades. In my book, I had emphasized the importance of making connections with those who shared my values and who responded to public policy issues by addressing equity and serving, that is, going where they were needed. The young woman's troubling question echoed a statement Jane had made to me in 1998, on my decision to become President of Morris Brown College: "Mom, they won't even know why you're there."

I felt challenged by the coed's question and began my response by referring to the building's historic past and the fact that W.E.B. DuBois had completed some of his writings within the very Fountain Hall Building where we were meeting. DuBois viewed the campus as a haven and dedicated his life to giving back what he had learned. Dubois might have responded to this student with a statement that reflected on his experiences and the challenges he encountered while navigating through a segregated society. The young woman's somber expression suggested I had not answered the question. She was looking for me to be more forthcoming.

I should have addressed her question with greater force and described the reasons rooted in my experience that led me to choose to accept the position as President of Morris Brown College. I should have gone on and on explaining to her the impact that the 1954 landmark Brown vs. Board of Education decision had on my own education. Success means staying in touch with who I am. I should have been more forthcoming. Should'a, would'a, as my mom used to say. I was in my role as president of the college. I kept in mind the fact that the college was in the process of seeking its reaccreditation; and I chose to avoid addressing the fragile financial condition of the college and what the institution was up against in responding to criteria for its reaccreditation. I also kept in mind my propensity to try to make a difference in tough situations.

I kept the focus on Atlanta's promise, Dr. King's dream, W.E.B. DuBois' legacy, and the rich history of Morris Brown College to let them know of the path others have taken to honor the wisdom and courage of the ancestors. I could have kept it real by acknowledging the shoulders on which I stand, and by speaking to my activism in the Civil Rights movement and experiences of addressing current inequities in higher education. And closing my eyes, imagining myself standing there, I can't hear the words, for I never would have said them. I came for victory at Morris Brown, not for defeat or excuse.

An alumna of the college who was a few years my junior, provided a disquieting response to my autobiography. She was quick to convey the lack of discretion in what I had presented about my life. I had written of the horror of being molested at age five and the anguish of being homeless at age thirteen. I had not spoken as a victim, but as someone who viewed life's test as a means to establishing a base for figurative marathons. I was frustrated by what she had missed, namely, the lessons learned from predominately white institutions where women and minorities were marginalized and bypassed for promotion and tenure; where people of color trained white people to whom they would report; and where the legitimate perspectives of women and minorities were ignored or picked apart. More, I felt the alumna just wanted to convey that I was an outsider who didn't appreciate or understand the culture of historically black colleges. The slate was empty. I had heard it before: "You're not one of us." "You weren't raised in the South. "You didn't attend a Historically Black College and don't belong to a sorority."

"No, but I am black" I would respond, first drawing a respectful silence, then laughter. I much preferred the silence.

I maintained physical resilience by running Atlanta's 10-mile Peachtree Road Race. The race attracts runners throughout the State of Georgia and nation. I ran it as well as the Atlanta Half Marathon while readying myself for a return to Chicago to run in Chicago's 26.2-Mile La Salle Marathon on October 16, 2000. The Chicago Marathon would be my 20th marathon in 14 years.

I flew into Chicago the night before the race that began in downtown Chicago's Grant Park. Thousands would be competing on what proved to be a cool, overcast day. An enthusiastic crowd was out to cheer the runners as we took off through the diverse ethnic areas of Chicago.

I viewed the venture as a statement of my resilience and experience in "going the distance." I joined runners at the 10-minute-mile pace. I started out slowly, taking few risks. I felt energized, yet not as well-tuned as I had been in previous races. Going the distance, though, had been my mantra in accepting the job as President of Morris Brown College, and nothing was going to stop me.

My shirt was inscribed Morris Brown College, and the bib on my shorts was stenciled with my age group. 60-65. I was beginning to relax and settle into a comfortable pace. I was energized with thoughts of both figurative and literal mentors, who had guided me through previous marathons. They would be making the steps with me.

I drew on the memory of relatives to propel me forward. My mother had waited in Harlem for me to pass as I ran the New York City Marathon. She expected me to finish and to make her proud. I think she was totally surprised when I spotted her mixed in with the onlookers, and slowed my pace to salute her.

No, on my marathon I was never alone. Ms. Malone always had a place reserved for her. She was the supervisor at my first job, and unlike others who told me to quit thinking about getting more education than a high school degree, urged me to go on to college. I smiled when thinking of a tutor who worked with me a year to help me complete a pre-college exam in algebra and qualify for college matriculation. I saw myself running side-by-side with several significant events in Black history: the 1954 Brown decision; the 1963 March on Washington; the Civil Rights Act of 1964; and the courageous accomplishments of the likes of Nelson Mandela, Rosa Parks, Martin Luther King Jr., Harry Belafonte, Shirley Chisholm, and Jesse Jackson.

Running the distance that day gave me time to reflect on how far the marathon team at Morris Brown College had come, examples of which included increasing the number of tenured faculty, implementing a technology infrastructure to transmit data to the Department of Education, and exceeding prior years fundraising levels.

Midway through the marathon I felt my energy flag. I anticipated the lift I would receive at mile 19, where the Rainbow Runners traditionally offered their inspirational presence, as they did during previous Chicago marathons. I had been running close to empty and was plodding ahead in a growing blur. I needed water and quickly received some from them.

I had been running over four and a half hours when I saw Grant Park and caught a glimpse of the finish line. Moving ahead, I heard the ripple of applause.

At mile 26, it was time to surge ahead and finish strong. I pumped my arms, lifted my legs and moved through "the chute." I was aware of the cheering for marathoners making it to the end.

After crossing the finishing lines, I walked alone on the busy overpass from Columbus Drive to Michigan Avenue, wrapped in the light-weight finisher's cape, wearing shorts and shivering in the cool of the second Sunday in October 2000. Within a few minutes I hailed a taxi to take me back to my hotel, where I showered, changed my clothes and prepared for the return to Atlanta where another marathon awaited me. This marathon, however, had no visible finish line and had demands that were just as great (if not greater) than the marathon I had just finished.

I flew back to Atlanta the same day. I looked forward to passing around my LaSalle Chicago Marathon finisher's medal at the next staff meeting.

I had experienced the exhilaration of going the distance. Now it was time to go the distance at Morris Brown. I felt we could achieve our goal and I needed to be clear on what lay before us.

I began the day with an image of the Deacons of Union Baptist Church assembled in the parlor of my grandpa's house on 50 Miller Street, Newark. Pa had come down the steps dressed in his black suit and stiff white shirt. He had a reputation for firmness and, while just 10-years-old, I knew the other Deacons had better not be wasting his time. I sat on the steps outside the parlor door and heard Deacon Jones clear his throat and solemnly proclaim, "Reverend Dr. Tucker, we need a Come to Jesus Meeting." Deacon Jones followed with an "amen." Pa raised his voice and said, "We'll end this session with an 'Amen' and not begin with it."

From the snippets of the conversation I could hear, I knew there was concern about the future of the church. It was two hours before I heard an "amen." I knew from my grandmother that a 'Come to Jesus Meeting' meant more than talking about a problem. You had to be prepared to take an action.

I didn't have Pa's cool in convening staff meetings, but I was going to give it my 'Come to Jesus Meeting' best. In rapid fire, I kept the focus on whether or not departments were keeping pace with new mandates, responding to external audits and meeting SACS deadlines. Prone to be impatient, grueling, and difficult, I pressed those around me to deal with the hurdles and keep moving ahead.

Some viewed the frequent reorganizations, expanded responsibilities and revisions in organization capricious and unwarranted. At times I could react with a short fuse to foot-dragging, in-fighting, and hollow excuses. I saw myself as simultaneously being out in the community, beaming the college up and at the same time working inside the college to have members of the team own their respective responsibilities as they responded to the college's vision for student success, the criteria for accreditation and government regulations.

The verse, "Lead me guide me, along the way, for if you lead me I cannot stray...." would sometimes ring through my head. Those words had been part of my early church experience. I smiled, recalling being in the church choir and rocking with choir members as we strolled down the church aisle to our seats in the choir stand.

At Morris Brown, we were faced with keeping pace with day-to-day management issues and needing to demonstrate unwavering progress in improving our financial stability and accountability, as well as improving opportunities for students.

The laptop initiative proved to be the most controversial. A statewide survey of parents and corporate leadership highlighted expressed concern about student preparation in technology. When our efforts to secure laptops at no cost to students failed, we proceeded in mandating laptops as part of a student's cost of education. I viewed having laptops as "leveling the playing field" for students. Not everyone agreed with what I considered an investment for students and the college. I invited Tony Brown, TV commentator of the show, Tony Brown's Journal, to speak to the college community on the role of technology in moving forward in today's environment. He impressed upon students the importance of investing in a laptop and that doing so was integral to their success.

In mandating laptops for all students, providing training for faculty in the use of technology to improve their teaching, and expanding computer facilities, as well as moving to a wireless structure, the college had taken bold steps and risked being faulted for the scope of our new directions. We were in a catch up mode in adhering to criteria for appropriate standards in all areas of our operation, yet we could not forego skill building to improve the retention and success of our students.

The bold move had its consequences. The college's external auditor called to my attention fiscal affairs' error in failing to reflect the acquisition of the laptops as a purchase in the budget, as well as flaws in the plan for repayment of the debt incurred. In response, we engaged an internal auditor to review the plan for monitoring laptop payments and distribution. He uncovered serious weaknesses in the management of the initiative. I invited my former Vice President of Information Technology at Chicago State University to visit Morris Brown and advise me on what could be done to improve the management of our overall technology objectives. He was impressed with the hard working staff at the college and excited about the opportunity to 'roll up his sleeves' and lend his expertise. He secured a sabbatical from CSU and joined the team to guide a task force in implementing interactive systems, improving the distribution of laptops to students, and moving us to a wireless campus. His commitment, enthusiasm and calm, 'no problem', approach perked us all up.

The board's decision to move the college to Division One Athletics required us to have an equal number of sports for women, build a new tennis court, address salary equity issues, and provide more scholarships and travel expenses. I was disappointed when, after reporting on the cost to the college in the move to Division One, a board member pulled me aside to say "Ms. President, you have found resources for technology and the laptop program. You can find funds for Division One." To his thinking, more alums might be drawn into the fold with athletics.

The growth of the program in Athletics was matched by the expansion of the college's marching band. The college was the first choice of many students who wanted to play in one of the best marching bands in the country. Alums formed separate committees to raise funds to secure instruments, uniforms and equipment, as well as to plan a football game classic to attract support for the move to Division One participation. The energy of alums and staff in getting behind the College's move to a new division matched what I saw in the enthusiasm for our new Center for Academic Excellence and Leadership and newly created computer lab that served the Atlanta community.

My understanding of the benefits of tradition at Historically Black Colleges was enhanced by conversations with my good friend, Dr. Tom Monteiro. Tom had completed his undergraduate degree at Winston Salem College. The academic and sports program there had contributed to his strengths and understanding of his history. Tom and I had taught special education students at P.S. 150, Brooklyn, been involved in New York City's African American Teacher Association and he encouraged me as I moved into higher education administration. I had been an advisor to him when he encountered resistance to his achieving tenure and promotion to professor at Brooklyn College, CUNY. He attributed his determination, confidence, and competence to having attended a historically black college in the South. His success story was not unlike what I heard from alums of other HBCUs.

A special spirit was evident when the college community gathered for the "Going the Distance Gala" to raise funds for student scholarships. The preparation and presentation were steered by the Vice President for College Relations. The Director of Special Events, a native Atlantan, was familiar not only with the protocol of Morris Brown, but with the expectations of Atlanta's fashionable and prosperous middle class. She was firm in offering advice to me, saying, "Don't worry about a thing, Doc" and comfortable in adding, "Do something with your hair. I want you to look drop-dead gorgeous when you enter with your student escort." I loved the humor, as she reminded me to take time for myself. I appreciated her candor, creativity and discernment in getting members of the college community in line to carry out well-scripted and inspirational events.

With the support of the offices of College Relations and Institutional Advancement, I took the lead in getting sponsors for the gala. As I had done at Chicago State University, I communicated the backgrounds and successes of students, as well as accomplishments of faculty, administrators and staff at Morris Brown College. The message was that of our needing to raise funds to help students meet the cost of their education without a heavy reliance on loans. I pointed out that the average amount of loans for Morris Brown graduates exceeded that of graduates of Harvard. Corporate leaders in and outside of Atlanta responded with sponsorships and donations. The refrain 'build it and they will succeed' played over and over in my head.

The 'Going the Distance Gala' was a huge success. Arrangements were made for students to escort me into Marriott's ballroom. Every table was filled and attendees stood as the music played and I proceeded to the front table on the student's arm. The fundraiser had brought in over $200,000 for the college and set the bar for galas we would hold in subsequent years. We used the occasion to communicate the college's progress and to honor students who were leaders and recipients of scholarships. The joyous black tie event brought alums, faculty and student leaders, as well as the Atlanta community together.

The Vice President of College Relations and her team were on the front line in balancing outreach activities of the President's office and coordinating, approving and promoting events and activities of faculty, staff and alums. The new spirit on campus meant more work for them. The college opened a Cyberlab to provide computer training for individuals in the community; renamed a Hall to honor a former faculty member; established an after-school program to train elementary school students in technology; enhanced traditions of the college. Meetings with the Vice President for College Relations were often held outside the Administration building as we toured the campus and discussed plans for moving the college forward. She joked about "keeping up with the president' as we talked and moved at a fast pace to communicate the Morris Brown College story and gain support for our efforts.

The college succeeded in getting the attention of the popular radio and TV talk show host, Tom Joyner. He identified Morris Brown College, as College of the Month for January 2001. This gave me an opportunity to meet Tom Joyner, his father and son. Their tight knit family had made a commitment to 'keeping it real' by extending the support and love that made them successful to Morris Brown College. Tom Joyner used his early morning radio talk show to introduce me and speak to the needs of Morris

Brown College students. His voice was electric with passion and caring for the success of black students and the success of Historically Black Colleges and Universities. Tom listened as we presented the challenges Morris Brown College faced and the actions we were taking to make a difference for students. His enthusiasm for the college reflected a deep understanding of the realities of the financial condition of Georgia's only black college founded by blacks for blacks. As a result of being College of the Month on Tom's show, we were able to reach people who had never heard of the college or its rich legacy. The spotlight contributed to students electing Morris Brown College as their first choice in their selection of colleges to attend in the fall of 2001. The college raised close to $70,000 in scholarship support for our students. Even more, Tom helped people understand that they could continue to help the college by directing their UNCF contributions to Morris Brown College.

The Vice President of Institutional Advancement announced a net of $20,000 for student scholarships from my donation of all proceeds from the sale of my autobiography, *Breaking Through the Wall: A Marathoner's Story*, to help students meet the cost of their education. Our travels to alumni meetings throughout the country, participation in alumni church and social events in Georgia, and insight from a dedicated President of the Alumni Association, led to alums setting new goals and exceeding funds raised in prior years. The alums understood that the college's legacy had to be supported. They responded by making resources available for the college's marching band and athletic department. Their support didn't stop there; they volunteered their time, working with students and staffing the alumni office. An alum whose mother had been a revered member of the faculty returned to the college from New York to donate full-time leadership to efforts of alums to support activities that had been signature events during his days as a student.

Our faculty had been the lowest paid in the AU Center. Through reallocating resources and leaving some positions unfilled, the salaries of faculty were increased by 10% and tuition and fees were maintained at the same level for students. The faculty had taken the lead in responding to SACS findings in the area of academic affairs by taking on extra assignments, instituting changes and responding to deadlines, as well as embracing the vision of the 'Learning Tree.'

I recruited and the board approved four new trustees. The recruits included CEOs from business and a foundation, as well as an educator.

They added influence and resources to facilitate the board's focus on fundraising and networking.

We didn't stop there. Bill Cosby agreed to be the college's commencement speaker. He set the pace for the event by calling on the band director and asking that he skip the traditional 'pomp and circumstance' music and lead the graduates in with a jazz piece. Cosby's presence signaled that despite our problems we were making progress in 'letting our light shine.'

I knew I was leading a college with church roots, and felt the energy of the references to God's lifting the college up through the power of prayer and inspired music.

I knew as well that should I be at the helm when the ship sailed to shore, I might be faulted for having pressed too hard, used too much fuel, or having slept and let the crew find their way. And should I be at the helm if the ship went down, blame would point toward the captain, even if the mates had on their watch, let the ship veer more and more off course. Whatever might happen, I would be held accountable, for the ship was Morris Brown, and I was the captain. I should have questioned why I was brought on board after four previous captains had been relieved of duty while sailing to shore. But I was so busy trying to get us safely to port, to see what was going on below decks.

AN UNPLEASANT FEELING OF A SEA CHANGE

In April of 2001, the Director of Student Financial Aid suffered a heart problem and was not on hand for several weeks. The College Counsel was assigned interim manager of his office. In the Director's absence, the Department of Education representatives were given access to managers and staff in his office. They had problems caused by what they viewed as the Director of Student Financial Aid's failure to delegate. In a meeting with me, the DOE expressed these concerns and suggested that the financial aid records be reviewed by an external firm other than the college's external auditor. I responded by engaging the firm the DOE recommended to review the management of student financial aid. Within six weeks the Director of Student Financial Aid returned to the college. It wasn't long after his return that he voiced complaints about my hiring a review team suggested by the DOE and staff discontent at his return.

The college also had to deal with new internal matters. The Director of Student Financial Aid faced allegations of sexual harassment. Former employees of the college presented their complaints to the regional office of DOE. He denied the allegations and the women refused to provide their names to the college. In a meeting with DOE on the matter and subsequent conversations I experienced the depth of the shift in their confidence in his leadership.

Before the start of the 2001 academic year, I met with the Director of Student Financial Aid and advised him of my plans to replace him. He was aware that the plan was to fast track a search, and find his replacement as soon as possible. At the same time, he knew that he was required to work with our external auditors as they reviewed the student financial aid operation as part of what the college would have to submit to SACS. In response to activities involved in the search process, the Director of Student Financial Aid asserted that he had been loyal to me and that I was reacting to the pressure directed at him by the regional office of the Department of Education and ill-founded complaints from some of his colleagues. He added that there were those, at the college, who were uncomfortable with his East Indian background. He continued to work long hours advising students and seemed oblivious to the deteriorating working relationship with his staff and the DOE. He also seemed to ignore the fact that interviews for his replacement were taking place I felt the tension heighten between him and staff at the DOE and involved them in an accelerated campaign to bring a new person on board. He also began forwarding signatures from students commending his helpfulness and made a point of communicating his loyalty to me and providing the impression he was staying on at the college by declaring: "Dr. Cross knows all about student financial aid and she and I go way back and I'll be working here in another capacity." Staff at DOE had been working directly with him and was not impressed with his attempts to turn away from his responsibilities, and present himself as more knowledgeable in the area of student financial aid than they were.

The summer and fall of 2001 were turning points in my relationships with key members of my staff.

The Vice President of Fiscal Affairs met with me in mid-June and delivered a letter on unbudgeted expenses. She seemed to be treating unanticipated expenses incurred in meeting SACS requirements, cost overruns for technology upgrades and fundraising travel as unnecessary expenditures by me as president. She appeared to miss the fact that much of the increase in the college budget came from the failure of her office to properly account for the laptop agreement. Her letter came after the external auditor's report on expenditures. In the absence of a functioning technology system, the college relied on bottom line reports from auditors for her analysis. I didn't feel she would resign and wanted her to stay on. The college had to submit its next report to the Association of State Colleges and Schools in October and much rested on our report from the fiscal area.

I provided a copy of her letter to the Provost. We agreed on the need to establish a task force of faculty and staff that would provide suggestions on cost-cutting and to make recommendations to improve our fiscal situation. I directed the Director of Personnel to develop various cost cutting options such as going to a four-day work week during the summer term, furloughs, hiring freezes, eliminating budget line items, and layoffs. As an immediate step, I eliminated raises for the executive staff and declined a raise of my own salary. I presented these cost-saving measures to the Board of Trustee's Personnel Committee Chair. The Chair of the Board of Trustees responded to my concerns on improving coordination of operations and agreed to the appointment of a Senior Vice President of Operations. We selected an individual who had worked as an administrator with my predecessor, and had held a variety of senior-level assignments during my tenure. Beginning in the fall of 2001, the Vice President of Fiscal Affairs and Director of Student Financial Aid, as well other phases of operations would report to him.

"Be careful what you wish for" was all I could think of when I was apprised of the report on the numbers of students who had listed Morris Brown College as their first choice. The diligence of recruitment initiatives by the Offices of Admissions and Alumni Affairs, as well as reports of our successes in improving retention and graduation, and establishing a wireless campus contributed to an unexpected surge in actual number of students who entered in the fall of 2001. I presented the dilemma to the Board of Trustees. We had hoped that the college would meet its target of 2000 students. The Chair of the Trustees made the decision to admit 200 more students and put the college in the position of having to provide services for students beyond the number projected in our budget. This approval resulted in the need to lease space to house students off campus, the planning for the construction of new residence halls and to provide spending plans to be monitored by the finance committee of the Board..

Additional students stressed our resources. Fiscal problems of the college were evident. In a visit to the campus cafeteria, I saw bins overflowing with garbage. After putting in a call to the head of facilities I learned that the college had not been able to pay to have its garbage picked up and had no working vehicle on campus to remove the trash. I requested a solution and was advised that a used vehicle could be acquired for $2,000. In response I wrote a personal check for $2,000 to pay for the truck. The garbage was removed and the Office of Facilities had a vehicle to improve waste management.

Matters got worse when I received a call from our SACS consultant that the college had not paid its dues of $4,200.00 to the accreditation agency. The bill had come to the president's office and been forwarded to fiscal affairs for handling. In response, the Vice President of Fiscal Affairs advised me that "she had too much on her plate," to handle the matter. I in turn demanded that fiscal affairs meet this outstanding obligation.

I sensed that things were breaking down when the Office of Fiscal Affairs began referring vendors to my office to resolve payment issue. While fiscal affairs was now reporting to the Senior Vice President of Operations, they wanted assurances from the President that payment would be made before they provided critical services to the college; for example, maintenance of the elevator in Fountain Hall. Without elevator service, students with disabilities could not make it to their classes.

On September 10th, the college received a letter from the Department of Education (DOE) pertaining to the seriousness of the problems in the management of student financial aid. The executive staff was called together to review the letter and develop steps for a response to concerns raised by the Department of Education. I pointed out that the letter needed to be treated as a confidential document because the DOE had raised, what I viewed might be construed as disparaging comments about the college's external auditor. After consultation with the Chairman of the Board of Trustees the college engaged an outside consultant to assist us in developing a corrective plan to respond to concerns raised by the DOE on the management of student financial aid in the Offices of Fiscal Affairs and Student Financial Aid. The consultant would review procedures in the offices involved in the management of student financial aid, bring all parties around the table to hold workshops, and develop a plan for the management of student financial aid for submission to DOE no later than March 2002.

When I learned that the DOE letter of September 10 had been given to the college's external auditors, I called a meeting of the executive staff and questioned how the information might have gotten into the hands of our auditors. I added that in checking with DOE, I was advised that it was not their intention that we provide the confidential letter of September 10th to the auditors who were conducting an independent review of the management of student financial. No one on the team admitted to having provided communication from DOE to the auditors. On the following day, it was determined that the Vice President of Fiscal Affairs had not been forthcoming and had, without my approval, taken matters into her own hands and transmitted the confidential letter to the college's external auditors. The disturbing questions I had were: 'why did the Vice President of Fiscal Affairs resort to insubordination?' and 'why had she lied about the matter in the executive staff meeting?' She answered by telling me of her responsibility to turn over all documents to the external auditor including DOE communication on student financial aid.

The Vice President of Fiscal Affairs worked closely with the Director of Student Financial Aid in the management of student financial aid. She relied on the Office of Student Accounts, which reported to her, for information on students verified as enrolled before any funds could be disbursed. In the turn of events, the Vice President of Fiscal Affairs appeared to be distancing herself from her role in making decisions about the management of student financial aid funds.

Following the September 10th notification to the college, DOE staff appeared on campus to talk to managers and staff in the offices of the Vice President of Fiscal Affairs and Director of Student Financial Aid respectively, about their responsibilities in the management of student financial aid. The two departments provided checks and balances in documenting student eligibility, receiving and disbursing federal student financial aid dollars.

In the fall of 2001, tensions heightened as I began receiving calls directly from vendors for payment and deadlines loomed for the staff to complete reports to SACS for a reaccreditation hearing in December 2001. Discrepancies in reports led to contentious executive staff meetings. The meetings of the executive staff were adversarial and divided. I needed help sorting out our concerns so I engaged an experienced budget director to review fiscal affairs. While his confidential report highlighted some of the Vice President of Fiscal Affair's management strengths, it also pointed out some possible deceptive practices driven by, among other things, hostility toward me. It was clear to him that she was no friend of the president and had said on more than one occasion that "the president doesn't know anything about fiscal affairs."

I weighed his report in light of her having successfully implemented new processes that addressed outstanding audit findings and the long hours she and her staff spent working on a response to SACS. I anticipated a change in her responsibilities and the leadership of fiscal affairs.

ATTACK OF 9/11

On September 11th, news of the World Trade Center attack created chaos on the campus, especially for students from the New York City area who were understandably frightened at being unable to contact their families and wanted to return home. What affected one, affected all, and they expected the college and its president to have answers. When word reached me, I went to address the visibly upset students in the residence hall, shared what I knew from news reports and communicated the importance of their staying on campus and not attempting to get on the highways. I invited students from the New York City area to my office to attempt to contact their families and used the opportunity to restrain them from taking off in cars. Former U.S. Senator Carol Moseley Braun, then a visiting scholar at Morris Brown, joined me on campus. She and other faculty and staff worked to provide the New York City-based students more information. The Senator spoke from her experience as a former Ambassador and cautioned them to stay put. We acted as a family in crisis.

The World Trade Center bombing brought about changes in our national security and changes in our expectations on all fronts. At a time when the college needed outside support more than ever, the priorities of government agencies, out of necessity, shifted.

A KIND OF MUTINY

Even though steps had been taken to make changes in the management of student financial aid, the Vice President of Fiscal Affairs and the College Counsel took things a step further. They met with the Chairman of the Board of Trustees to express what they perceived as my blind loyalty to the Director of Student Financial Aid, my disregard for the hard work of members of the administrative team and flaws in my administrative style. The Chairman listened and referred them back to me.

In the meeting that followed they told me that they were responding to the Chairman's open door policy and didn't feel they had to advise me beforehand. I felt them back tracking as they underscored the Chairman's support for me. I listened knowing full well that they were not in my camp and were working on their own agenda.

The College Counsel was aware of the Trustees' decision to replace him with a Counsel reporting directly to them, which meant he would have to return to his faculty position. They were aware that I would be making changes in the executive staff as well. I did not confront them with my thoughts on what motivated them to go past me to the Chairman of the Board of Trustees. As I listened and observed them, I felt the depth of a divided executive team as the Vice President and College Counsel underscored their love for the college and their frustration at my "just not trusting" them to do their jobs. I also sensed that they viewed themselves as having the wherewithal to rescue the college from its president.

All this time, complaints from students were mounting. They ranged from complaints about problems with financial aid and on-campus housing, to alleged administrative abuse of student activity funds and perceptions of bloated administrative salaries.

There were also complaints about students. The Director of Residence Life advised us that there were some students living in dormitories and attending classes who had not enrolled. I learned that historically some of the students delayed completing the enrollment process to defer being billed. The depth of pre-existing problems continued to unfold. I set up an Enrollment Task Force, chaired by the Vice President of Student Affairs. I directed the Provost and Registrar to work with faculty and staff in identifying non-enrolled students who were attending classes and to get them to complete the enrollment process. I directed follow-up of concerns raised by the Director of Student Financial Aid regarding what he viewed as processing problems by staff in other offices. The offices of student financial aid, fiscal affairs, registrar, faculty in academic affairs, as well as residence life staff had to take steps to ensure that students completed the enrollment process.

There was also the problem of current students not meeting their financial obligation to the college. Millions of dollars were identified as owed to the college but uncollected from students who were in attendance. I was told that letters had not gone out to students because the college could not pay for postage; I directed payment for postage. A debt management process was set up and the word was out that students had to be in a payment plan before registering in the spring of 2002.

The SGA leaders who toured the campus with me in the fall of 1998 had graduated and moved on. Our enrollment had increased, as had impatience for change on the part of new student leaders. There were not enough gains visible. Student leaders knew that their predecessors had been involved in preparing the campus for a visitation by SACS and spearheading improvements in the condition of the campus. Yet there was more to be done beyond beautifying the campus. While the executive team was responding to requests from external auditors, preparing for more frequent Board of Trustee meetings, seeking solutions to fiscal issues as well as handling time pressures to get data to SACS, students sought greater involvement in the direction of the college and our decision making. Often there was a mere two weeks between meetings with the Trustees and various board committees. I also had my weekly meetings with the Board Chair. Talks were also underway to get support for a technology center on campus and new residence halls. Our achievements had raised student expectations for greater improvements in the quality of student life at Morris Brown College.

In the fall of 2001, the worsening dissatisfaction among the students became clear during a ceremony before the second-half of a football game at the football stadium. As I was speaking, officers from the student government association turned their backs to me. Initially, I was unaware of the affront as I proceeded with the welcome to the crowd, then I heard the jeering, but continued to speak. I was fazed, yet managed not to show it or respond.

I sensed a change of attitude on campus, when at an earlier student forum, student leaders assailed the administration. They laid out problems with their student financial aid, unfulfilled promises for additional student housing, and inadequate discretion by the Student Government Association (SGA) in use of student activity funds by the SGA. Students also expressed their displeasure with the hiring of, as they viewed it, "highly paid consultants." They presented details about administrative and executive matters that students would not, in most cases, be privy to. Student dissatisfaction and anger was mounting. It was no secret: if you want to take out President Cross, use the students. I sensed the meeting had been orchestrated by key members of my staff, given the tenor of the meeting and what had been obviously misconstrued to the students. I felt betrayed. Whoever had encouraged the students had identified my Achilles heel: losing the support of students. I was visibly shaken when I took my place in the front of the room. I faced the audience of close to 300 students, faculty and staff and did not respond to the anger in the room. I requested that the students remain in the room and meet with members of the executive team on specific concerns on student financial aid, student budgets and use of activity fees, housing and student services. I tried to convey a positive message of unity and convince them that this was not the time to turn on each other. Even so, as I returned from the meeting, I felt my spirits slump more as the Vice President of College Relations, confided that there were rumors that "confidence in the administration was eroding," and I was being viewed as not being true to my mantra: "Students Come First."

MILE 20

We were pressed by a deadline on November 7, 2001 to submit our report to the Southern Association of Schools and Colleges. I had contacted their office to receive two extensions. The Office of Fiscal Affairs was pushed to meet the third deadline. The Vice President of Fiscal Affairs worked until the last hour of the extension. The crunch was such that there was no opportunity for the Provost to review the final document. The driver sped to get to the office before it closed. It was heart-pounding. We anticipated that our having to develop a corrective plan for the Department of Education would be an issue. Within a few weeks we would learn of our accreditation status.

In late December 2001, the college was formally notified that we had successfully complied with 65 of the original 68 SACS findings and would be placed on Probation with Cause to address the remaining criteria for reaccreditation. I contacted the Associate Director of SACS. She reiterated the importance of the college having an interactive technology system and acknowledged the progress the college had made. The remaining recommendations were significant and related to areas such as strategic planning for fiscal viability as well as the management of student financial aid.

Faculty, staff and administrators in academic affairs had been on the frontline in responding to SACS findings for reaccreditation, responding to opportunities for faculty development and revising the faculty handbook. Dissatisfaction with the Provost and Vice President of Academic Affairs contributed to his receiving a faculty vote of no confidence. He agreed to step down from the post while remaining at the college as special assistant to me as we continued to document responses to outstanding SACS findings. I appointed the popular Dean of Faculty to his position. My decision to have her predecessor maintain a liaison role with the AUC Provosts was a deal breaker for her. She declined the job and I engaged an interim Vice President of Academic Affairs who had been Registrar.

She was a Morris Brown College alum. Her appointment was not well received.

We had to keep things on track. Changes were underway in academic affairs, fiscal affairs, student financial aid, facilities and in the counsel's office. The shifts, among other reasons, were in response to complaints, consultant reports, and our concerns for cost effectiveness. We had identified a new Director of Student Financial Aid who declined the position before her anticipated December 2001 start date. A second highly qualified candidate required time to transition to the position at Morris Brown.

The Board of Trustees was now holding meetings two and three times a month and I met weekly with our Chair. There was intense focus on our developing a spending plan that included meeting the laptop obligation. Increased efforts in fundraising and cost cutting were also presented to the Chair of the Trustees. With the new constraints on spending, rumors of layoffs, and additional organizational changes, campus discontentment continued. It was difficult to appear unruffled in the midst of it all. What the students failed to see was that change had to be made to improve the conditions that had prevented change in the past. To repeat an old saying, you can't make an omelet without breaking eggs, and the eggs were deeply entrenched beliefs and assumptions about Morris Brown. The omelet was the steps we had to take to complete the accreditation process and achieve some degree of financial solvency.

Before Christmas, I traveled to Rio Caliente to take a badly needed break. On a daily call to the office from Mexico, I was alarmed to learn from the college's counsel and registrar that the FBI had requested the names of all Morris Brown College students with Muslim surnames. I realized that in the aftermath of 9/11 the government had passed acts and new measures to uncover terrorists residing within the United States, and that a broad net was being cast. I regarded the request as outrageous and directed the counsel and registrar not to turn over names. I wanted to ensure that the students' civil rights were not being violated. There was intense discussion in the higher education community about this issue, and it would be weeks before I gave the go ahead to comply with the request. Nevertheless, I was on record for having initially opposed providing a list of names of Morris Brown College students with Muslim surnames.

In mid-January shortly after her dismissal, the Vice President of Fiscal Affairs returned to campus to vehemently vent her displeasure at the actions of my administration. She was given an opportunity to make a presentation at an impromptu faculty meeting convened by the faculty representative on the Board of Trustees. The agenda of the meeting was a secret and not shared with me. When the Provost and other key members of my executive staff arrived and were acknowledge as unwelcome guest to a meeting attended by approximately 40 members of the faculty, the dismissed Vice President of Fiscal Affairs alleged that a member of the executive staff with the same last name as mine was related to me, that her pay increase was hush money, that I had deducted the amount the college received from the sale of my autobiography as a personal tax deduction, that I had blocked her communication with DOE, that my loyalty to the Director of Student Financial Aid was at the heart of the complaints in his area, and that I had interfered with her doing her job as Vice President. There was no mention of the fact that her office, as well as the office of student financial aid reported to the Senior Vice President of Operations in the fall of 2001. I would learn much later, that prior to her dismissal, she had spent valuable work time behind the scenes campaigning for my dismissal as President, prior to her dismissal as chief fiscal officer. Her contemptibly unsavory allegations confused and destabilized a community already reeling from the disappointment of having just been placed on Probation with Cause by SACS. The spectacular nature of her assertions and charges only seemed to underscore the truth of an old saying—that destroyers often masquerade as moral sanctifiers, especially when covering their own insecurities and failures.

The emotional meeting led to a faculty vote of "No Confidence" for the president of the college.

News of the vote of No Confidence was circulated throughout the campus. When hearing the news of the vote, I realized that no matter how much I struggled to take the college forward, I could not survive a vote of no confidence without full Board support. At the same time, I could not let her allegations go unaddressed. I circulated a response to the faculty community that soundly refuted her allegations. Unbeknownst to me, the Trustees had received a letter from the Vice President of Fiscal Affairs that repeated the allegations she had made to faculty. It also underscored the view that problems in the management of student financial aid were attributable to my support of the Director of Student Financial Aid and an inadequate investment in a technology system. There was no mention of her responsibilities in the management of student financial aid and the checks and balances I had directed to ensure appropriate processes were followed before any funds from federal student aid were disbursed.

I had joined the college to provide experience and hope. While Morris Brown had not lost its accreditation and was given time to address the remaining 3 of 68 findings, I had failed to take the college to the distance. Dismissed, disgruntled and weary employees fed negative assumptions about my honorable intentions. Employees began to distrust me. I learned that distrust is a virus that needs very little to start spreading. Back stabbing and professional rivalries helped worsen an already tense and distrustful environment. I was viewed as the cause of all the distrust. I was viewed as the culprit. It became impossible for me to battle whispers among the campus community that were tantamount to the view that I had taken the college off course and was steering it toward a steep cliff with a sharp drop off.

On February 7, 2002, a Morris Brown trustee called me at home and urged me to step down: "It's not worth the fight," he said. On two prior occasions, I had written the Chair of the Trustees of my wish to step down as president on June 30, 2002, and urged the development of a plan of succession, yet each time I was asked to stay on and "fight the good fight." I yielded, venturing back into the fray. Yet this time, my gut told me it was the right time. I knew that our accreditation status, pressures to manage the six million dollar reported debt, and the view held by some, that our troubles should be attributed to the actions of the Trustees fractured my relationship with them. The board was prepared to ascribe all stewardship responsibilities to the president and were ready to accept my resignation.

At the board meeting on the following day, I addressed allegations made by the Vice President of Fiscal Affairs, related progress the college had made in responding to SACS findings, DOE issues, and reported on the work ahead for the college. I faced dispassionate faces and few questions. Dolores E. Cross had become the agenda. The board accepted my request for administrative leave to begin on February 8, 2002, with June 30, 2002, as my official resignation date. I could not go on. It was time to step down. In interviews with the press the Chair of the Trustee spoke of regretting my resignation. He mentioned as well that I had apprised him more than a year before of my intention to step down as president in 2002 and he had urged me to stay on. There was no inference, as would be presented in subsequent press reports that I had been "fired."

I contacted a former university president who had experienced an untimely departure, and sought advice on how to make a graceful exit. He suggested I make a list of "Lessons Learned" for sharing with my colleagues and added that I should keep it light. I couldn't bring humor to bear on the situation and came up with the following statement:

Lessons Learned

Learning is one of life's greatest gifts. Those individuals who manage to continue learning over the course of an entire lifetime are the most fortunate of all. Already a veteran president when I arrived at Morris Brown College, I learned more than I expected and, in some instances, more than I ever felt I wished to know. I could cite several cases in point:

- I learned that many quality academic programs and outstanding terminally degreed faculty populate historically black institutions, despite a history of severe resource limitation. While many Morris Brown faculty members could have achieved appointment in prominent, mainstream institutions, they chose to devote themselves to the success of Morris Brown College students.

- I learned that a THEM versus US (i.e., administration versus faculty) mentality that unfortunately existed at Morris Brown served to provide a fertile breeding ground for acts of deception and sabotage by disaffected faculty members and employees dismissed for cause.

- I learned that well meaning, but naïve Board of Trustee members fell short on due diligence by a blind acceptance of lurid allegations by disaffected faculty and dismissed administrators, ultimately endangering the entity they are entrusted to protect, as they give unwitting credence to those allegations.

- I learned that women presidents of HBCUs are held to performance and appearance standards not generally enforced upon their male counterparts.

- I learned that even when one takes great care not to become the agenda by planning a graceful departure from the presidency, one nonetheless becomes THE AGENDA, if the Trustee Board has not put in place a well-thought out plan for presidential succession.

- I learned that a rogue cry for leadership change in the absence of determining the validity sets the stage for failure.

- I learned that a history of long standing problems left unexamined can make fiscal (and other) crises at HBCUs almost impossible to comprehend when examined by the news media.

- I learned that relationships with federal and state agencies are tenuous at best, when there is a history of various problems, and that DOE operatives do not admit to making mistakes.

- I learned that Morris Brown College, in spite of malingering historical racial inequities, is a "best buy" alternative, rooted in the African Methodist Episcopal Church, that provides a welcoming extended family setting and a haven for intellectually "hungry souls" in search of a quality education contextualized in community service.

I resigned after being president for three and a half years. I was the fifth President of Morris Brown College in the space of almost 14 years. It didn't matter. As they had done almost half a dozen times in the past, the Trustees knew it simply was time for another change of the regime and Dolores E. Cross would just be a woman who failed to resuscitate this historically black college. My Senior Vice President of Operations was named interim President of Morris Brown College.

After my resignation, I left for California to attend a meeting of the American Council on Education. While away, my successor, who had never established a track record of relationships with the College's regulatory agencies and accrediting body, set as his first order of business the dismissal of all of the surviving members of the highly experienced executive team. This flew in the face of SACS' clearly articulated directives to the College to maintain a stable executive team. The loss of so much talent in such a brief span of time mortally wounded the College and crippled any chance it had to implement the debt reduction, and fiscal and financial aid reorganization plans put in place prior to my departure.

It didn't stop there. My desk and office were cleared out and my belongings packed. I returned from my trip to find boxes on the front porch of my home. I was later advised by a security guard that if I were to return to the college, he had been given an order to have me escorted off campus.

I was unsure of whether to laugh or cry. What was my successor afraid of? What harm would have come from my having the opportunity to retrieve my things? What message was being sent to the Atlanta community by these actions? I sought humor to dispel what I was feeling, and began imagining what if I had done something absurd and totally outrageous before leaving for my trip – something like storing a half-empty pint of Jack Daniels in my front file drawer or better yet several bottles and some breath mints? I had to make myself laugh to keep myself from crying.

I got a glimpse of where things were going when I received word that my successor lost no time in giving the impression that "President Cross had sat on her hands" and not acted assertively. My successor acted as if he could simply jump in at mile 20, pick up the finisher's medal, and declare he had what it took to go the distance. I thought of the lines from "H.M.S. Pinafore." He "polished up that handle so carefully. That now he is the Ruler of the Queen's Navee!" And where was I? On a lifeboat watching the ship sail on.

A Second Home

At pivotal points in my life I have withdrawn to a place I have come to view as my second home, a spa in Rio Caliente, Mexico.

I had been visiting Rio since 1994, most often with my daughter. From the moment the plane landed in Guadalajara, Mexico, until the cab took us to the desk at Rio Caliente Spa, we never heard more than a smattering of English. It was all, "Buenos Dias and welcome back, Senora Dolores and Senorita Jane."

The spa was an oasis. Flowers, bushes and trees flourished among guest quarters. Horses and donkeys moved through the grounds of the ranch-like atmosphere. While there were no TV's or telephones in guest rooms, there was the crackle of wood burning in the fireplace at night, and from my window I could see the sun rising over the mountains every morning.

The time away gave us both a chance to relax and just be.

I had visited the spa twice during my 40 months as President of Morris Brown College. As I turned up the path to the entrance, I caught a glimpse of the guest house where I had completed my autobiography, *Breaking Through the Wall: A Marathoner's Story.*

On this day, I arrived in time for the afternoon meal. It was the big meal of the day and followed by rest, relaxation and time for the guests to chat. I easily embraced the Mexican pace and felt quite relieved to have taken a week off to get some physical distance from professional matters of consequence and have time to catch up on friendships and even a little time for myself. Caroline, the owner, was one of the first to join me after lunch. An Englishwoman, she made Mexico her home after deciding not to complete a doctorate in sociology in London. Caroline was a year younger than I, and I was accustomed to referring to her as Lil' Sis. It had been close to a year since my last visit, and I was eager to hear more about how she was doing implementing programs to improve finances and prospects for her Mexican employees.

She spoke passionately of her concern for the workers who lived in villages close to the ranch; and it was not uncommon for grandparents, parents and children to be working together in a close-knit family of employees. Caroline had set up a pension plan for her employees, subsidized down-payments for many to purchase their first home and lent support and provided guidance to women who were victims of domestic violence. She was independent, feisty and didn't give a damn if her 'share the wealth' approach was viewed by some as socialist.

That afternoon, we talked about my resignation from Morris Brown College and my plans for moving ahead. In speaking with Caroline, I talked about hitting the wall in marathon terms (i.e., failed to check the course and missed opportunities to relate to the terrain). I told her of having imagined a field of marathoners with a shared vision of the finish line and what it would take to get there. I spoke of surging ahead without a full sense of where others were in the race."

Our conversation drifted into a discussion of our early experiences with individuals racially different from us. Caroline told me about her own challenges growing up as a child in World War II. "We'd been having such a hard time with the bombing," she said. "We weren't allowed to go into the underground shelters. As my mum said 'You will not bow your heads before an illicit tyrant and crawl underground like rats,' so that summer she took my brother and me to Cornwall, the deep south country of England, to spend a couple of weeks at a farm. On the way home, I had a memorable experience with the American troops who were just arriving to defend us. Our train stopped at Plymouth to pick up these young soldiers and sailors, and the rule was that they got to sit on the seats while we civilians stood in the corridors. The corridors filled, and we found ourselves standing in one of the carriages between two rows of seated, uniformed men. And suddenly this exquisitely beautiful man, his black skin shining in his white uniform, picked me up, put me on his lap and gave me hugs and candy. I hadn't yet heard about the kindness of strangers and could hardly believe the generosity. And it meant even more because I had an Afro doll I was very fond of, dressed in a lovely striped-colored waistcoat and shiny evening suit, who I had named Gentleman. And there began a lifetime of gratitude and friendship with other ethnicities. But I'll never forget that very special gentleman who cared for me on the long, long train ride back to London."

My own views of the war had been shaped by newsreels. I would watch the screen light up with a black-and-white newsreel. The music would blare as we'd see white male American troops dashing onto foreign shores, smiling, and appearing victorious. The newscaster's voice would rise as he spoke of our brave young fighting men on heroic missions abroad. There were occasionally clips of white women WAVES and WACS in crisp uniforms. These 'women are supporting the war effort.' But the newsreels never showed black men fighting or appearing resplendent in their uniforms. I felt that living a world away, in England, Caroline's image of Blacks in uniform was more positive than that of her white counterparts in my country.

I shared with Caroline how, at age six, I had been given instructions by my mother that should an air raid drill happen, my sister and I were to find shelter in a closet in the apartment. My mother's instructions included completing a list of chores while she worked long hours at a war plant, making munitions for troops engaged in World War II. One day I was given instructions by my mother to go to the corner store and purchase food for our lunch. Fearing an air raid drill, I wanted to move quickly. I ran down three flights out the court and down Orange Street to the corner store and purchased ten cents worth of baloney and a large fifteen-cent loaf of bread. I didn't have money and expected the store owner to bill us by listing 25 cents on a paper bag beneath my mother's name. My mother would have to stop by and pay the bill. I stood in the store and pointed to the baloney. I was a stutterer and the words wouldn't come out. Tears filled my eyes as I pointed to the baloney then to the bread. The burly white man at the meat counter had seen me before with my mother. He smiled broadly. "Don't worry," he said. "I understand. I have problems too: my English no good." I had heard these white store keepers speaking a language different from my own. I knew they were different in skin color and language. I felt only this immigrant's kindness. I told Caroline how I would come to think of that experience as "my moment on the train."

I went on to tell her of the opposite realization of kindness, when, at the age of eight, I traveled south to spend the summer with my Aunt Lucy in Raleigh, North Carolina. My uncle Noah, her husband, had taken my sister and me into a local grocery store. It was hot and I reached into the open freezer for an ice pop. Before I could touch it the white store owner yelled, "Nigger, get your hands out of that freezer!" His rage frightened me to tears. My uncle tensed and led us out of the store. Outside, he tried to calm me, saying that the man was ignorant, but I had seen the hatred in the man's eyes.

As Caroline and I talked, I thought it was probably unlikely that our mothers could have had a similar conversation. Yet, we had come together in the 1990s, friends from different countries and cultures, yet who could share experiences about compassion and race, experienced as children who grew up in the 1940s.

I thought of my experience teaching a class on "Multi-cultural Perspectives in Education." This was the single most important class in all of my time in higher education. I tried not to fill students' heads with "stuff" or polemic; instead, I wanted to open their eyes to seeing, feeling, understanding, and believing in the experiences of others, whether they were close or far-removed.

Thanks to talks with Caroline and Jane, and long walks in the desert, I left my retreat in Rio Caliente knowing I would move on and God willing return to my first love, teaching.

HYDE PARK AGAIN

When I returned to Atlanta, my family and friends urged me to "get out of Dodge," to move on. Yet leaving Atlanta was not an easy decision for me. I loved the house in Midtown Atlanta and hated to abandon all the improvements I had made to convert the space into a 'president's residence.' The location in central Atlanta allowed me to benefit from the presence of the Midtown community and to make excursions to nearby Piedmont Park. I'd envisioned a future with balmy evenings on the front porch swing, continued running in Piedmont Park, and the company of neighbors and my dear friend and housekeeper Ms. Wilhelmina.

I couldn't help feeling anxious about how my dog Cassie would fare dealing with elevators in Chicago and not being free to chase squirrels in the backyard. I had rescued Cassie, a mixture of sheep dog and border collie, at a local Petsmart. I called her bright and shining eyes "Bette Davis eyes." She barked in the open cage, and I decided on the spot to adopt her. She seldom barked after the rescue. Cassie was more of a companion than a pet or a protector. I learned this after an early morning break-in on the first floor, which resulted in stolen items from the kitchen counter as Cassie watched and perhaps greeted the intruder as one might a guest, without so much as a bark.

In June, I held a party for Johnnetta Cole to celebrate her move to the presidency of Bennett College, an all-women's HBCU in Greensboro, North Carolina. More than anyone, Johnnetta knew what I had been up against at Morris Brown. It would be the last event I'd give in the president's residence. The turnout of women friends was extraordinary. I was pleased to receive Coretta Scott King and Shirley Franklin who had announced her plans to run for Mayor of Atlanta, as well as close to 30 women and men from the civic and corporate leadership of Atlanta and a few colleagues from Morris Brown College.

I was thrilled that Coretta Scott King had joined the celebration. She wasted no time in taking me aside and telling me that her husband had not always been embraced by folks in Atlanta. Her comment added to my sense of having connected with some good women in Atlanta.

The gathering was a salute to Johnnetta and my farewell as well. In the guest book, Johnnetta wrote:

"Sister President, my dearest sister-friend, Dolores, as each of us 'gets out of Dodge,' let us pledge to stay in each other's lives. For surely, we must continue the very special sisterhood that we share."

Other women signed with words of encouragement:

"Dear Dolores, As much as I hate to lose you, I know that your next step will be extraordinary. I still am in awe of you as a runner, administrator, and phenomenal woman." "Fondly, Patty."

"Atlanta and Rotary will miss your upbeat attitude and your fabulous smile, along with all the energy and expertise you have brought to the community. We will be cheering you on as you continue on your running, winning way! Jean."

"Thank you, Dolores, for inspiring me to run. I, too, will run my first 5K when I am 50. It first dawned on me that I could do this when Johnnetta introduced you at Rotary. Do you know that when you address a crowd from the podium that you are absolutely angelic. Best wishes, Angel Dolores. Always, Astrid."

"Wow...I can't believe you are leaving but I am so glad we had this time together in Atlanta! Thank you for all you did for Morris Brown

College. Your leadership was very much needed and was very special. Love, Ingrid."

These women from Atlanta were heroes and friends. We had given each other lasting energy.

My friend Eunice Holder flew in from New York to help me organize for the move. Eunice had always been there as I moved along. She'd voiced concerns about the risks I took in responding to my passion to make a difference and was aware of the costs financially. She could sense the investment and was aware of my generosity. Eunice worried about the ease with which I seemed to give things away. She shook her head throughout the yard sale. "Dee, you're not selling this for enough" and at several points yanked back some items I'd put out for sale with "I'll take this," or "Dee, you are going to need this. I won't let you sell it." We laughed as she tugged items out of my hand and returned them to my closet.

Mary Hazel, a friend from Newark, New Jersey, visited to help me prepare for the move to Chicago. Mary had been proud of my taking jobs in the North and of my successes since leaving Newark's housing projects, yet she never understood my decision to accept the position at Morris Brown; and I was accustomed to the fact that she pulled no punches. In rapid fire, Mary let me know her views: "Dee, you never should have gone to Atlanta in the first place. These niggers don't understand, never will. We've gone backwards, not forward. It's not like it used to be. Folks just don't understand and these folks haven't been taught the way we were. It's a damned shame. After all you've done."

Mary would go one step further to tell me: "You were too nice to those people. You should have cussed them and showed them you were from Newark, New Jersey. That's your problem, Dolores, you're too nice and niggers don't appreciate it." Mary could hit hard and not miss a beat and used the "f" word like a chronic hiccup. I would imagine coming out with a more colorful response at staff meetings. There were times when listening to what seemed like endless whining about woes of the college, I visualized Mary standing at my side and urging me to blurt out, "Shut the hell up" or "Get your worn out butt out of my office" or "Are you talking to me, loser?" I got a laugh as I thought about what the reaction might be if I'd lost my mind and spoken in Mary's manner. While I would miss living in Atlanta, I was happy to have the support of friends, who, in Mary's words, wanted me: "To get my raggedy ass out of Dodge."

In July 2002, I returned to Chicago. My apartment was on the 21st floor of a building that faced Lake Michigan, the lakefront beaches and parks, all in walking distance to museums and the University of Chicago. People from diverse backgrounds enjoyed the unpretentious environment in that area of Chicago.

My friends James Willis, and Renee Williams, and her children Sara Jefferson and Salim Jefferson, were present in Chicago to assist me in my move-in to an apartment in Hyde Park. James had joined Renee and another friend, Marva Jolly in traveling to Atlanta for my Morris Brown College inauguration. Through thick and thin they had remained my friends. In 1995, Renee had presented me one of her finest paintings, titled 'Reconnections'. On the day of the "move", we with great care, placed the 3 ft. by 5 ft. artwork on the wall. I was reconnecting and acknowledging a need to connect with friends.

Home in Chicago, I would be a seven-hour drive from St. Paul, Minnesota, and my son, Tommy, his wife Patricia and my grandchild, Jackson Tucker Cross. Being Jackson's "Nana," was wonderful. I loved down-hill sledding, catching and chasing butterflies with him and watching Scooby-do for hours, things I missed or just didn't do with my own children. The best was hearing my grandson exclaim: "Nana, you're the best grandmother in the world" and believing it.

When I returned to Chicago, I made an appointment with my physician, Dr. Daniels, to follow up on the recommendation from my physician in Atlanta. An MRI scan confirmed I had likely had a series of minor mini-strokes months earlier.

To improve my health, I added alternative approaches to health issues and sought recommendations for an acupuncturist. My cousin, Francine, was quick to recommend an acupuncturist named Dr. Deng, in Lake Forest, Illinois. After making an appointment, I found Dr. Deng upbeat and positive as he provided dietary supplements for the brain and anti-aging. While the needles were used to balance my chi and energy, the sessions were meant to relieve stress and rejuvenate my body. I wanted to remain strong, improve my memory and enhance a sense of well being and harmony.

My plans included taking up running again and preparing for another marathon. The Lakefront would prove ideal for getting me running again. The running would also be good for Cassie. I had spent weeks getting my dog to adjust to the elevator. She was terrified of the box that took her up and down and would whine, vomit and look generally miserable. At one point I called my former neighbors Stacey and Tracy in Atlanta and inquired if they might adopt Cassie. They knew this was a tough call for me and were supportive. I cried for Cassie and for me. When people say "dogs don't understand," it is because they haven't owned one. After my tearful bout on the phone, Cassie began to simmer down. I provided a treat and she began to eat it and fix her eyes on me as we descended in the elevator. I laughed, hugged her and called Jane on my cell phone to communicate the good news. With Cassie at ease, I was really home.

Word of my resignation from the college led to my receiving offers to join education consulting firms, consider nominations for senior-level administrative positions and to participate on national educational panels. At the same time, I wanted the continued connection with students and opted to return to my first love, teaching. An opportunity came through after my call to the President of DePaul University in Chicago. He responded enthusiastically. I was interviewed and was offered a visiting scholar position in education. I liked the service mission of the University and the different pace. DePaul University's urban campus on the north side of Chicago was located a few blocks from the L-train. In driving to the campus I realized how infrequently I had seen the Lincoln Park area of Chicago. I could not help but wonder if students at DePaul ever traveled south past McCormick Center, let alone to the south side to Chicago State University.

My position at DePaul University entailed responsibility for coordinating the doctoral program in education and teaching a course called Perspectives of Multi-Cultural Education. I found that the approaches I had used in teaching a similar the course at Northwestern University some 20 years earlier would have to change. I found that student views about multi-cultural education were shaped by their experiences with people from different racial, cultural or linguistic backgrounds. Some had specific ideas about they might improve the interaction between various ethnic and cultural groups. My strategies required them to understand social, racial, and economic constraints faced by various groups and the fact that groups were not all equally oppressed. I would have them uncover the different situations faced by black males in this country, the issues Hispanic women faced, and discrimination experienced by women in the workforce. Some students in the class expressed a desire to expand our discussions and include issues faced by groups such as gays and the physically challenged. Student journals provided me with information about the impact this approach had on them.

In response to a student's questions about my travels to South Africa and policies in the United States, I read excerpts from my April 16, 1996 presentation before the Chicago Council on Foreign Relations:

"My first visit to the University of the North in South Africa was a reminder of how, by permitting a level of mediocrity, by failing to create viable opportunities for the poor and underserved minorities, we serve our own apartheid. The experience had a powerful impact on me because it made me realize not only what was at stake for the University of the North, but it deepened my sensitivity to what's at stake at other urban colleges and universities in the state and nation......Just as we are concerned about South Africa, we must also be vigilant about policies here. The chipping away at affirmative action, unemployment, health care, and urban higher education are symptoms of a larger illness. They represent a retreat from the belief in a level playing field."

"We are seeing it daily, the move to cut back on safety nets, for example, to close college doors to high risk students, a general backing off from the ideals of access and equity that have guided higher education for two decades......Whom are we to penalize if persistence falls short, if retention is not where it should be? The student is an easy target. Or how about the schools, institutions that seek to serve underprepared students, that unashamed and courageously continue to struggle to address the needs of urban students and communities. I submit that we look not where to place blame but rather where support can be garnered."

"We and our students need the support of business, of government, of people who make higher education policy. We need them to support and help us fight the pressure to pull back. We need them to help us continue to change urban higher education in a positive way. We must come together in our priorities...Hope is an expectation and a desire felt with confidence and trust. The expectation and desire to create hope, develop from a vision or dream that one or many have —something to be that isn't. That "something" might be equal access to a quality and affordable higher education."

In reading this and other excerpts from my writings and those of scholars, I heard the voice I had used before colleagues in higher education associations, before legislators at the State and national levels, and before audiences in the wider community. I was happy, moving on and doing what I loved best: teaching and relating to conditions facing poor underserved and disenfranchised students in our communities.

The interaction with students renewed my spirit. I was in a different administrative area and required to be hands-on in communicating with graduate students and faculty on program requirements for the doctorate in education. I was moving ahead in doing what I loved, yet continued to be dragged down by articles that spread misinformation and threatened the future of Morris Brown College and other struggling historically black colleges and universities.

In the past, I taken the responsibility of reacting to news commentary that promoted misinformation. In October, 2002, I captured my thoughts on the worsening crisis at Morris Brown College by submitting an article for the "Opinion" page of the Atlanta Journal Constitution:

"As I survey the response to the struggles of HBCUs, specifically Morris Brown College in Atlanta, I catch myself alternating between bemusement and dismay, not recognizing stories now emerging as being anything close to the image of institutions, upon which teams of administrators, faculty, students, alums, and Board of Trustees lavished their passion, vision, and energies."

"Reports of the $23 million debt now facing Morris Brown College seem to have created, even for some longtime supporters, a sadly premature rush to judgment. Some have questions how I could have presided over such an outcome. Was it a lapse in judgment or the breakdown of my moral compass that led an inveterate university president with many years of experience to deliver Morris Brown College, a revered, A.M.E. church-related institution, into such a low estate? What is clear is that it is time to paint the bigger picture of the contextual reality of making progress to achieve excellence while in the absence of a 'level playing field,' being accountable to federal and state regulators. This accountability extends across all facets of an institution's operations-educational programs, students and faculty performances, funding, fiscal efficiency, financial aid, physical facilities, and board of trustees' oversight. Historically Black institutions of learning have achieved heroic academic outcomes, despite inadequate funding, inadequate and aging physical facilities. They have reversed a century of compounded inadequacy. This circumstance brings into sharp focus the complex web of stresses that regulatory oversight imposes."

"The crux of Morris Brown College's dilemma lies in its ability to resolve in a compressed period of time what has taken decades upon decades of resource-starved circumstances to create. The heavy regulatory burden experienced by the college at this juncture only adds more layers of a daunting and onerous complexity on top of the culturally-evolving system that an HBCU already is. The $23 million debt now being reported reflects in large part the withholding of financial aid income by the U.S. Department of Education until the college undertakes an extensive effort to reconstruct student financial aid records and appeals to the Department for recovery. As a consequence, the college has not received millions in financial aid income that it would normally have collected."

"What's lost in the reports of Morris Brown College and other HBCUs is how closely these institutions work with the Department of Education officials to provide information to improve the processing of financial aid and, provide as well, information on how the process is often a barrier to receiving financial aid. Federal student financial aid was meant to remove cost as a barrier for eligible students, yet many of our institutions are pushed to the edge (as in the case of Morris Brown College) by delays in releasing funds. These delays arise in part by a misunderstanding of HBCUs and the vital role they play in closing the gap between the haves and the have-nots. Morris Brown College and many other HBCUs are tuition-driven and a vast majority of their students are eligible for financial aid. This unique class of institutions labors against the widespread illusion that America has by now achieved the free and just society, where all who have the potential and determination to earn a college degree can do so. They labor as well under the illusion that as a class of institutions they are not dispassionately affected by the current economic and political climate. And despite how well and how much these institutions work with federal officials to avoid sanctions when problems occur they are viewed as having brought it on themselves."

"While recognizing that those who report the news are constrained by both time and space requiring that they select only a minor fraction of what they have seen or heard for presentation, articles on Morris Brown College and other struggling Historically Black Colleges and Universities miss the point when they focus only on 'mismanagement' and fail to establish the credibility of these institutions. HBCUs create diversity where it counts; after graduation, their graduates either matriculate in the work place or at the nation's top graduate and professional schools. Enrolling only 16 percent of the nation's African-American students and comprising only 3 percent of the nation's 3,688 institutions of higher education, a mere 103 historically black institutions award over one-third of all African-American undergraduate degrees. They are also responsible for the bachelor's degree training of more than one-half of all African-Americans who earn doctorate degrees. HBCUs do this, in spite of the severe resource limitations under which they operate."

"These journalists and columnists miss the point as well when, as in the case of Morris Brown, they fail to point out all of the positive things the college achieved the past three years as it responded to recommendations for reaffirmation by the Southern Association of Schools and Colleges. As examples, the college responded to an outstanding financial aid audit which would have cost the college millions; retired a $4 million line of credit in 6 months; implemented a state of the art technology infrastructure (Y2K readiness); raised $6 million in restricted funds; improved student retention; instituted under-monitoring of the Department of Education, new processes in the fiscal and financial aid offices; improved faculty salaries; increased the number of tenured faculty; implemented a year-round pre-college program; established in partnership with the City of Atlanta a community cyber lab; and satisfied 65 of 68 recommendations of the Southern Association of Colleges and Schools (SACS) for reaffirmation."

"Given these achievements, I am confident that Morris Brown College can address issues remaining for reaffirmation and successfully undertake a reconstruction of files and an appeal for the recovery of student financial aid dollars."

"At the end of the day, those who report the news have to be able to look in the mirror and know the very process of selection on what to report can transform what appear to be facts into an interpretation of reality that may or may not catch the essence of events or situations." Dolores E. Cross

The Atlanta Journal Constitution (AJC) was interested in hearing more from me. I took their bait and responded to a request for a profile article. When the reporter and cameraman arrived, I was candid in saying Morris Brown had much to be proud of and deserved to survive. In the space of an hour, I shared what the college had achieved in addressing long-standing problems, satisfying 65 of 68 reaccreditation findings, as well as taking administrative actions to rectify issues in the management of student financial aid and fiscal affairs.

Following the interview by the AJC, I was dismayed when an article appeared which was titled "Cross and Singh as key in the Morris Brown College debacle." The article referred to my having waited too long to "fire" the Director of Student Financial Aid and Vice President of Fiscal Affairs.

The former Director of Student Financial Aid called me at home to challenge the fact that I had announced his replacement as tantamount to being fired. He continued with how the article was negatively impacting his success in a new position in California. The former Vice President of Fiscal Affairs immediately went on the offensive, repeating to CNN in Atlanta the allegations she had made to the faculty. She focused on what she viewed as my lavish lifestyle. CNN was not made aware of the anonymous grant that supported my compensation or the extent of my financial contributions to the college. There was also the implication that I was involved in an illegal draw-down of 8 million dollars in student financial aid funds to the college. I was devastated, but later relieved when a reporter from the New York Times said he would investigate and set the record straight. The Times reporter interviewed individuals at the Georgia Finance Authority and determined that, as president, I had not ordered a draw-down of eight million. The funds had been electronically transferred to the college based on a review of the fall 2001 files. The correction took a small space in the New York Times, yet a big place in my heart. I felt hope and gratitude that the Times had gone beyond conventional reporting in their investigation and the issuance of a correction.

After what was my only interview with the press in October 2002, I understood that reporters may see their job as simplifying complex issues and in doing so mislead by omission and misinformation. My vision for underserved students would be viewed as lofty and ambitious. Moreover, the fiscal condition of the college and problems that preceded me would be dismissed and trivialized. Reports about me were also happening in a post-9/11 environment of duplicity and deception. I happened to be at Morris Brown College at the wrong time.

After reading the article that followed my interview with the AJC reporter, I thought the betrayals and grief accompanying the swirling political maelstroms had created in the news media an over-emphasis or spin that would—incredible as it may seem----ensnare me the looming crisis at Morris Brown College, as well as threaten the dismissal of civil action suits brought against me by the former Vice President of Fiscal Affairs and the former Executive Vice President of Facilities.

I was further unsettled when I learned of attempts to serve me with papers at my apartment in Chicago. I would leave my apartment building, looking over my shoulder, and avoid cars that seemed to be idling in front of the building. I was terrified at the prospect of being stopped at home or the university and being served with documents. On Jane's advice, I contacted Atlanta attorney, Randy Gepp whom I had retained to handle Civil Action Lawsuits. Randy was familiar with Morris Brown College and there was mutual respect between us. I arranged for him to receive any official documents on my behalf.

Yet it didn't alter the reality of my being pursued.

Inauguration at Morris Brown

Dr. Johnnetta Cole, Inaugural Speaker at Morris Brown College, gives my cap an 'attitude' tilt.

Ted Turner, speaker at Morris Brown College Graduation in May 1999 is presented an honorary degree by Dolores Cross as Provost Grant Venerable observes.

Michael Bivens of CocaCola presents a check of $300,000 to support
Morris Brown College's pre-college program

Lighting a candle in Bethlehem,
Israel on June 29, 2000, the day my
grandson Jackson was born

Finisher's photo for my 20th marathon
in Oct. 2000 (Chicago)

Jackson age 3 months and I

A photo opportunity with Oprah Winfrey during a reception at
an awards benefit in Atlanta, GA.

Tom Joyner with me during his January
2001, month long campaign to raise
scholarship funds for Morris Brown
College students.

Bill Cosby and I at 2001
graduation at MBC

Jane, Jackson and Tom Jr. in 2003

Jackson, age 4, giving a big hug to his Nana.

Clinton McRae and Jean McRae

Chapter 4

In the summer of 2004, I was stunned to receive a phone call from a representative of the United States Office of the Inspector General requesting that I go to their office on Court Street in downtown Chicago to be fingerprinted and to provide writing samples. It was a brutal wake-up call and an alarming signal that efforts were underway to implicate me in a Grand Jury Investigation of criminal wrongdoing at Morris Brown College.

On the day of the appointment, I arrived early at the federal building and was met by a representative of the office of the Inspector General who escorted me to a room where I was fingerprinted. Then I was led into another small room where I was seated and directed to repeatedly write out my name, phrases and the names of other individuals employed at the college. The process went on for an hour. At the end of the session I was drained. Sweat dampened my body. I felt incomplete at not knowing the reason for the strange requests -- and where things were leading. I felt sweat as it dripped and dampened my jacket and armpits. I had been given instructions by my attorney not to answer questions, yet I wanted to raise questions of my own.

Soon, I learned that colleagues and friends were being called to testify before the Grand Jury in Atlanta. The former Vice President of College Relations at Morris Brown had been awakened before sunrise by spotlights on her home outside Atlanta. Her children had been frightened. With the last name of Cross, she and her husband had been subjected to intense questioning about their relationship to me. The situation was bizarre. Cross was my married name and my ex-husband had been adopted.

A close friend, James, had responded to banging on the door in his Chicago apartment, to find an agent from the Inspector General's Office ready to serve him a subpoena to testify before the Grand Jury in Atlanta. James had merely traveled to Atlanta to visit me and participate in events at the college. It was devastating to sense his tension and concern as he made plans to comply with the order.

A consultant to the college who had been interviewed at great length shared that the FBI interviewers compared the situation at Morris Brown to that of "Enron" and how in doing so they were attempting to coerce her with a scenario they had created.

In late October, a contingent of more than a dozen individuals representing the Office of the Inspector General, United States Attorney's Office and the Federal Bureau of Investigation faced my attorney Drew Findling, and forensic investigator, Joe Pagani in the Atlanta Courthouse on Spring Street. Drew and Joe were there to present information that would, I hoped, persuade the representatives of the United States Attorney's offices not to move forward with an indictment.

Drew was direct in asking, "What would motivate Dr. Cross to commit crimes?"

The room was stilled when a black female FBI agent blurted, "Her ego!"

Six weeks later, on December 2, 2004, the decision was made to indict me for crimes against the government. The decision came without my having ever been personally interviewed by the FBI, the Office of the Inspector General, the Grand Jury or Assistant U.S. Attorneys. The 36-page indictment stated that I was co-defendant with the Director of Student Financial Aid and had knowingly and willfully embezzled, stolen and obtained by fraud, false statement and forgery, funds and property provided and insured by the Department of Education under Title IV, that is, loans for ineligible students.

The report concluded "...defendant Dolores Evelyn Cross was an organizer, leader, manager and supervisor in the criminal activity."

Standing in my apartment staring at the 36 pages being sent to me by fax, I scanned the seemingly endless indictment as it emerged from the fax machine. I felt disoriented and overwhelmed as though the accusations concerned another person with the same name as mine. I paced the apartment and settled in a chair near the window. I sought calm as I gazed at Lake Michigan. The lake had not frozen and the dashing of the waves reminded me of the realm of things out of one's control. I would have to surrender control to a defense team and a supreme being. I could not play attorney and I could not play God.

I was haunted by the FBI agent's response to the query on my motivation for committing criminal acts.…..acts which would put black students in harm's way. With abandon she had raised her voice to exclaim: "It was her ego!" It was disturbing to know that these words came from a black woman. With sadness I realized that the FBI agent and the attorneys for the prosecution knew nothing about me.

December 14, 2004 was set for my indictment. My attorney Drew Findling had seen it coming as investigations ensued and the Atlanta Journal Constitution had rushed to implicate me in the college's demise as early as October 2002. Drew felt as well that the U.S. Attorney in the Northern District of Georgia seemed intent on persuading the media and the public that as president of the college, Dolores E. Cross had orchestrated illegal activities in the day-to-day operations of financial aid in the Offices of Fiscal Affairs and Student Financial Aid. I learned that the U.S. Attorney was a George W. Bush appointee and had heard that his appointee had never tried a case.

I was terrified of the unknown, unpredictable, and foreign terrain before me. Through e-mails and phone calls I struggled to put the pieces together. Drew's candor, energy and sense of humor relieved the tension. We could talk with pride about our roles as parents, politics and my views on education, as well as his New York roots. I recalled seeing him on Fox News providing liberal commentary on legal issues. He came across as quick, feisty and well-informed. He communicated impressions he had gained from reading my autobiography, "Breaking through the Wall, A Marathoner's Story." In turn, I retraced experiences at Morris Brown College by referring to having assumed the presidency at a time when the college was pressed to respond to criteria for its accreditation, government mandates, outstanding audits, as well as strategic planning. Drew listened and made it clear that given his read of the environment the odds were that I would be indicted. He added that the attorneys for the prosecution were not skilled in the complexities of higher education. Further, it was not about truth. It was about winning. His response was sobering and I was pleased that we had engaged Joe Pagani, a well-known and respected forensic investigator to review my financial records and statements and court documents.

What was driving the indictment? How and why had I become the target of the Grand Jury investigation, indictment and media reports? It didn't make any sense. The DOE had full access to employees at the college and had not reported to me or the Board of Trustees any suspicion of criminal activity. The college's external auditors who reviewed the Offices of Fiscal Affairs and Student Financial Aid met independently with the Trustees and submitted their findings to SACS with no indication of fraud.

I was taken aback when a colleague repeated a rumor of the AME Bishop, Chair of the MBC Trustees, having strong connections with the George W. Bush Administration and that the Board appeared to want to keep any perception of wrongdoing focused on Dolores Cross. He added that the Board had resolved its problems in the past by throwing presidents to the wolves. Those close to Morris Brown College knew that I had relied on subordinates to carry out the day-to-day tasks in the management of federal funds and that I had provided open access to DOE staff and our external auditors to uncover problems for their reports to the college.

The impact of indictment of the president of the college on students was the greatest tragedy. Their college careers would be interrupted and a swarm of negative attention attending the indictment would denigrate the college's heroic efforts and its message of hope. I knew that I would have to remain focused to fight the invisible force that seemed to have filled my life and now would not go away.

In phone calls, Drew heard in my voice that I was devastated by the onslaught of horrific and frightening charges. He gave me the okay to fax a copy of the indictment to Jane who was vacationing at the Spa in Rio Caliente, Mexico. As her Christmas gift to me, my daughter had bought me a plane ticket to Rio Caliente; and I planned to meet her there on December 15. Drew advised that Jane should not travel to Atlanta, but that he would request the court to permit me to travel to Mexico after the indictment proceedings. I was elated, for Jane counted on my being given permission to take the scheduled trip. I knew I needed distance and the support of friends in Rio Caliente.

As Drew had cautioned me not to discuss the case and make myself vulnerable to charges of obstructing the process, I discretely avoided talking about the legal events looming over my life. My cousin Francine, James and I, arrived to meet with Drew and Joe on the morning of December 14th. We gathered around Drew's conference table in his office in the Buckhead section of Atlanta. The meeting provided an opportunity for Drew and Joe to discuss logistics for the day.

We then had to wait for hours as Drew negotiated my not being handcuffed at my appearance in court. The possibility of being brought in wearing manacles was humiliating and yet another slap to my senses.

Drew continued discussing the sequence of events from the moment of my arrival at the court in downtown Atlanta, to what I should expect in the courtroom, and the subsequent process of being fingerprinted, photographed and interviewed by a pre-trial officer. The situation sounded surreal.

We left his office at 1 p.m. for the 30 minute drive to the courthouse on Spring Street in Atlanta

Despite the briefing in Drew's Office I was not prepared for the crowd at the courthouse, the stares and comments announcing my arrival. Some of the faces were expressionless and others clearly showed hostility. I was focused on getting inside and was comforted by the presence of Francine and James, Drew and Joe. I felt the intensity surrounding my presence as we passed through the lower level of the Federal Building to the elevator. People in the courthouse were gaping as we passed through the gray marble lobby to the elevator. Two former Morris Brown employees pushed in to join us on the elevator. I acknowledged their presence and faced ahead. There was no indication that they were present to give me support. I recalled that they had not received favorable evaluations from their supervisors and had been long-time employees at the college. I surmised that they had come to see "Cross take the heat."

As I moved on to the courtroom, Drew pointed out three attorneys from the United States Attorney's Office in the Northern District of Georgia assigned to represent the prosecution. The two females and one male were white, attractive and appeared to be in their mid-forties. I waited as Drew went to greet them. Returning, Drew led me inside the austere and somber courtroom, where I heard the buzz of chatter as I moved to a table on the left, facing the raised lectern where the judge would sit. Hearing voices, I turned and noticed the co-defendant, the Director of Student Financial Aid, sitting with his wife and two defense attorneys in the row behind me. Drew sat on my right. The three U.S. attorneys moved to the table across from Drew.

Abruptly, the bailiff appeared, saying, "All rise, Judge Julia Carnes presiding."

As we rose, Judge Carnes entered the courtroom. I judged her to be in her early 50s. From searching the internet I had learned that she'd been appointed by the first President Bush. She had a slim frame, stood approximately 5'5," had short blond hair, a soft voice, and projected an unassuming professional presence.

I felt my stomach constrict as she dispassionately read the government's allegations against me, the President of Morris Brown College, as co-defendant with the college's Director of Student Financial Aid. I was being charged with conspiracy to commit fraud, the embezzlement of student financial funds and concealing information from the college's Board of Trustees.

As she continued reciting the list of charges, I found myself drifting off to recall the words of a spiritual we'd sung in my grandfather's church: "Precious Lord, take my hand, lead me on…." The situation was out of my control and I had to trust I would somehow find my way back to the life that had been mine until now.

I was numb yet attentive as we listened to the judge's pronouncement of a bond and a ruling that I would have to surrender my passport, plus pay a special assessment. I would be referred to pre-trial offices for monitoring and periodic urine and drug tests, while I awaited trial. I would not be permitted to travel out of the Northern District of Illinois without approval from my pre-trial officer.

Drew went up to the dais to plead for me to keep my passport. Minutes later, an agreement was reached to permit me to join Jane for planned travel in Mexico and for me to surrender my passport when I returned after a seven-day stay. When agreements were reached on all points, I was required to sign certain necessary forms. As quickly as it started, the session was adjourned.

The attorneys on both sides seemed relieved in having gotten through this first step. I glanced at the U.S. Attorneys to my right, then giving in to an impulse; I approached a lead attorney for the prosecution and surprised her by reaching out to shake hands. Things had gotten this far and she had not ever met me. I was saddened when she looked away without a word.

The meeting in the courtroom had taken less than 45 minutes. Almost immediately, I was introduced to the intake process of the criminal justice system. I was interviewed by the pre-trial officer in the courthouse. She verified my address, raised questions about my physical condition and requested the names and addresses of family members. I was then escorted to another floor to be photographed again. We were buzzed in to an area that had a jail-like appearance. I filled out forms and provided information on everything from my driver's license, to the car I owned, and my weight and height. Then I was photographed face front, then right and left sides. Once the forms were completed, I sensed I had crossed into the criminal justice system.

Outside the courthouse, the media was in full force as photographers angled for a view of me leaving the courthouse. Pausing on the steps, Drew read a brief statement stating that the facts would exonerate me. I stood tall and avoided questions as we moved to a waiting car. As we drove away from the courthouse, I didn't cry. I didn't feel the attention had much to do with who I was, my life, or the true circumstances of what had occurred at Morris Brown College. It was a hard, cold introduction to stepping into the line of fire of the media.

I later learned that while Drew was giving his statement to the press, the U.S. Attorney in the Northern District of Georgia was announcing an 800 number for Morris Brown students to call for assistance with their financial aid. The reporters were caught up in the fact that the former President of Morris Brown College was co-defendant with the college's Director of Student Financial Aid and had been charged with conspiracy to commit fraud in the management of student financial aid. I was the target of the media reports. The reporters and photographers were in search of a story, headline and something topical to serve up for the evening news. Getting a photo and sound bite were all that mattered. The possibility of feeding the flames of rumor and false accusations didn't matter.

I was in the grips of the prosecution, the press and public perception of a villain. Did the truth matter?

My son called that evening. Tommy had been wrestling with questions of what had happened to me. He reminded me of a conversation that he and his sister had some years back when he recalled that I had made numerous appearances before Congress to testify on the importance of financial and program support for low-income students. And that I had, as Vice Chancellor of CUNY circulated my opposition to competency testing in the absence of equity in school funding.

To my son's thinking, I had raised my profile then and raised the likelihood of "being taken out by people who I had made uncomfortable." I knew, however, that I was not alone in promoting programs for low-income and high-risk students. Yet no matter how certain Tommy was that I had been set up for "coming from the North and making too big a name of myself," I refused to believe that a connection existed between my advocacy and my having been indicted for crimes harming students, let alone any crime.

118

The indictment had happened and I felt myself shutting down. A lifetime of words to convey who I was, to express my values and intentions throughout my life, no longer seemed to matter. The accelerating pace of my situation was terrifying. I still couldn't accept that I was charged with having committed crimes. After the indictment, I traveled back to Chicago. No sooner was I at home in Chicago than I began to experience the onslaught of professional and personal "disconnection."

It was clear to me that professional distancing had taken place when the President of Chicago State University denied access to an NBC affiliate looking for footage of a Chicago State interview with me they had completed as part of a Public Broadcasting System (PBS) documentary on my mentor, Dr. Peter Drucker. I was furious, yet got the message: connections forged would be severed and my past service would be invisible or disregarded.

Given the response at Chicago State University, I should not have been surprised when reporters interviewed a faculty leader from CSU who discredited my leadership at the university and scoffed at the notion of improvements under my administration. Of course I was angry at what he said about me, but more so for his debasing what faculty, staff, the community and students had achieved during my tenure.

While there were takers for my "tar and feathering", the press was not interested in the 'opinion' submitted for publication by Morris Brown College's former Provost and Vice President of Academic Affairs in which he equated my predicament with that of a "lynching." He wrote:

"Lynchings were always the result of a public need for a scapegoat to fulfill a deep, unconscious need for blood sacrifice and revenge for actual heinous crimes for which there is no easily identifiable explanation or culprit. But the driving force behind a lynching is an attractive member of a disliked group as sacrificial victim. And whether or not that individual truly committed the crime is irrelevant, if it is believed that the sacrifice will impart to the people a kind of temporary sense of relief and redemption. Plus, a good, dramatic lynching—especially by fire—provides a major source of entertainment and community bonding that nothing else will. The ideal sacrificial lamb is a high-profile leader, and the more intelligent, powerful, or glamorous, the better in terms of relieving the collective grief and guilt felt by classes of human beings besieged by the storm-tossed seas of life. The central figure in Christianity was the most famous scapegoat in all of history. Atlanta's own Rev. Dr. Martin Luther King, Jr. gave his life in the title role of scapegoat for the Civil Rights Movement. Government, as local sheriff or in the present case, the U.S. Attorney, faithfully acts to place its stamp of approval upon popular lynchings—as FBI Director Hoover did with his unseemly, public persecution of Rev. King, as U.S. Special Prosecutor Kenneth Starr did in his unseemly assault on President Clinton in what began as simply the White Water case; and as the news media did in its Yankee-rooted ridicule of President Carter for his down-home Georgia honesty."

"Now comes the U.S. Attorney for Northern Georgia and a viciously unfair, even un-American, revisionist interpretation of everything that the Cross Administration stood for—as a way of condemning a national champion of the right of poor black youngsters to attend college, who would otherwise have no opportunity to attend. Short of taking the stand to personally rebut every single facet of a cleverly worded, if incoherent, indictment (someone should nominate it for a Pulitzer best work of fiction)—I can only ask: 'Where in the **** did he get his information?'"

"Certainly not from me or anyone else legitimately in the know—but clearly from someone who had an axe to grind about the changes that the College had to make in order to survive. And folks were readily available and lustily preyed upon by the "esteemed hometown boy" who grew up to become U.S. Attorney, so that they could air their gripes. And he could put another feather in his cap, this time for being the first member of his boss John Ashcroft's inner circle to boast that he brought down a (former) college president. That tells this career scientist that real, self-critical fact-finding was far from the agenda at hand—and that the staging of a lynching was the priority du jour. Furthermore, an African-American constituency was to be delivered to him and his political handlers by his painting himself as the new champion of black youths victimized by members of their own race. Just call my 800 number!"

Former Provost, Morris Brown College

I had caught a glimpse of the U.S. Attorney of the Northern District of Georgia at the indictment and envisioned students looking to him for help in dealing with a situation that they felt I had caused. In his appeal to students to call his 800 number, I heard the cry of "hang Dolores Cross."

I was anxious, sad, engulfed in an onslaught of events. Years earlier a colleague had commented that I operated as though I had no fear. He was referring to my dealing with resilience in my pursuit of legislation to assist part-time students. I had also held several administrative positions in areas dominated by white males and was successful in persuading predominantly white boards of directors to undertake research to uncover inequities for women and minorities. He viewed me as having equipped myself with values, passion and an abiding propensity to believe in the power of "We shall overcome." It was different now. I was overtaken by feeling alone and abandoned. My resilience was increasingly compromised as I saw how I was being portrayed in the press. I was caught in a media maelstrom already judging me in the court of public opinion.

Chapter 5

Following the indictment, I received a call from the Dean of Education at DePaul University. She had been besieged by reporters from the Atlanta Journal Constitution who wanted to interview my students and to take photos of my office. She requested a meeting off-campus. I recalled meetings with her in her office in which she had expressed the support she felt for my presence on the faculty. She said that I had been helpful in her outreach for fundraising and participated in a variety of staff meetings.

When the indictment occurred, she had telephoned and read an inspirational verse from the Bible. It was different now. From the beginning of our off campus meeting, I saw in her demeanor a shift in her approach to the situation. She held her back straight, leaned slightly away and avoided looking directly at me. I listened carefully as she described the university's position. I observed a clearing of her throat, shift in her tone and body as she described what was best for me and the university. In the few days since the well publicized indictment, I had become familiar with gestures of "banishment" "aloofness," and "superiority." While swelling inside, I remained as regal as I could. The Dean had been in conversation with the president of DePaul University and the decision had been made to reassign my classes and terminate my relationship with the university. She added that it would be best if I cleared out my office over the weekend. I wanted to ask her if she thought that an "indictment was tantamount to a conviction?" It didn't matter. The university had acted as if it was. I thought of the graduate students whom I would miss motivating and learning from. Despite the ups and downs in the past two years, the classroom had been my world. I managed a smile when the Dean advised me that a young Hispanic woman whom I had worked with at Chicago State University and encouraged to go on for a doctorate would be replacing me in the classroom.

Taking my cue from DePaul's action, I resigned from the boards of the National Center for Public Policy in Education, Institute for International Education, Field Museum and the Board of Northern Trust. Feeling despondent, I knew I needed distance, so, with the approval of the court, I prepared to visit my daughter in Rio Caliente.

On December 22, 2004, I took a direct flight from Chicago Midway Airport to Guadalajara, Mexico, and arrived at Rio Caliente at midday, only five days behind Jane's arrival. When I emerged through Customs and headed to the exit, I saw Jane. She was carrying a large bouquet of flowers, smiling broadly and calling out, "Over here, Mom." It was a surprise. I was expecting to take a cab from the airport some 50 minutes to the spa. Caroline, the proprietor of the spa, had arranged for Jane and her driver to meet me.

During the ride back to the spa, Jane and I chatted about the guests at the ranch. Jane's Spanish was fluent and she and the driver conversed about spots she wanted to point out to me along the way. I had passed those places in the past yet I didn't know much about where the roads led or about the region. I felt less like a tourist and more in tune with a place I had referred to as my second home.

We turned off the highway onto the dirt road leading to Rio Caliente. I had taken the road before on morning hikes in the mountains that surround the spa. We approached a brightly painted entrance gate to the spa/ranch that was opened by a middle-aged Mexican man who, seeing us, waved and smiled broadly to greet a familiar returning guest.

As we proceeded toward the registration and dining area, I noted how little had changed. The grounds were immaculate, with blooming flowers and the areas around the single and adjoining guest quarters spotless and inviting. It was serene and soothing.

Caroline was waiting for us as we arrived at the small registration cabin. We had arrived at the ranch before the end of lunch. She was there to give me a hug and to accompany Jane and me to the dining room where I was greeted by broad smiles of familiar guests and friends who, like me, had spent holidays in Rio Caliente. I heard, "You were supposed to be here two days ago" and "Are you going to do the long hike tomorrow?" And "We have really enjoyed Jane and her wonderful sense of humor." Most guests knew me as a veteran marathoner who liked to hike, enjoy a good joke, and interview them. Although, to be honest with myself, I knew this trip wasn't so much about having fun as it was about regaining balance.

I felt a sense of peace in the room reserved for me near the steam room and soothing mineral pool. The space was light, airy, and cheery. There were floral prints on the wall and pottery vases and candles on the mantle above the wood burning fireplace. With the exception of Caroline and another friend, Sylvia, Jane had not shared the news of my indictment. I had met Sylvia, a black female executive leadership coach from Oakland, California during one of my many trips to Rio Caliente. She had been invited to lead periodic workshops at the spa, where she provided insights as guests sought to balance their personal life with professional demands. When I returned home from Mexico, I continued to communicate with Sylvia on subjects we had discussed during sessions at the ranch. Our conversations had helped me to move through the thicket of events involving Morris Brown.

On my first night, Sylvia and Jane joined me for a 'clearing ceremony' in my room. Together we meditated as Sylvia guided our focus to the strengths of our ancestors and honoring the gifts of endurance and clarity. Jane supplied music from her tape recorder and we joined hands dancing and singing. I was "in the moment" and had briefly detached from the arraignment in Atlanta a few days earlier.

Two days later, I was eager to join Jane, Sylvia, and other hikers for a slow, yet steady two-hour climb up the mountains. I had adjusted to the altitude and was ready for the gradual ascent. The terrain was rough and we needed hiking boots for our footing. Along the way we enjoyed festive flowers in a rustic setting amid streams of hot water flowing from the mountains. The conversation on the walk was about where we were in the calm of our getaway. We talked about the aspects of Rio Caliente that remained constant. It was unpretentious, relaxed and sort of spiritual. The food was great….mostly organic, always fresh and nutritional, as well as low fat. "You can always count on dropping a few pounds at Rio,"

As I walked along I realized I had come to Rio Caliente to dispel inside tears and replace them with smiles. I listened to my breath as I inhaled, held, and exhaled slowly. I felt my body relaxing and my feet gathering the energy of the earth beneath. The sun caressed my face and I was soaking in warmth where there had been cold.

With each step I felt the purpose of my life was to respond to my strengths and remain in touch with the lessons I was absorbing in Mexico.

Listening to my friends, I felt a smile filling my face. We helped each other up the mountain, pausing to check on the hikers bringing up the rear. The slow ones in the group realized they wouldn't be left behind as others cared about their making it to the top. It was the wisdom that guided my life and who I was; I sensed my endorphins accelerating as I moved back to encourage a slower hiker, then ran up again to find my place. I was guided by the heels of the hiker who walked ahead of me. I knew to look at the place where I would plant my foot. I was focused doing what I was prepared to do. I had found my center again. My confidence was kicking in and uncertainty lifted. The view from the summit was breathtaking. There were no villages in sight. We saw only treetops and roads in the distance where horses grazed. All around us was serene, and for a while there was no talking, just us listening to the birds and slight wind moving through the trees. I was gladdened by the silence, for I was surrounded by nature's perfection. I accepted what was there before me and remained aware of what I couldn't change. When we reached the top of the mountain, we gathered to look back and to marvel at the road that had taken us here. We considered the narrow path, rock-strewn road, and obstacles along the path down to the ranch. Someone called out "our heroes' journey" to which I smiled, yet thinking --- the journey is not yet over.

During the week's stay at Rio Caliente, I learned that I could be happy despite the dark clouds of events building in the distance. I would return home with new strength and focus.

Chapter 6

Returning to Chicago, I discovered my foes in Atlanta had not been idle. In conference calls, Jane and Tommy sensed the anxiety I was experiencing. There was no more joking or light talk about which path to take or even what lay ahead. I was distressed by the impact on them of what had occurred.

Jane was deliberate in responding to the crisis. She had many questions and wanted to get right to the point and get on with what I must do. She asked me, "Mom, what documents can you produce?" "How will you meet the costs of your defense?" "Who are your allies?" "Who gains by your indictment?" "Who wants to see you hurt?" "And why did they wait until now, after you resigned as president over two years ago, and then after serving three and a half years?" "How can we help you stay strong?" "How are you going to go about confronting your fear?" "What are you doing to get a handle on what went wrong at Morris Brown?" And finally, "Mom, you should know that when you elect to work against the odds for the public good in today's political climate, you risk becoming a target and in your case indicted for a crime. It is quite routine for someone who has achieved a high-profile and been an advocate for minorities and the down-trodden. Angela Davis, Shirley Chisholm and even Oprah have been under fire. I know it's not the same, but you must stay in touch with who you are and pull through."

My children clearly saw how the ordeal of the indictment had jarred me.

The energy was gone from my voice and body. I recalled people saying how when almost dying they saw their life float by. I felt the same way. Everything I had experienced began returning as memories. I was in the grips of the criminal justice system. I was reliving the past in the present. I tried to overcome insomnia by reliving the hope and happiness of early years, only to be interrupted by horrible nightmares of racing with no end or being assaulted by formless creatures in my sleep. Where would this journey lead me?

The ancestors were there to remind me how in 1986, a hundred years after my grandfather, Reverend Thomas T. Tucker traveled by foot from Virginia to New Jersey, I made the decision to run my first marathon in New York City. I came from a family of strong men and women who had figuratively completed marathons. As grandchildren of slaves my uncles and aunts established themselves as entrepreneurs, politicians, skilled laborers and community leaders. I would have to rerun their lives and mine to connect the dots of their moving from strength to strength. When in November 1986, I collected the NYC Marathon Finisher's rose and had the Finisher's medallion placed around my neck, I was feeling invincible; my mother, my children, my sister and her husband and their children greeted me at the finish line. They were also with me as I moved at marathon pace to higher education faculty and administrative positions in Michigan, Illinois, California, New York, Minnesota and Georgia.

Jane followed my path into education and became a Law Professor at Nova Southeastern Law School, in Ft. Lauderdale, Florida. She was also Director of their Caribbean Law Program, advisor to black law students, and the author of articles on legal writing, black bar exam pass-rate studies and gender issues.

Tommy followed his finely tuned ear to a career as a teacher of music. He majored in Music at California State University, Sonoma; and took part in Broadway musicals, tutored other students and played the saxophone and clarinet in local jazz groups. He began teaching in California and moved to Minnesota, where he become a band teacher at a predominantly minority high school. Tommy embraced life without prejudice in spite of subtle and not so subtle racism.

I thought of my children's unwavering strength in standing by me. When I made the decision to move to Atlanta, Tommy had been quick to say, "Mom, you've adjusted to working in higher education in five states in the U.S. and also consulted in South Africa. Mom, you'll have more of a black experience in Atlanta." From my son's perspective, I had signed up to lead a college with one of the best marching bands in the country. In his view "Music was the key to greatness" for a marathon in a different city.

When not visiting, I now communicated with them through conference calls. I heard Tommy's anger. His voice boomed as he expressed how difficult it was to try to do your best as a black educator. He pointed to his personal experience of receiving a three-day teaching suspension for loudly admonishing a white student for stealing a musical instrument. The student had admitted the theft, then, probably intimidated by Tom's loud voice and six-feet, four-inch-frame, complained to Tom's supervisor, who criticized Tom for confronting the student in front of other students in the class. Tom had been deemed the problem; and he felt that I, too, had been simplistically presented as the problem in a much larger situation.

Jane shared her alarm at how the U.S. Attorney in Georgia was inciting the situation by giving student "victims" an 800 number to call. His act gave the impression that I had betrayed students. She remembered as well what she had learned as a law student about the depth of the FBI's invasiveness.

Tommy responded with concern over how I was handling the situation emotionally. "Mom, I worry about you and want you to stay strong," he said.

My children were helping me keep in touch with the courage I'd given them in not being constrained by discrimination directed at minorities and roles prescribed for women. I questioned: How far had I really come? Had my moving ahead been an illusion? How different had I made life for my children? I was reminded of how Jane lost out to a white male when she went up for a new position at her law school. I knew from other black women in higher education that they had pressures in securing tenure and they were challenged with having to publish in the face of administrative and service responsibilities.

Tommy responded, "How many people from the housing projects of Newark, New Jersey, manage to earn a Ph.D. from the University of Michigan and go on to be a college and university president? And "How many moms over 60 are still running marathons? And remember when you raced Jane and me as children, you beat us to the finish line," he added. "Look at what you've accomplished in writing and presenting papers on policies impacting women and minorities. Don't let them shrink you down to fit in their bottle, Mom."

In her customary fashion, Jane cut to the chase. "Mom, nothing much has changed for women, especially black women. You're likely to get trashed and 'dissed' at every turn. Don't let them take your power.

Being afraid is not going to help." Jane's voice softened, "Mom, I love you. You're not going to like this but I told you not to go to Georgia. Don't worry about Tommy and me. It's not that we don't need you. We just need you stronger. Get started running again. Give yourself some quiet time. You keep going over and over documents and reviewing materials on the college. You are more than this bump in the road and your resume. You have a genuine love for people, you care, and your true self will get you through this. Tommy and I know you didn't break the law. In truth, you were addicted to giving back and caring outside of yourself." I knew she was trying to help but I was feeling stranded and down from having to lean so heavily on my children. I knew as well that they were not going to join me in a "pity party." and they encouraged me to move to a position of strength and get past the fear.

In my heart, I felt that many others cared, may have felt helpless or just didn't know what to do and think. A positive answer came when I received an editorial written by Dr. Joyce Ann Joyce, Professor of English at Temple University and Editor of the Temple University Faculty Herald. Her March 27, 2005, editorial. *Sins of Omission*, drew attention to the March 18, 2005 issue of The Chronicle of Higher Education that included two stories on controversial college presidents, Dr. Elizabeth Hoffman of the University of Colorado and Dr. Manny Aragon at the New Mexico Highlands University. In the editorial excerpted here, she contrasts the situation they faced and mine:

> "Their experiences pale in the face of those that describe the last year of Dolores Cross, the former president of Chicago State University and Morris Brown College. Dolores Cross, one of the most devoted academicians I have known, now faces at least thirty (30) criminal counts of fraud, provoked by investigations and lawsuits that result from the firing of incompetent faculty and administrators. Cross is indicted to stand trial for her "alleged" role in a financial aid scandal."
>
> "Like some of the women in President Hoffman's faculty who fail to support Hoffman because they disagree strongly with her handling of the football players' sex scandal, Dolores Cross does not have the support of a circle of women during a period in history when women celebrate Women's History Month, but fail to ask the important questions that probe beneath media hype and to address the realities that describe

the long-range financial problems of Historically Black Colleges and Universities (HBCUs) as well as the consequences of being a black female Yankee outsider in the deep South."

"The comment Bruce Benson, a former Republican gubernatorial candidate in Colorado makes about President Hoffman very adequately describes Cross's situation. He says, "The press beats on you long enough, pretty soon the perception becomes reality." Andrea Jones's piece in the Atlanta Journal Constitution, which she entitles "Tarnished Record," contains the masterful tricks the media plays on those of us who do not understand that there is no free press. And it is most disturbing that Jones is a woman reporter, who plays a game quite characteristic of the patriarchy who trained her in her coverage of Cross's indictment."

"The slanted coverage begins with the picture, which introduces the story, capturing the picture of Cross on her autobiography Breaking Through the Wall, A Marathoner's Story as she finishes a marathon. Jones says that in Cross's autobiography, Cross describes herself as a visionary. But we soon see that the use of the autobiography is a set up. Jones asserts, "Yet, for all her vision, Cross time and again has faced questions about her competency and criticism for her autocratic leadership style. At both the schools she led, critics say, she surrounded herself with an inner circle of friends, closing ranks against detractors. And even as her high profile projects were propelling her into the limelight, the schools were sinking into fiscal disarray.".......

"None of the newspaper, magazine, or internet accounts of Cross's story have given a detailed account of Cross's accomplishments. Rather than mocking the fact that she sees herself as a visionary, I would like to demonstrate the manifestation of her vision. I would like to focus on the media's sins of omissions. While Andrea Jones cites the comments of some of Cross's disgruntled faculty at Chicago State, Jones forfeits the opportunity to highlight how one black woman president could have accomplished as much as she did at Chicago State University. From a list of her accomplishments, it becomes clear that Cross left Chicago State University because she is a change agent and, like President Hoffman, she knew that the time had come for her to resign. A faculty comfortable with the status quo cannot take too much change."

"It is my hope that other women of all ethnicities gather together in the courtroom during her trial in Atlanta, Georgia, particularly those of us who understand that there is not one HBCU that is not struggling to stay afloat financially and because if Dr. Cross, who has spent her entire professional life serving the underprivileged, is under siege, any one of us could be next."

I was uplifted by the courage Dr. Joyce had taken in the midst of the negative press I was receiving to write an editorial in my behalf. Her help came at a time when I needed a public expression of fairness.

From a friendship that had developed from her leading seminars in Rio Caliente, Sylvia had volunteered to help me learn more about myself and deepen my inner emotional strength and to be there for me throughout the ordeal. She scheduled phone sessions every week and assisted me on the path of understanding: how, after rising to the heights of my profession, I found myself in my present situation. I experienced her prompting me to describe what really wasn't working for me and how I found myself in this situation. Initially I was uncomfortable with what she was encouraging.

I was taking an inward look, achieving clarity and discerning limiting beliefs. In making herself available every week, Sylvia put me in touch with the strengths of those who had preceded me. One of the assets of looking at those who had preceded me was to sense the depths of their struggle. My own struggle had become an addiction for me. Sylvia helped me understand the mistakes I had made when I failed to step outside my struggle and see it in perspective.

Responding to Sylvia required me to stay in touch with what it would take to overcome my fear. From her path in the corporate world and through her interactions as a professional black woman who never felt constrained or limited in ways that others may have viewed her, she was there to guide me. I was stuck in how others were viewing the 'me' wrapped in the cocoon of my resume. I needed to evolve by uncovering and resolving issues. It would be an arduous climb from the abyss that sought to overtake me. I always wanted to help and now I had to start with my own life. I couldn't turn away from myself. The important thing for me now was self-preservation and I had to feel worthy of preservation. My mother needed me to be a hero. When I was 13, I encountered the landlord, Mr. Amberg, after being evicted with my mother from the housing projects. I didn't realize the significance of confrontation then. I confronted him with the unfairness of evicting my mother when illness led to her not paying the rent. There was no thought in my mind of Mr. Amberg's values and constraints caused by the social condition of the late 40s. He must have been astonished as he watched me, a Negro girl of 13, stutter through a protest I wanted him to understand. Yet the situation was piled against me. He dismissed me and my effort to make a difference. Well, now I was back in front of a room full of Mr. Ambergs and I needed help to discern the situation and stand up for myself.

In daily phone calls, I listened to Jane, realizing it was as though my daughter had now become my symbolic mother as I was now her child. I could not help but think of my holding my mother many years earlier and trying to fuse strength into her. I had to draw from my own well now. Jane could always sense when I needed the infusion of confidence, for day after day she would tell me how I couldn't give up. I had to fight -- as I always had.

"Mom, people have piled up to deal with you and you tried to get them to like you. You have a lot of work to do for yourself now. There are too many folks in the black community who don't understand." She was adamant in communicating that to make it through the next step I had to be strong and it would take more inner work to reach that point.

I ached, felt pain everywhere and I didn't feel I could move ahead. How could I stay strong? Except now, it wasn't my body that was in pain. It was my heart and my soul. There were days when I was gripped by sadness and would plunge into deep depression. I saw my life crumble before me and my reputation ruined. I didn't feel worthy. The despair filled every corner of my mind. I didn't want to talk to anyone. I didn't feel attached to anything. I forced myself to return phone calls. I pushed myself to get out and walk or run with Cassie. Sometimes, I called Jane two and three times a day.

My cousin, Lillian would not be put off by my evasiveness. Despite having problems of her own as she alone managed and ran 'Focus on Fun' entertainment business in New York City, Lillian called often. She made a point of being there 'for and as family." She understood what it meant to have to fend for yourself and urged me not to become too self-absorbed.

.

Yet no matter how hard I tried to suppress worrying about the indictment, I kept hearing the Dean of Education at DePaul advising me that my service at the university had ended and my feeling that my life as an educator had ended. Not a day went by when I could forget the implications of the indictment.

In telephone sessions with Sylvia, I practiced joining her in meditation to try to relax and let go of an "if only" pattern. What caused me to forge ahead with so much assurance? Maybe that black female FBI agent was right. In failing to slow down and question where I was going, I had been led by my ego.

Sylvia helped me to understand what it would take to rid myself of the notion that innocence alone was armor against the onslaught of the media and the prosecution.

I had to enter a marathon unlike any I had ever run before. I would be running with only one goal in sight: to prove my innocence of all the charges. For this new marathon, I had to be strong, centered and prepared to run to win. There could be no giving up, no stopping, and no time-outs. This was the marathon of my life, and, strangely, no one would see it but me. I realized that if I were stuck in my training for a marathon within the walls of my apartment, I would seek the help of Sylvia to get me ready.

In reaching out, I was responding to the need to develop inner emotional strength. I would have to let go of believing my previous accomplishments would get me through if I wanted to develop the emotional clarity I needed throughout the coming ordeal.

I was frustrated and didn't want "my light" to be snuffed out. There were days when I started humming "This little light of mine I'm gonna let it shine, this little light of mine I'm gonna let it shine."

Chapter 7

I reported to my pre-trial officer in Chicago as scheduled. She maintained communication with her counterpart in Atlanta. The visits were reminders of the status of having been indicted as a criminal. For the first time in my life I was subjected to having to provide a urine specimen before a stranger who watched me fill a cup and leave it for analysis. The pre-trial officer took time to repeat what I had learned in court in Atlanta. She provided a map of the Northern District of Illinois and stated I was restricted inside that area. I would have to request permission to travel anywhere outside those limits; and I would be subject to unannounced visits to my residence, as well as periodic meetings with her. There was no negotiating. She was doing her job and presenting the rules I would have to follow.

I began to fill my days volunteering as I had worked before in community organizations and schools. The opportunities to serve came in unexpected ways. On a morning walk with Cassie, I met Sue Duncan, a woman about my age with two dogs. We had seen each other often on the path behind the Museum of Science and Industry.

> In a conversation she asked, "What do you do, Dolores?"
> "I'm retired," I replied. "I was an educator."
> She asked if I would be interested in tutoring.
> Without a moment's hesitation I responded, "Yes."

Within a few days I showed up at the Sue Duncan After-School Program at Jackie Robinson Elementary School. Sue simply introduced me as Dolores and a marathoner.

She assigned me to a group of youngsters to help with their homework. I completed the necessary paperwork and became a regular tutor with other parents and students from the University of Chicago. On warm days I trained some of the children in running. They were amazed that this gray-haired lady looking like their grandmother could outrun them. I taught them how to pace themselves and make the best use of their arms. I learned that Arne Duncan, Chancellor of the Chicago Public Schools, was Sue's son. I learned also that she had been working largely with minority and low-income youngsters for over twenty years.

A second opportunity to serve as a volunteer came through my church, The First Unitarian Church in Hyde Park. A representative from the Midwest Workers Associations (MWA) made an appeal before the congregation for volunteers. I made a donation and accepted some of the reading material. Within a few days I appeared at the Midwest Workers facility in Englewood to inquire how I could help. I was assigned the task of gathering and loading my car with groceries at the local co-op and delivering them back to the center. I joined staff in unloading the goods and packing them for the distributor who was waiting to make deliveries to the MWA members. My day there continued with canvassing for donations and updating contact cards of sponsors. It felt good to get away from my problems and return to what I liked best: helping people.

A few days later, I was contacted by a former graduate student from Northwestern University. She headed a literacy program and called to request that I read from my book on marathon running to inspire her students. A reading was arranged at Simpson Academy for teenage mothers. The Principal, Dr.Beverly Bennett was a member of my church. Her office provided a view of her appreciation for African art. She was dedicated to the school's mission and we quickly became friends.

The volunteering gave me energy. I was feeling purpose in being needed and being able to continue making a contribution, however small.

On the advice of my attorneys, I avoided responding to specific questions about the indictment. When asked about my situation, I referred to the accusations as totally outrageous, unfair, and untrue. When people were particularly insistent, I would ask them the same question: What if every president who headed a college where there had been an audit disallowance had been charged with conspiracy? Who would be running the colleges and universities today?

I thought again of a statement expressed by the Vice President of Government Affairs of the American Council of Education: "It was a far reach for the government to link the president of a college or university to issues in the day-to-day management of student financial aid." Yet there were those who believed that if the government said, "She did it. She stole funds" that would be all they needed.

Word of the indictment had no boundaries and was repeated throughout the country. I received a call from a cousin who questioned why I had not taken the time to take in what was available on the internet and the negative press reports. I responded, "If you've read them, what do you think?"

She snapped with impatience, "Based on what I read, you "fucked" with the government's money."

Her remark stung and I hung up.

After a week, we resumed our communication. She had taken a risk to provide me with an impression of what was 'out there.' Despite what she said, I knew she sought to keep it real and help me deal with the devastating reality that most folks believed I had committed a crime. She was pushing me to move ahead and not permit the vortex at Morris Brown to create an image of Dolores E. Cross that has nothing to do with who I am. After all is said and done by others, what counts is what I say and do. I learned that truth as a child and had never forgotten it. I knew if I began to listen to the rumors, I would crumble under the weight of public ridicule and humiliation.

What hurt most during the dark tunnel of days after the indictment was the misperception given all the students I've cared about. For me, it had been about working to make a difference and working against the odds in situations where many would not venture. I didn't want others to be discouraged and not take on jobs where they were needed – especially if they felt that I had led to their disillusionment. I didn't want to see 30 years of giving erased by a perceived violation of my values.

Despite the adversities I'd faced growing up and the challenges of reaching the summit of my profession, nothing prepared me for the vilification that preceded and followed my indictment. I felt like I was being judged by criteria that had to do with my beginnings and not who I had become. What in my life would have ever suggested I would betray the ancestors?

I learned too late, "Never give an interview when the spin is in." Better yet, never give an interview! "No comment" was best. No matter how much you invested, it is almost impossible to set the record straight. If you're bent on telling your side, run it past your attorney. Never let your ego do the talking. The situation I faced was presented within the context of "Black on Black" crime. There were pockets of hatred ready for what a newspaper columnist described as "Cross burning." It was not a double-entendre I was comfortable with. An Atlanta newspaper printed a horrid cartoon of me as the Grinch Who Stole Christmas, and printed editorials that assumed my guilt as a foregone conclusion. I felt incredibly sad.

Chapter 8

A few months after the indictment, Caroline and Ev announced that we three would form the Diva Defense Team. I was moved, for I knew how similar we were in how we reacted to injustice and always tried to use humor in facing our troubles. Ev was a frequent guest at Rio Caliente. As a trio, we shared progressive politics, experience in male dominated fields and a raucous sense of humor. They understood the seriousness of what I faced and the irony of my fighting against inequities faced by others and struggling to have financial resources to face the injustice I was experiencing.

I shared my feelings, reactions and joys in our e-mail letters. The voice we shared was that of women who entered history about the same time. Our mothers were women who, because of their gender, were given social ranks and professional positions below those of their male counterparts. It was not likely that the paths of our mothers would have crossed given geographic, racial and class differences. Yet we three have come together as friends and I could share my innermost thoughts with them.

We conversed about what we viewed as our propensity to take risks in difficult situations. We'd taken on battles beyond our own in fighting for the underdog and speaking for those who had no voice. Just as in a marathon, we delved into reserves of strength and, after finding out how far those would take us, delved again.

Caroline had reached out on behalf of abused women in Mexico and established funds to support the education of Mexican children. Ev was her financial consultant. She had acted as a mentor to young men and women entering the world of finance, and maintained a network of friends throughout the world. With them, I could speak of my values and commitment with ease. We were not judgmental of each other and supported our respective choices. It did not occur to Caroline or Ev to ask, "Dolores, how did you get yourself into this mess?" They were politically conscious and understood how choices could put you at risk.

The spirit that ignited our friendship at Rio Caliente continued across the miles by e-mail to provide an oasis in what would otherwise be a desert.

Dear Caroline and Ev,

> *Growing up, I remember hearing stories of others who'd attended Historically Black Colleges and Universities in the South. They were proud of their education and connections made. I was inspired by the sit-ins and demonstrations I witnessed on TV. I imagined the community and determination of the Freedom Fighters. My experience in visiting the South had been painful. My sister and I worked with cousins in tobacco fields. We slept together on a pallet on the floor and used an outside toilet to relieve ourselves. My cousins could not imagine what it was like for me to attend school with whites in Newark and to have access to books. They'd ignore my stutter as I retold stories I'd recalled. The rides back from the South meant segregated train cars, drinking water from fountains labeled Colored and White and seeing restaurants along the way that you dare not enter to be served. Most white folks looked past you or seemed annoyed by you, others looked charitable with smiles of apology. There are days when I feel black folks are looking past me in much the same way as the whites I encountered then.*
> *Dolores*

In her reply, Caroline wrote:

Dear Dolores,

> *Thank you for responding so fast as well as sending me more about what you have been going through and thinking. I hope you will include it in your book to inspire others just as you inspire Ev and Me.*

A few days later, my spirits slumped and again I reached out to my friends thousands of miles away, yet for me, it was as though they were watching from across the room, encouraging me not to give up.

Dear Caroline and Ev:

Realities came crashing with comments from a former colleague who wrote: "Dolores, they want to see you broken and in despair and too depressed to be out here. Their perception becomes reality. Even if you are exonerated, there'll be a cloud. It won't be the same and you must tell your story. You've gone through the wall of marathons. You've gone the distance. You've been strong. And the scandal, the perception of wrongdoing and media frenzy is to have left you broken, confused, and never to rise again."

In response, I must train as in a marathon where age is no factor. It is lonely. I'm motivated by the shoulders on which I stand, the notion that my children need me to survive, inner strength and truth.

The spiritual quest is important. In a real sense, the crisis has put me on a path in which I have taken steps inch by inch not to become a victim of fear and to find joy where there's sorrow.

I've been given an opportunity in this crisis to add meaning and depth to the phrase "Stay and Be Strong."
Dolores

Day after day, writing to them from my apartment, I felt that the only thing that kept me from slipping out of sight of everything that mattered was a tiny white screen on which the words of people whom I loved kept appearing — notes in a bottle that kept washing up, day after day, all the while setting my own notes adrift in the white sea.

Each showed me that I was at the center of someone's loving thoughts. No matter how far my life seemed to have drifted, I was still anchored in someone's heart.

A poem from Hal Edwards, a dear friend and former Executive Director of City Quest, Illinois, that came without explanation or introduction, simply words rising up evoking in me what they were offering:

Awakening
In a moment of peace
I gave things
To the source of all peace.

As I set forth
Awakening
In a moment of peace
I gave thanks
To the source of all peace.
As I set forth
Into the day
The birds sing
With new voices
And I listen
With new ears
And give thanks
Nearby the flower called Angel's Trumpet
Blows
In the breeze
And I give thanks.

It was hard, though, to give thanks. My gratitude seemed like the water at the bottom of a barrel. What little there was I needed to give to the few loyal friends whose presence never wavered. It was hard giving the kind of thanks I had been accustomed to dispersing.

Then a letter arrived unexpectedly from someone who must have known how marooned I felt. She had been one of the few black female educators to be elected a college president.

As I focused on excerpts from her letter, I felt as though she were speaking from the vantage point of seeing my career merged with those of all the black women educators who had struggled to reach the pinnacle of responsibility.

"Dear Dolores:"

"As college or university presidents or chancellors during our era, we tried to "magically" keep our colleges or universities afloat and our students in school – even though most could not afford college tuition. The challenges were absurdly difficult yet the boards of trustees, alumni, etc, expected us – with little real assistance from them (except for running motor-mouth) – to cure all, to solve all problems, and to not ever make a human error. After all, we had to be superhuman just to take these jobs. But our commitment and dedication would not let us do otherwise, and

the truth is our "magic," (i.e., our tireless efforts and attempts at unique solutions) could never be enough in many cases."

"Sister, do not put your head down. You profited not one iota from your efforts to keep Morris Brown afloat. Wasn't it apparent to those who brought charges against you that something else was at work there? Why weren't they prompted to ask, "Why has Morris Brown been in its financial predicaments for so long? What is the constant for all the long-standing problems at Morris Brown College?"

"I will lift you up in prayer, and remind you to read Isaiah 40:31 "they that hope in the Lord shall renew their strength; they shall take wings as eagles; they shall run and not be weary; they shall walk and not faint."

Dr. Dolores Cross shall be strong, take her wings as does the eagle, shall run and not be weary, shall walk and not faint, for in reality, she knows of what she is made."

"A Sister President."

I didn't want to ever forget the words meant to encourage me, especially in the light of the events I would be facing in the days ahead: people and accusations would be trying to strip away my wings, feather by feather, until I fell from the sky.

I wouldn't let them. I wouldn't allow what I have given my adult life to achieve be taken away. It wasn't fair, I thought, and then shook my head at my naïveté: when had it ever been fair? One had to fight for equality, one had to fight for justice, one had to fight for the truth, and I would fight for all of them in the name of Dolores E. Cross. If I didn't, who would? Yes, I had Jane, Tom, Jr. Yes, I had Caroline, Ev, and yes, I had my colleagues and friends spread out across the country like candles whose flickering light was encouraging me on. But I knew when it came time there was only one person who would have to carry the day to save Dolores E. Cross. And that was one anxious black woman, eligible for social security, standing at a window looking down at the deserted shore of Lake Michigan.

I walked through the apartment, stopping to turn off light after light. Alone was one thing, but alone with all the fears of the trial was another. This is the big world Ma was always struggling against, the one I feel the full brunt of now. I understand the sighing and the silence, as well as the concern lines on the faces of my grandparents.

Well, now it was my turn.

Before crawling into bed at night, I would sometimes reread papers I had once written to inspire others.

Now I had to keep myself lifted up.

Chapter 9

"The marathon tears down the body that has been built up for months in anticipation of a strong effort. Injury and illness are frequent not only during and immediately after the marathon, but also in the weeks following. The body is weak, and the mind is undisciplined because the immediate goal has been achieved. A post-marathon runner is very vulnerable."

I looked at the words I had written in *Breaking Through the Wall*, wondering, vulnerable to what? Was I vulnerable to giving up running again? Until now, I always felt my marathons made me stronger. But then the figurative marathon of the indictment was unlike any I had ever run before. I felt myself floating into a cloud, moving into a frightening nightmare. Thoughts collided; twisted images blocked my vision and the feeling of falling made me want to scream. I wanted to wake up and be relieved of the horror that engulfed me. I hadn't prepared for this marathon and simply had to endure an out-of-body, mind experience until the end. In the nightmare I was living, I tossed and sweated through the fright of forces meant to humiliate, disgrace and shame me. I had to press on.

Most often, I got out of my bed and looked out the window at the path along Lake Michigan where I had run so many times in the past. Now it was deserted. Where was the team? Where was my anchor?

"Guess what, Dolores?" a woman's voice uttered, "you get to be your own anchor."

"Well, I don't want to be," I heard myself answer. "I've been strong for others. Why can't someone be strong for me?"

"Lots of people have, Dolores," the voice replied. "Lots of them you don't even know. Many died before you were born. They were strong for you. Now you gotta be strong for them and you."

"So, I'm the anchor, huh?" I asked, shaking my head. "When's the race starting?"

The voice didn't answer.

Silence would have to do for now.

When the alarm rang at three a.m., I didn't get up. I lay motionless, savoring the warmth of the quilt. Then anxiety stirred and my brain started to turn. In an instant, a thought was prodding me: today I had to fly to Atlanta to prepare for my defense.

I quickly showered and dressed in clothes prepared the night before. After driving Cassie to her sitter, I drove to the airport, parked, and was through airport security by 5 a.m. for the 6:00 a.m. flight to Atlanta. Much as I tried, I couldn't sleep on the plane. There would be much to accomplish in Atlanta.

Joe met me as I moved up the escalator to the arrival area. He was dressed in his usual long-sleeve, open-collar shirt, and greeted me with a reassuring smile. He chatted as we walked to the car. We would be going directly to the Federal Building to review documents which might be referred to in the case.

We parked in the lot outside the Federal Building. The area close to the building had been barricaded since 9/11 and we had to search through the crowded area for a parking space. We entered through the rear of the building and proceeded through a long line of employees and outsiders who presented identification, placed hand-carried items on a security belt and proceeded through monitors. We stopped for coffee, then proceeded to the 15th floor where we waited to be escorted into a room to begin reviewing the documents. There would be close to 150 boxes to sort through as we prepared for trial.

An FBI agent had been requested to escort us to the room. I recalled Drew mentioning her name from the pre-indictment hearing. I was surprised to be facing a black female. I studied her closely. She looked to be in her mid-40s, medium build, about my height, with a short natural hairdo and of average appearance. She smiled upon meeting me, a smile both pleasant and not overly friendly. I detected her measured indifference as she wheeled in the first of many boxes for us to review. I had heard how she had grilled associates at the college and been angry when their responses failed to damn me as she wanted. A former employee had confided how the agent had angrily banged his desk and threatened that he would be pulled into the line of fire if he weren't more "forthcoming." He was clear in communicating, "Dee, she's out to nail you," he warned me. He was referring to the FBI agent who had been present at the pre-indictment hearing with Drew and Joe. More than anything I wanted to ask the agent, "Do you really believe I am guilty?"

The answer came to me as I recalled what had been related to me of her interview with the former Provost. He received a late evening visit from two federal agents at his Vice President's office at Lincoln University of Pennsylvania. He was interrogated under fairly threatening pressure for 3-1/2 hours mainly by the woman sitting before me. She was "fishing" for a case and seeking specific answers from him. Her frustration built as he easily explained or rebutted the entire litany of allegations against me. In doing her 'job,' she had seemed bent on concluding I was guilty and bent out of inventing a case from hearsay offered up by those who did not mind seeing the destruction of the College or the reputations of fellow human beings.

I turned to the task that lay before us. It was going to take time for Joe, Drew and me to sort through all the evidence and the weight of what I was dealing with. I had to use the rigor I had employed in advocating for students. This was the first of what would turn out to be a dozen trips to Atlanta to meet with my defense team. They would have to spend a great deal of time reviewing documents, government interviews, as well as interviewing potential witnesses.

Keeping it all together was draining. There were e-mails from attorneys to answer, documents to review and trips to Atlanta to meet with my defense team. The situation was with me every minute of the day as I replayed events at the college and found words to respond to the indictment. I sat at my computer reviewing well over 90 hours of tapes of board minutes. Listening to the voices and contents of the tapes drew me back into the situation at the college and the tenor of the board meetings.

At home in Chicago, I worked six-to-eight hours a day at my computer communicating with my attorneys. The government interviews of faculty and staff at the college were most unsettling. I attempted to understand what had been presented as their take on what went wrong at Morris Brown College. In some cases those interviewed appeared to be responding to the spin in the press and pressure from the FBI and government's investigators. I tried to imagine the impact of the Trustees seeing government agents coming to campus to empty files and seize computer hard drives concerning the interviews I was reviewing. They must have sensed that something terribly amiss had taken place at Morris Brown, and the former president, Dolores Cross, had, to the government agents' way of thinking, created a problem that not only endangered the college but its actual existence as well.

I picked up similarities in their responses to government interviews.

- "Dr. Cross knew about everything that was going on at the college."
- "She defended inept administrators."
- "Dr. Cross made frequent changes in the organization."
- "She was impatient and would sometimes get angry."
- "She had a lavish lifestyle."

Once a rumor picked up speed, it was difficult to stop. Staying focused was not easy. I longed to write about the achievements of the college and plead to the community to fight back and not let the government diminish what had been achieved by letting them have their way with me.

I realized that by implication, what had happened to me at Morris Brown College would perhaps forever impact the professional careers of dedicated administrators, staff, and students. I shuddered to think of career hopes dashed by association with me. I prayed I could only stay strong and hold my head high until I could clear my name and release all those close to me from any negative association being directed at them.

Chapter 10

In April 2006, I left Chicago for the trial in Atlanta. Jane joined me in a leased apartment not far from my attorney's office. I had driven alone from Chicago with my dog Cassie and my Toyota Matrix loaded with clothes and food for what might be two months in Atlanta. I felt the weight of a few allies in Atlanta and the wider community. Jane joined meetings of the defense team, and would be in the court as prospective jurors were interviewed.

The team was now led by Attorney Dorothy Kirkley. While Drew and Joe continued to review documents and interview potential witnesses, Dorothy took the lead in implementing the defense strategy and responding to government inquiries, as well as communicating with my co-defendant's attorneys. In adding Dorothy I gained the involvement of a highly competent paralegal, Emily Healy, and a law partner, Tom Hawker. Dorothy had also hired a jury consultant to review responses from prospective jurors.

I kept my eyes on the door through which candidates for the jury would file. I was seated at the table closest to the judge, only once nodded at her and said nothing. From the interviews, I learned that many individuals in the pool of jurors had seen media reports on the case and a few admitted their bias. I expected a good number might be disqualified. I made notes that would be compared with those of the jury consultant and my attorneys after the interviews.

When we returned to the office, the jury consultant reflected on what he perceived were good candidates for the jury and, given the negative media coverage, any overall problems in getting an unbiased jury pool. He wasn't very optimistic.

As things turned out, we were faced with a more serious problem. After days of interviewing prospective jurors and four days prior to the start date of the trial, the Director of Student Financial Aid admitted illegal improprieties to secure more financial aid than the college was entitled to receive, struck a deal with the prosecution and agreed to be its star witness against me. He had concocted a scheme that had gone undetected by auditors from DOE and the college's external auditors

He was prepared to say words to the effect that "he did it and the President knew all about financial aid transactions occurring in his office, and that they were done under her direction." The prosecution could no doubt parade witnesses who would concur and seek to convince the jury that as president I had orchestrated criminal activities in the management of federal student financial aid.

This man, I thought, is my Iago. I am his "stay out of jail" card.

As discussions continued about the jury pool, my defense team weighed possible outcomes. If the jury found me guilty on multiple counts, under mandatory federal guidelines, I faced ten years in a federal prison without possibility of parole. My thoughts darkened when I considered what I'd seen as the relentless posture of the U.S. Attorney in Georgia, the abandonment by the college's Board of Trustees and the silence of members of my family and some former colleagues.

The nightmare of being left to fall even farther than I had was too dismal to contemplate. Never once in my life have I ever given a thought to suicide as a way out of a problem. But at that moment, I have to admit I did.

My mind filled with worrying questions:

Would the prosecution be successful in redefining the role of the president of the college to the jury?

Would the prosecution be successful in assigning a sinister motive to my acceptance of the position of president of Morris Brown?

Would witnesses for the prosecution view a Dolores Cross conviction as a means to gain government or DOE favor in their efforts to save the college? If so, how might such a possibility impact their testimony?

What was behind the government's granting of immunity to some potential witnesses?

Why had the government been steadfast in refusing my defense team's request to have my case separated from that of the Director of Student Financial Aid? What did they seek in "joining us at the hip" in allegations of fraudulent behavior that had caused the college to receive more financial aid than it was entitled to receive? And what was the basis for their alleging that as President of the college I orchestrated a scheme and conspiracy to embezzle student financial aid funds?

How far would the U.S. Attorney in the Northern District go to fold me into a fraud and embezzlement scandal at Morris Brown College?

Was the death knell for me or for the college?

Would the weight of the community's grief for the loss of accreditation be what it would take for the jury to grant a "pound of flesh?" and return a verdict of guilty that would send me to prison for ten years?

All the questions, like dangling nooses, and not one knife of an answer to cut them away.

The proverbial light at the end of the tunnel was about the size of a match in rising wind as Jane and I spent a long night trying to sort things through. Looking at Jane, I saw the anguish despite her attempt at being composed.

Before retiring at night, I called my friends Betsy and Hal Edwards. Hal understood my need for clarity through spiritual guidance and prayer. He called upon me not to lose faith.

The next day, the possibility of my making a plea surfaced.

Initially I viewed it as making a deal with the devil. I listened as my attorney spelled out the possibilities of a plea and went back and forth with assistant attorneys for the prosecution. Given the situation, they envisioned a short term of probation for me. There were no promises. The judge was told of the fact that I was considering a plea.

I felt trapped by having allowed the idea of the offer of a plea to persist. I knew that an admission of guilt could not be retracted. I could not escape the feeling that everybody but my children and a few dear friends had stepped back to see what was going to happen to me.

Then as though encapsulating all that I needed to hear from the outside world about what I believed true about myself, an editorial by a former doctoral student at Claremont Graduate School and professor at Chicago State University appeared in the Black Commentator.

"Tomorrow, a trial will begin in Atlanta, Georgia, that should receive nationwide attention. The trial I speak of is the trial of Dolores Cross, the former President of Morris Brown College, who has been charged with fraud and the embezzlement of funds from the college she once headed. This is a long story, so I won't go into a lot of the details here. I am simply writing at this time to urge you to look into giving priority coverage to how the government has targeted this prominent black educator in order to silence her from speaking out about the conditions of black higher education in this country today."

"If you give this issue a moment's thought, you'll quickly recognize that there are virtually no black college presidents who have been willing to consistently speak out against the travesty of the sabotaging of black higher education today. The evidence for this serious charge is rather apparent: the paucity of substantial government funds needed in order to elevate the quality of education at most black colleges; the cuts in loan programs for financial aid; the cuts in Pell grants that disproportionately hurt minority students; and the egregious support of laws that require black colleges to meet a quota of white "admits" in order to receive money for their operation budgets. I could go on, but my point is that if you look around you'll see that most black college presidents have been cowed into an ominous silence of consent. Dolores Cross had the courage to speak out and is being targeted unjustly as a result."

"If the government is successful in silencing her by conviction in a public trial, the United States, I believe, will be one step closer to the police state that W.E.B. DuBois, Martin Luther King, Cornel West, Marimba Ani, Angela David, Derek Bell, and many others warned us about. We must not allow this targeting of black leaders to go on unabated."
Sincerely
Bartley McSwine

But the lone sweep of the lighthouse beam was brief solace for the darkness that ensued as I thought of those who might have stepped forward to attest to my integrity, and at the same time might be reluctant to bear witness on my behalf when the United States Government had arrayed its legal forces against me.

In high school, I recalled watching documentary footage of the McCarthy Hearings and remembered realizing how blatantly unjust were the accusations that ruined countless lives. Yet for all the people who knew it was wrong, few were willing to gather round friends and colleagues who had been summoned to testify. I kept thinking that "innocent until proven guilty" sounded so noble, yet it was hollow compared to what ruled in its place: guilt through accusation of rumor. Like spilled mercury, my reputation, once fallen, couldn't be picked up. How could I draw back from people's minds an unjust attitude they had formed of Dolores Cross simply from having read newspaper articles or rumors? The truth was I couldn't. I would have to go through the gauntlet of the trial and hope to emerge standing.

Jane had been present at meetings with the defense team and jury consultant. The options were to present what I saw as a limited plea or to move forward with a trial. In considering whether I should go to trial, I thought of my children and the journey they had made with me from birth. They didn't deserve the trauma of a trial or the possibility of having to visit me confined in prison. I didn't want them to live my nightmare. And, I didn't want them to see me fold and fail in going the distance.

The next morning I went for a long walk in the park near where Jane and I were staying. The vision of my mother seated on the courtyard bench in the housing projects floated before me. That day she seemed hunched over with fatigue as she told me she had done her best. I fixed on the vision of her and recalled that she had been evicted without a hearing. Her contributions in supporting the war efforts by working in defense plants, having to leave her children alone with prayers to protect them, and providing as a single mother, didn't matter. She had been judged, evicted, and we'd become homeless.

The gloomy visions from my childhood didn't end there. I saw my mother coming with her stacks of Civil Service examination cards, indicating she had qualified for placement to various positions. But I quickly learned being qualified didn't mean placement in jobs. She had to sit and wait despite the rules and promises of fairness. I recalled traveling with her to meet with attorneys when she fought against being passed over for the job of supervisor of telephone operators.

And here now, all these years later, I sat alone on an Atlanta park bench with visions of my mother's presence and asking myself, "How far have we black women really come?"

Had this one woman come anywhere? Or had I merely been making an enormous circle back to where in some strange way I was actually behind all the steps my mother had taken to move forward?

Was it, as some would say 'karma,' the sum of my mother's actions or my actions in a previous life that had led me to this fate? Or was I experiencing the madness of racism and sexism in mean times? Snapping myself out of my reverie, I realized I didn't have the time to ruminate about karma or the political environment. I was presented with the option of going with a plea or going to trial.

What if no matter what I said or did, no matter what was shown in my defense, the jury found me guilty? What did Drew say could be the maximum punishment? Ten years in a federal prison with no option of parole.

Blackmail, I thought, and then I couldn't help smiling, no: black female.

Yes, one 68 year old black female, trying to decide to keep on running or to throw up her hands and say okay, you got me. I give up, so I don't have to give away the remaining freedom of my life.

I could have pulled the slats from the bench from the way I was gripping them, rocking back and staring at the sky, then getting up to pace back and forth, before dropping back down as though it were the only solid place left in the world for me.

Finally, I dropped my head and hoped that if my father and mother were watching they would forgive me for what I was going to do.

It hit me: The time I had seen my mother sitting on the bench, all the life gone from her eyes, and I had wondered "Where's her fight?"

What was it I had heard so often? "Dolores, you're just like your mother." While defeat did not define her, I was haunted by what I had seen in her breakdown when I was 13. I was scared and terrified of losing it. I had seen my mother's achievements dismissed and folks who knew better had called her "crazy Ozie'. As in her case, the spin was in and there was no referee.

I felt violated. The buried memory of being of five years old, living in Baxter Terrace and being molested by a stranger while my mother worked nights emerged and trapped me in a vat of helplessness. I was gripped with fear. Could I endure an ugly trial? Could I bear days and nights of waiting for an outcome that might mean losing my freedom for ten years? Were there enough years left to recover?

I decided to enter a plea and avert a trial that might end in a conviction and ten years in a federal prison. Jane accompanied me as I met with the defense team and indicated my plans to go with a plea. She was confident that under the circumstance, I had made the best decision. I wanted to believe that the one stain wouldn't ruin the fabric I had been weaving all my life.

On May 6, 2006, Attorney Dorothy Kirkley read our statement to the court:

"AS DR. CROSS' COUNSEL, I AM SATISFIED THAT THE GOVERNMENT COULD OFFER AT TRIAL THE EVIDENCE IN ITS FACTUAL BASIS. HOWEVER, MUCH OF THE EVIDENCE WOULD BE DISPUTED AND THE FACTUAL BASIS DOES NOT PRESENT THE COMPLETE PICTURE OF THE FACTS.

DR. CROSS IS PLEADING GUILTY TO COUNT 27 AND ALL THE REST ARE BEING DISMISSED. SHE IS PLEADING GUILTY TO THE MISAPPLICATION OF $25,000 IN FEDERAL LOAN FUNDS ON APPROXIMATELY DECEMBER 27, 2001, AT THE END OF HER PRESIDENCY OF MORRIS BROWN COLLEGE. ALTHOUGH THE INDICTMENT DOES NOT SPECIFICALLY USE THE WORD "MISAPPLICATION," TITLE 20 USC § 1097 INCLUDES MISAPPLICATION. MISAPPLICATION IS THE MOST APPROPRIATE TERM TO APPLY TO THESE FUNDS. LOAN FUNDS WERE WIRED TO MORRIS BROWN AND $25,000 OF THESE FUNDS WERE USED FOR OPERATING EXPENSES AND NOT RETURNED TO THE DEPARTMENT OF EDUCATION. THE PERIOD OF RELEVANT CONDUCT WAS SEPTEMBER 10, 2001. THE REQUESTS FOR THESE LOAN FUNDS WERE NOT FALSE OR FRAUDULENT WHEN SUBMITTED TO THE DEPARTMENT OF EDUCATION. ON SEPTEMBER 10, 2001, DR. CROSS RECEIVED A REPORT FROM THE DEPARTMENT OF EDUCATION PUTTING

HER ON NOTICE OF THE IMPROPRIETIES IN THE FINANCIAL AID OFFICE. SHE FAILED TO MAKE AN ADEQUATE INVESTIGATION AND REMAINED DELIBERATELY IGNORANT OF THE SEVERITY OF THE PROBLEMS. AS A RESULT, ON DECEMBER 27, 2001, SHE KNOWINGLY AND WILLFULLY AIDED AND ABETTED CO-DEFENDANT IN MISAPPLYING THESE FUNDS BY ALLOWING THEM TO BE USED AS OPERATING FUNDS FOR THE COLLEGE'S OPERATING EXPENSES. AS THE GOVERNMENT HAS STATED, THE FUNDS WERE USED FOR THE COLLEGE, NOT DR. CROSS PERSONALLY.

ALTHOUGH NOT SPECIFICALLY STATED IN THE PLEA AGREEMENT, THE AMOUNT OF RESTITUTION AGREED TO BY BOTH PARTIES IS APPROXIMATELY $11,000."

Though I had agreed to plead guilty to one charge, and the prosecution had agreed that there had been no personal profit, I felt I was staring into a bottomless pit that had opened following my plea. Even though the prosecution agreed that there had been no personal profit, I felt hollow and haunted by sadness.

On May 6, 2006, I appeared before the judge to indicate that I understood the conditions of the plea.

As the two attorneys stepped forward to speak with the judge, I imagined hearing the voices of every student I had ever taught and the voices of every colleague with whom I had worked. In unison, they were saying: "Dr. Cross is pleading guilty."

And I, who had never pleaded guilty to anything in my life, trembled.

Within minutes it was settled. By pleading guilty to Count 27, all the other charges would be dismissed.

The judge ordered a recess.

When my attorney returned to where I was sitting, Drew could see I had been crying.

He leaned over. "Dolores, I understand you're upset. But we did the right thing here."

I looked up at my attorney. "But I pled guilty."

"Yes, only to one count, the remaining 27 counts have been dismissed."

"Was it clear that I hadn't taken a penny of that money for personal use?" I doubted that the press would focus on what the government had acknowledged:

That Dr. Dolores E. Cross, while willfully misapplying the funds for the college's operating expenses, did not take any of the money for her personal profit.

That, I thought, is what matters most. The public, my peers, my former students, my family, friends, and, perhaps most of all, my ancestors, must know that I did not steal one cent. I was taking responsibility as president at the helm of the college. Yes, I was wrong in taking for granted that certain student financial aid management concerns in the Offices of Student Financial Aid and Fiscal Affairs were being addressed and naïve in relying on the college's external auditors or DOE auditors to alert me to illegal and fraudulent activities in the management of student financial aid at the college. As I viewed it, while the auditors were accepting no responsibility, I was accepting responsibility for failing to pursue the possibility of criminal irregularities in the overall management of student financial aid after receiving the DOE letter of September 10th, having permitted the disbursing of funds for the operation of the college to go on as usual without determining if the checks and balances I had put in place were working. I wanted to rant: "If this can happen to me, it could happen to anyone else in higher education!"

Thoughts were swimming in my head. Could this have happened to a female president of a small woman's college in the North? Is their a subtle form of racism in the South's system of "justice" at work to undermine a college that through sheer audacity was founded by and for blacks? How convenient was it to target a woman from the North to stall and attempt to dismantle what former slaveholders never meant to be? And given what descendants of slaves know of the history of pitting us against each other permit and encourage the persecution of Dolores Cross? In making the decision to enter a plea I had to answer the question of "How far have we come?"

It would come as no surprise to individuals from my generation that I would become fearful and paranoid, when I learned that efforts were being made to implicate me in a Grand Jury Investigation, and that I would suffer sleepless nights as I learned of repeated visits and threats by the FBI. I grew up when segregation was the law of the land and had narrowly escaped being arrested in the Lakeview-Malverne integration drama. I had seen former Newark neighbors join radical movements and suffer one indignity after another and I had read the fine print in Bush's Patriot Act. I was trapped by my fear. I became guarded in personal and phone contacts and avoided media reports that might heighten stress.

I had heard of threats against my life. Were they real or merely someone venting anger? I didn't know. My core trust in people had been shaken. I realized as well that the power of the government could cause family, friends, and associates who had urged me on in the past, to disown me and doubt the credibility of honors and accolades that had been bestowed upon me.

In an instant, what had been the bright, life-long road of my marathon had become a darkened swamp in which my path to the present had been swallowed without a trace.

Chapter 11

I was numb when I was called forward to acknowledge my understanding of the plea. It was an admission of guilt for which there could be no legal retraction. I signed documents prepared by the prosecution that contained sentencing possibilities of up to a $250,000 fine and five years in prison. My attorney advised that while the prosecution would prepare documents for a harsh sentence, she was prepared to refute the allegations in her pre-sentencing report.

I anticipated the possibility of six months probation, yet my attorney could not promise an outcome. Reports from attorneys for the prosecution and my attorneys' defense would be presented to a consultant to the Judge for a sentencing recommendation to the Court.

My plea was still plunging through me like a stone. Regardless of extenuating circumstances, my statement was an admission of criminal wrongdoing. Seeking to sensationalize the verdict, the Associated Press and other newspapers declared erroneously, "Cross embezzled millions of dollars."

The details, circumstances, and issues didn't matter. I took responsibility and admitted to behavior that happened during the semester the college was to present its report to SACS. There was no secret or concealment of steps taken to meet the college's obligations.

I was admitting in my plea that, given the letter from the DOE dated September 10, 2001, I should have raised more questions of administrators in their management and disbursement of $25,000 in student financial aid funds for operating expenses of the college.

But all the "should haves" in the world were behind me.

In the days following the plea hearing, I learned that a guilty plea to one charge had avalanched into reports of my having admitted embezzling millions of dollars. For me, the plea was an appeal to stop the emotional bleeding and to end the lingering stress on a grieving college community. I saw the plea as a way to move on past the hurt, lies and persecution. The plea reflected my deep-rooted distrust of the system being fair to anyone who dared to be an advocate for the underserved and oppressed. I recalled how, during my early years, injustice had driven my mother into despair, how my uncles had sacrificed their business interests to get blacks registered to vote, and how I had seen TV reports of freedom fighters who had been beaten, jailed, and even killed. I also recalled how in the course of the past few years I had seen my values, contributions, and service trashed by a system intent on crushing me. And now my pain and sadness joined theirs. Where they had hoped to find justice, they found worse than none, they found the opposite.

Despite how it might be viewed, I had also relinquished any future right to appeal. The stigma would always be there. No matter what I did with the rest of my life, there would always be that place in the road, that marker saying, Here, Dolores E. Cross pleaded guilty to a crime.

As much as the guilty plea burned through me, I knew there was one tiny balm: the government had agreed that I had not personally benefited from one single dime. That essential fact had to make a difference to the students.

My failure had been to look ahead and not around me. In failing to check the course to determine the pitfalls and hurdles, I missed a step, and from that missing step, slowly lost my balance and, later, fell.

I failed to fully absorb the instability caused by the college's having four presidents in a span of 10 years. In retrospect, I was too self-assured in believing that I could achieve what my predecessors had failed to achieve: stability for Morris Brown College. I had been driven by concern of losing re-accreditation and had forged ahead despite crumbling support, betrayal, and lapses in accountability.

But to the press, there were no mitigating factors. Like a cave that had opened up, everything could now be rolled back inside the sentence: Cross guilty.

Part III

Chapter 12

I was reminded of what happens to those who bring up the rear of a marathon. The crowds have gone. There may be a few family members and friends still waiting for one to appear on the way to the finish line. But though one is still trudging on alone, the marathon is over. Then I caught myself, realizing I was wrong in seeing what was happening as a marathon. "No, Dolores," I told myself. "If anything, it is a gauntlet. And if there is one thing you don't do inside a gauntlet, it is to fall down. You gotta go on to the end to be free."

Jane described the plea as an act of self-sacrifice on my part. To her way of thinking, I had fulfilled the need for a scapegoat, taken a lot of folks off the hook and had, in accepting responsibility, gone way beyond the limits of responsibility for college presidents. But I felt I had let everyone down by pleading guilty.

It hurt to think about those who had expected me to stay in the fight: my Diva Defense Team, Caroline and Ev. They had provided financial and emotional support when my resources had been drained. I wanted to go the distance and be exonerated, not give up. I was lifted up when Caroline told me she understood and realized the odds I faced. She applauded my strength.

The rise and fall of my tide of moods, swirling with optimism only to recede away, exposing the rocks of pessimism, must have been apparent to my friends. Not content to read my astrological charts on her own, Caroline even went to consult a professional astrologer on my behalf.

Dearest Diva,

The astrologer lady from Chicago was here looking at your charts last night. And she spoke for about an hour, more like a psychologist really, about the inherited trends and your spiritual path. Bottom Line, she couldn't see what precisely would be the outcome of sentencing, but identified this part of your life as a lesson in standing alone, as yourself, caught between your values and those of your parents, being a major part of a changing paradigm from the ancestral patterns. It's more about your internal journey. Barbara says your soul is dealing with a long history of betrayal and injustice and learning to break this – but without attacking or being unforgiving. Just needing to get rid of it in order to live in a world that's peaceful despite individual differences. As in the case of Nelson Mandela, what's important is how you'll come out at the end! And the outcome can be alchemical – base crap turned to gold – so long as you release betrayal, injustice, etc., rather than making yourself another symbol of such abuse. You have a very important mission.
Caroline

Yes, my mission. What had happened to my mission? Had I lost it myself? Had I misplaced it? Had I taken it for granted? Had I forgotten that it was a gift, an attitude, an awareness that had to be called upon each day? My mission, my mission, I kept thinking, imagining it like some gold ring I had taken off momentarily only to turn back and find it gone, forever.

I didn't know what to tell my friends and family. I knew to outsiders that it wouldn't make sense that I would sacrifice my reputation and career to avoid a trial. How could I have done it? I could hear people asking.

I was tired. I had reached a time to let go, to release and move on with what was left. But that was an excuse, and excuses didn't hold up when faced with a guilty plea. I didn't expect to be understood. Some things no longer mattered. People would either line up on one side or another: with me or against me. I had said "enough". I'd been out in front taking on challenging jobs, attempting to make a difference, working against the odds, and in the process losing sight of my limitations.

"Enough." I was done. Just let me keep what is left, I said. But there was no one to say it to… except God, and I had to pray that He wasn't in on what had happened to me. Worst-case scenario, he merely watched what had taken place, or had something else more important to tend to than Dolores E. Cross's trials and tribulations.

So I stepped back inside my life and waited for the sentencing. It seemed like everything was suspended until the date when I would learn what would be my punishment. Week after week I waited to hear when I would be sentenced.

In early summer 2006, I wrote Caroline.

Today was difficult. As I may have shared, I have real difficulty sleeping, the drama keeps coming back, it's uncomfortable dealing with all that has happened, i.e. the betrayal and disconnection. I'm working through it and writing helps.

I cringed when you used the words "my demise." I know you are describing what others see and this is an apt description for some. I see myself still standing and fighting back and advocating. This time it's for me as I try to set the record straight.

I encountered some impressions when I went to get my hair cut this morning. My barber has been a long-time supporter. She is a good woman and has had to deal with customers who seem to get delight in sharing the bad news about Cross. Her name is Margaret and I've been her customer since the days when I was president of Chicago State University. Margaret doesn't understand how people have forgotten my contributions to Chicago and its students and would have liked to see Chicagoans reach out to me in support. Where is Oprah? She says, and Jesse Jackson and Farrakhan in speaking out? I explain to her that for some it's part of a ritual. "Provide a sacrifice and say thank the Lord it's not me." She shares how customers bring in Jet Magazine and point out the story on Morris Brown College and say "Cross should go to jail." Yet they have no answers when Margaret asks, "What did Dr. Cross do?" She wonders why Jet Magazine did not contact me. They are part of Johnson Publication and located in Chicago. They accepted the story as expressed by the Associated Press and failed to investigate. Margaret realizes that for many blacks, Jet Magazine is the gospel truth.

I hear how the stress of defending me is affecting her and know as well that all I can do is to represent strength throughout the ordeal. Margaret is concerned about the sentencing. She knows what the jail experience is like from customers. She knows as well that a black woman will not be treated like Martha Stewart. We both know that there are folks who want to take me down and want to see me hurt and can't wait to throw stones.

I do not want to be a martyr. I do not want to pay a higher price for refusing to compromise my truth, but I do want to tell my story and to recount events from the vantage point of having been President of Morris Brown College. I want to communicate why I went there and the 35 years in education that led to my three-year tenure at Morris Brown College

I am concerned about making major strides on the memoir before the upcoming sentencing hearing. I honestly don't think I could survive incarceration. The thought makes me depressed for hours. Yet this passes and I visualize a better outcome. There's a real sadness at times, a disconnection from much of what seemed important in the past. I feel numbness as if my life is on hold. I worry about memory loss, forgetfulness and a lack of interest in things I once enjoyed. I go through the motions and wait to achieve the next hurdle, sentencing. Probation is an option and can happen. It doesn't make me feel good when friends I counted on to be positive and wish for the best tell me "serve your time proudly" or "it is only your body and not you." I want them to visualize me free and moving on with my life. I don't want to be a martyr for them. Strangely, I also feel an inner peace in my life. I understand and appreciate the gains of the journey and the opportunities presented by the crisis. I bounce back again and again, yet tire of the struggle. I value my solitude.

I'm starting over, yet staying put. My relationship with my sister is complex. She works full time and is caretaker for her ailing husband. It's too stressful for her. I know she loves me and I want to keep up a good front with her.

I keep moving on despite it all and learning how much standing up for yourself really matters and the importance of relationships grounded in who you are as a person is formed, yet not constrained, by history or defined by immediate circumstance.

The sentencing has been rescheduled from August 23rd to September 14th.

What do you see in the charts?

Dolores

That night, Caroline replied.

My Dear Dolores,

From my astrological hunting, I remember always seeing September as the worst time.

And now you are coming up inside it for your judgment in court. How easy for any of us, not in your position, to talk about what we think or guess will be happening, without going through all this horror and stress you have, all the time worrying that you will be handed a sentence at the end.... jeez.

However, we did ask over and over, could it be prison and the answer was continually NO.

Just restriction and repression – but at a lighter level. What a reward for all that work on instruction and empowerment of the needy. Where's that 40 acres and a mule, come to think of it.

I feel so bad for you, Dolores, and I just don't know how to express it.

Happy 4th of July to you – if that's not too ironic.

And love and healing thoughts.

Caroline.

In her communications I could always hear Caroline's soft British accent and lively spirit.

Dear Dolores:

A major friend who also came here a lot was Grace Halsell, the woman who wrote Soul Sister (and many books and pieces on the Middle East too). Do you remember her? She dyed her skin dark and lived as a Black woman for at least a year, in NYC and the South, and wrote out exactly what happened - she having come from a well-heeled Texas family.

As the color faded, she then posed as an American-Indian and wrote a book about how she was treated. She also joined a Jerry Falwell trip to Israel and wrote about the crazy fundamentalists who long for a major Armageddon so that they'll be wafted up to heaven to have front-row seats to look down and watch the planet burn.

A great woman with a passion for Justice - as are you. I have one or two extras of her books left and will give you one when next you can visit. Or mail you one if you're hot for a read?

On the sentencing hearing: The advice of the pillow, always clarifying, is that the restriction (Saturn) and oppression (Pluto) are ongoing and, with the help of a shuffle or two of cards, my best guess is that you're going to be given 3 months of house arrest.

I don't know quite what that means, but I imagine you are allowed out to work, or walk, or do the shopping?

Definitely no prison, but not as soft as probation either.

Restriction is the word of the day. A face-saver for the authorities/authoritarians. (I'm surprised the Statue of Liberty hasn't tipped over yet.)

Was talking with an old friend at breakfast and she'd just seen a movie about the McCarthy era - you know, she said, when they just pointed the finger at anyone, without any evidence, and cut them off at the knees!

Yep, beginning to recognize that. But I'm repeating it to you as perhaps the comparison may be used in your defense for this next case.

Admirable Diva, it just brings tears to my eyes every time I consider what is being done to you. But you'll get them one way or another if only by maintaining your stature and strength. Hugs to you,
Caroline

When I finished the letter, I looked up and knew I was trapped in a place where my entire life was on hold while I waited for my sentencing.

In late July, the government had filed its sentencing memorandum for review by the consultant to the judge. My defense team prepared a statement commenting on portions of the government's report and describing my background as well as what could not be proved.

Within a few weeks, my attorneys called to say that the consultant to the judge had recommended a far harsher sentence than they anticipated. We would have to take our case to the judge and have it weighed in light of the report from the judge's consultant. The consultant had responded to the government's presentation which persuaded her that my role in what the government regarded as a "scheme" went beyond the limited scope of my plea.

There was a stretch to go and I visualized someone cheering me on, most often heroes I have admired.....Nelson Mandela, Rev. Martin Luther King Jr., and Malcolm X. I also find myself talking to them, as well as members of my extended family who supported me through the crisis I faced when we were evicted when I was 13. It keeps me going to know there are others who understand the complexity of my journey and encourage my resilience.

The August and September dates for filing a response to the consultant's recommendation were delayed when Dorothy suffered a break in her right arm that required her to postpone filing a follow-up response to the consultant to Judge Carnes.

Despite the setback, Dorothy remained steadfast as she communicated her objections to the pre-sentencing report of the consultant to Judge Carnes. Through phone calls and e-mails Dorothy and I discussed the basis for our objection:

> Morris Brown College was not "in the black" when I began my tenure. The college had trouble paying vendors when I arrived and the school's audits from DOE were three years in arrears. The largest expenditures during my tenure were for unexpected costs to obtain the school's reaccreditation, technology infrastructure to meet DOE's requirements, repairing school facilities which were badly maintained, the laptop program to improve educational opportunities and payments to DOE for audit disallowances

in student financial aid from findings that pre-dated my presidency.

The government consistently overstated my knowledge of the detailed day-to-day application of the DOE regulations concerning students and my relationship with the co-defendant. As president of the New York State Higher Education Services Corporation I had legislative oversight of an agency with close to a thousand employees that provided student financial aid to over 750 institutions in the State of New York. I had no direct management responsibilities for the operation of the State's Tuition System Program or the Federally Guaranteed Student Loan Program. In the 1980s, the co-defendant was a member of a committee of student financial aid directors convened by the agency's Vice President of the State's Tuition Assistance Program. When the Director of Student Financial Aid moved to Indiana in 1995, he applied for position of Director of Student Financial Aid at Chicago State University.

The government argued that I occupied a position of trust in a Program Participation Agreement that Morris Brown entered into with DOE relating to student loans. Their simplistic position is that because I signed the Agreement and was the President of the school, I was a personal fiduciary. The Program Participation Agreement describes a fiduciary relationship between DOE and the institution, not the President or the signatory.

What is more, Morris Brown College's Director of Student Financial Aid had admitted to criminal wrongdoing by management practices that brought excess funds to Morris Brown College. He sought leniency by claiming what was not true, when he stated that, as president, I knew all about financial aid and his criminal wrongdoings.

The government held that I had aided fraud by placing the Offices of the Registrar and Student Accounts under the supervision of the Director of Student Financial Aid. However, the Registrar reported to Academic Affairs and the Office of Student Accounts reported to the Vice President of Fiscal Affairs. I had not given the Director of Student Financial Aid authority over these areas.

The government attributed the college's loss of accreditation to me, while in fact; Morris Brown lost its accreditation 22 months and two presidents after my resignation in February 2002.

Despite all we did and could have presented, I realized that in this emotionally-charged environment I did not have the support of the Board of Trustees had not heard from colleagues I had worked with on higher education boards who knew my values and advocacy for students. I stood alone.

I had difficulty sleeping and finding enjoyment in the simplest of routines. How could this be? The government simply did not have the case it believed it did when the indictment was returned. Their pre-sentence report relied on new government theories on the case and its expected evidence. The prosecution was now theorizing that when in the fall of 2001, as president, I responded to reports of students attending classes and living in the residence halls who were not enrolled by taking administrative actions to ensure that students were identified and enrolled, I had sought to enroll students with uncertain status. When in fact, as I would later learn from reports of the college's external auditor, there were longstanding system problems in determining student status caused by inadequate systems that predated my tenure as president. I had stepped into the fray when no else would.

Without ever interviewing me on what had occurred in the fall of 2001, the government relied on distortion and misinformation to create its case for presentation to the consultant to the Judge that would fit their conspiracy theory and keep me on the hook. The government was highly motivated. They had sensationalized the case in the press providing a point of view that joined the co-defendant and me at the hip. They were not about to admit they did not have the case against me that they alleged at the time of the indictment. The relentless posture of the U.S. Attorney in the Northern District of Georgia didn't stop there. The Department of Education in Washington, D.C. was asked to investigate possible wrongdoing in the management of student financial aid during my tenure as President of Chicago State University. They found none. The government had reviewed college records and my personal records to determine if any student financial aid dollars had gone to personally benefit me. They found none.

Not a day or night passed when the situation was not on my mind. In a trying state of "limbo," running with Cassie was the only thing that got me through the day.

Chapter 13

On the second Sunday in September, 2006 after the deadline for filing had closed, I made the decision to run Chicago's Half-Marathon. A field of 11,000 had registered to go the distance of 13.2 miles, and the starting line was only a block from my apartment. I called the marathon office and learned it was too late to register and get a number.

Yet if ever I was going to run another marathon, now was the time to do it.

It was Chicago's 20th Half-Marathon and I'd completed 20 full marathons during the past 20 years. I wanted to be in it and experience the runners and the pace on what turned out to be a glorious, perfect day. I needed to finish the race to feel that I could still do something important that mattered in my life, to feel that not everything was lost. Not everything that mattered had been taken away.

My clothes were set out the night before. I'd removed a number-bib from the hall bulletin board from the 2005 half marathon and pinned it to my shorts. As I hadn't registered, there would be no official record of my time and having gone the distance. With luck, though, I'd be allowed to finish and receive a coveted finisher's medal.

I found my place among the runners and set my mind to slow-run the entire 13.2 miles. The goal was merely to finish and experience the energy of the commitment and joy, and to follow my bliss. I noted a few outsiders like me without numbers and felt relaxed far in the back.

From where I was placed, it took me four minutes to pass the start line.

I had been running sporadically for more than six months, confining myself to long walk/runs with my dog. When asked where I had been, I explained a "loss of passion for running hard." I had maintained my running weight, yet not my muscle tone. Being in the marathon felt like I had stepped back into a river of energy I had wandered from.

My body instinctively recaptured the flow, and I soon found myself running ahead with scores of other runners. What am I doing? I wondered. Entering the race was not my intention, yet I felt ready and had no doubt about going the distance.

I was getting in the groove, moving at an easy pace and listening to my body. It's okay, I felt my legs telling me, with each rise and fall.

I was running and humming, "I surrender, I surrender, Lord...running relaxed and attracting the best outcome. I'm not struggling to be free. I am free"....feeling the truth of my energy sustaining my body. I was conscious of being one with people, pavement, sun, trees and voices about me.

It was an occasion to see more young black women running alone and in teams. It was different from what I experienced 20 years before. I was reminded of how the best continues whether I was in it or not.

I'm okay, I repeated to myself. I accepted the past and the present and visualized the best outcome for this race and the one waiting with my sentence. "I'm moving on," I whispered. I repeated the chant I used in training runs:

"Relax, release, relate,

Relax, release, relate,

Relax, release, relate."

With each step, my fears diminished. As I focused on the feet ahead of me, I settled into a running groove and greeted familiar marathoners. Yeah, I told myself, I can do this.

I finished the half marathon in 2 hours and 30 minutes, received a finisher's medal, returned home, phoned Tommy and Jane with the good news, and then took Cassie for a walk.

Why couldn't life be so simple all the time? I wondered, and then realized, it wasn't life that was complicated, it was people, and not all people, but just a few. Among them it took only one or two to undo all that I had accomplished.

Chapter 14

In November 2006, I was at home in Chicago when I received a call from my defense team concerning an offer from the government. The attorney general's office was prepared to recommend a sentence of one-year home-confinement at the sentencing hearing scheduled for January 2007.

Attorney Kirkley viewed the prosecution's offer as a good deal. She reminded me that the pre-sentencing report had supported a harsher sentence and, after all, "this was Atlanta." I didn't know what to make of her view that this was good news. I heard her saying "among her colleagues this was considered a good outcome" and "given the jail time received by former Mayor Campbell, Cross got a good deal." The merits of my case didn't matter. Even more, the U.S. Attorney for the Northern District of Georgia was not budging.

The government seemed to be holding the view that as the president of Morris Brown I should have been aware of what the "Blue Book" called for in day-to-day management of student financial aid and that in signing a program participation agreement I would be personally managing the timely refunding of student loan funds. The government attributed sinister motives to what it saw as my receiving reports on enrollment levels and cash-flow projections from federal student financial aid. Their presumption was unjust. What would happen, I wondered, if the government were to apply these conditions to every president who monitored the recruitment and retention of students, as well as expected revenue from student financial aid and fundraising in fiscal planning? The allegation or notion of a conspiracy was embedded in the government's view of my faith and confidence in the expertise of the college's managers of student financial aid.

At the end of December 2006, Caroline e-mailed a philosophical criticism of my situation which she told me was based on a book written by her uncle Professor Charles Vereker. She'd often spoken of him and I felt her concern in what she had prepared for me.

Caroline wrote:

Plato defines the four cardinal virtues as wisdom, courage, temperance and justice. He is looking to find these qualities in certain groups of people, citizens, in order to create and maintain a moral and harmonious civil society.

But where his civil defenders must have wisdom and courage, the society really depends for its purpose and consequent happiness (Eudaemonia, the Good Life, translated as Happiness in later centuries) upon there being people within it capable of making right judgments "because it is this sense of deciding wisely rather than pronouncing according to law which is nearest to the Greek term translated as justice."

And this ruling virtue, to be shared with and by all citizens already enjoying a political as well as an economic relationship between their groups, will create happiness and harmony amongst the citizens – with a moral life determined not by belief, or custom, but by wise and just decisions. "Political life is an essential means to a moral end."

Where do these basic ideas leading directly to the Pursuit of Happiness within the American social framework – and its Constitution - touch on the life and actions of you, Dolores Cross?

You have dedicated your life to the education of a previously discriminated, enslaved class of people who were not in any way empowered as citizens or integrated within the civil framework. They contributed economically, but got few citizenship rights or rewards and minimal integration-based happiness in return. You, who have dedicated your life to educating and empowering young people to enable integration and higher development to the good of all society, now stand unjustly accused of fraud and conspiracy in student financial aid.

Where, we must ask, is the Wisdom of this decision
as opposed to facile finger-pointing and the unresearched
application of Law. What has happened to Justice?

Caroline was saying what we both knew. In the likelihood of a
politically-motivated agenda against me, there need be no correlation
between an abstract concept of justice and a concrete manifestation of its
antithesis: injustice.

I was soon to live the reality of the antithesis.

On January 3, 2007 Jane and Tom Jr. met me in Atlanta. We talked
about earlier times and prepared ourselves for the court appearance. Dorothy
Kirkley explained that the appearance should be brief. We discussed my
personal statement to the court. It was clear that I would not have my
full say in court and that letters of support provided her for forwarding
to the Judge would not have a bearing on the agreement reached with the
prosecution. Dorothy had pared down what I had presented to her and
provided her own version for my approval and which was subsequently
agreed upon by the prosecution. She was, to my thinking, done with my
defense and had negotiated a tightly scripted statement for me to read in
court.

I didn't want to pass through the gate from which there would be no
return. I told her that I did not want to go forward with a plea. She was
clearly frustrated as she explained the repercussions of retracting my plea.
Drew was called in to explain the dilemma and efforts were made to reach
Jane. Were I to retract my plea, I could face charges of perjury and I had
sanctioned the course that was in motion.

Fear and despair had taken me to this place and I would have to accept
the consequences. I reread the statement and prepared to go into court.

When we entered the courtroom, I felt secure with Jane and Tom Jr.
with me. With his 6'4" frame Tom's presence was comforting. I was proud
of his protective posture. He glanced at me and stood at the door watching
people fill the seats in the courtroom. Jane sat next to me, checking out
attorneys for the prosecution.

With my children were a cluster of colleagues and friends. My eyes met
those of a friend, Dr. Gloria Jackson Bacon, a physician who had traveled
from Chicago to give her support. I had joined Gloria in efforts to establish
a clinic for residents of the Altgeld Housing Project in Chicago. Sitting
next to her was Grant Venerable, who had been on my team in various

administrative positions. While he'd gone on to distinguish himself as vice president of Lincoln University, I was aware that his support for me had undermined his hopes of ever achieving a college or university presidency.

I took note of Marcia Cross, Anita Whatley, and glanced around for others who had been on my executive team at the college. I realized that if things went bad for me, they, too, might suffer professionally from their close association with Dolores E. Cross. In front of them sat Dr. Joyce Ann Joyce, Professor at Temple University. Looking at her, I recalled how she had written an editorial, "Sins of Omission" in the Temple Faculty Herald in March 2005. Her article spoke to how the Chronicle of Higher Education reported on women and what had been missed in reporting on the situation of Dr. Dolores E. Cross. I had committed the conclusion of her editorial to memory: "It is my hope that other women of all ethnicities gather together in the courtroom during her trial in Atlanta, Georgia, particularly those who understand that there is not one Historically Black College or University that is not struggling to stay afloat financially, and if Dr. Cross, who has spent her entire professional life serving the underprivileged, is under siege, any one of us could be next."

I saw Joyce's dignified demeanor and took strength from the presence of faithful associates who joined me in the crowded courtroom. I was not alone.

The room was austere, with walls and chairs of dark mahogany. To offer a glimmer of hope, the ceiling was white with sunlight showing through the high windows.

Abruptly, Judge Carnes entered the courtroom.

Everyone rose. I focused on the surreal experience of having the course of my life determined by a judge, instead of by myself, as I always had. Had every day of my life led to this day? I tried to absorb every word cascading forth in a jumble.

Standing there listening to myself described in the third person, I thought of how far things had come since my attorney had appeared before the court a year earlier and had read the statement upon which the plea had been based and recorded. I waited, already knowing that the sentence would include my being fitted with an electronic bracelet. I had discussed with Drew the anguish of wearing an electronic ankle bracelet. It was a symbol of being shackled as a slave. In response, Drew said he would passionately state that I was not a flight risk and that I should not be required to wear an electronic ankle bracelet. What had motivated the prosecution's insistence that I wear an electronic ankle bracelet? What point was the U.S. Attorney in the Northern District of Georgia looking to convey? There was no negotiating on the point, the judge said, staring at me, "Dolores E. Cross is to wear an electronic bracelet."

I looked down at my ankles. "Which one's it gonna be?" I couldn't help wondering.

Then came "my moment in court." I paused for a moment, trying to draw on the strength of the ancestors, my friends in the courtroom, and my children sitting behind me. With a step forward into what I sensed would be the hardest marathon I would ever run, I walked to the front of the courtroom and prepared to read a statement which had been reviewed by the prosecution and presented to the judge prior to sentencing.

> Standing as tall as I could, I stared directly at the judge.
>
> "Your Honor, I am very sorry for the conduct that caused me to plead guilty. By mid-September, 2001, I knew from the DOE that Morris Brown College was not refunding all the student loan funds which it was legally required to return. I was keeping up appearances. I allowed this situation to continue even though I, as president, should have addressed it immediately. At the end of my presidency, I grappled with the tension between the visible flaws in financial administration and the need to keep up appearances." I shifted my stance, so that I could acknowledge the people in the courtroom, all the while being able to still see the judge. "To the students, alumni, faculty, staff and parents of Morris Brown College, I apologize for my failure of leadership with respect to financial aid. Morris Brown is an important historically black college."

For a moment, I paused, trying not to give in to the pain I felt. I forced myself to look back up. I don't think I have ever heard a space with so many people inside be so silent. A pin drop would have sounded like a boulder in that room. A heartbeat would be more like it; and I sure could hear mine, beating faster and faster.

> "I want to thank the faculty, staff, and board members and friends who worked so hard with me to try to address the many problems that existed at the beginning of my presidency. When I joined Morris Brown, the school was already on probation with the Southern Association of Schools and Colleges. There were approximately 68 findings of default when I started my

tenure. With the help of many, we were able to remove 64 of these findings. We also established the federally-required technology infrastructure and improved facilities where maintenance had been neglected. Funds were also required to settle earlier DOE complaints about financial aid. These initiatives did require the use of previously unbudgeted funds. I will always regret that we were unable to fix the financial aid and other management issues at the school."

This time I couldn't help brushing away a tear that had disobeyed me – sliding loose and making its way half-way down my cheek, before I dabbed it up with my index finger. I forced myself to look straight at the table of prosecutors, not scowling or smiling, merely letting them see me looking at them with an unbroken gaze.

"My family and defense team have stood by me throughout this ordeal and their support has helped me through this, so I want to thank them."

"Your Honor, I do want to contribute to my community after this is over, and I am more than willing to perform 500 hours of community service. When I stopped teaching, I volunteered with the Simpson Academy for Girls, Sue Duncan's After-School Program and the Midwest Workers Association. I am also active with my church and would like to teach others, maybe seniors, distance running in order to improve their health and well-being. I will continue these or other volunteer activities as permitted by the Court. I still feel that I can help disadvantaged girls and women negotiate the academic and other challenges they face. In order to fully participate in helping others and because I am so humiliated by this experience, I ask the court to order that I not be required to wear a bracelet for monitoring. I have been completely cooperative with my pre-trial officer and will be with my probation officer. Electronic monitoring is really not necessary for me to follow the rules set by the Court and my probation officer."

I paused, wanting to see if the Judge would make any sign of listening. She merely shifted in her chair, so I went on.

"Your Honor, I appreciate the depth of your review of my forty-year history as an educator, my health and the set of circumstances I faced at the end of my presidency. My conduct was not meant to benefit me personally, and the government has agreed it did not. I believe I have some contributions left to make and home-confinement with community service will allow me to do that. Thank you for your consideration of these remarks."

Pausing, I lowered my head, and then caught my breath, stood up tall and looked back up at the judge. "That is all I have to say, your honor," I said, walking back to my seat. I could feel every set of eyes on me as I walked down the aisle. I prayed that some of them were those of my parents and grandparents. I needed every set of loving eyes I could count on.

The judge asked for presentations by others who wanted to address the court. A Morris Brown College graduate responded on behalf of alums of the college. I was not surprised by his repeated linking of my name to the Director of Student Financial Aid. It was clear he was alleging we were "joined at the hip." His voice resonated in the courtroom as he placed the blame for the demise of the college on "the defendants." He was clearly asking for a harsh sentence. There were no other presentations in court.

Before issuing the sentence, Judge Carnes referred to the long-standing problems at the college when I assumed the position, stated that this was not just a case of mismanagement and that the sentence here should not indicate a judgment in pending civil action cases. She also questioned the government on the number of responses they had received as a result of the U.S. Attorney in the Northern District of Georgia's announcement of an 800-number for students to call for help. There was a low murmur in the court when the attorney for the prosecution stated that less than a dozen students had called and most were not from Morris Brown College.

I listened as the Judge addressed what the case <u>was not about</u>. It was not about Cross pleading guilty to embezzlement. In legal language, the charge at hand was a technical violation called misapplication of funds. She added that it was reasonably doubtful that the body of evidence that had been gathered would support allegations of embezzlement, given that Cross had never enriched herself at the expense of the college.

In issuing her sentence the judge was asked by my attorneys to consider health issues. I didn't want the details made public. Pity would be added to ridicule. It was too much to endure. As requested my attorneys approached the bench and presented medical records from a neurologist. The MRI report affirmed mini strokes and signs of trauma and evidence

181

that my condition required monitoring as well as medication and a specific regiment.

The judge proceeded to issue her sentence. I was to be given one-year home confinement with an electronic bracelet for the first six months, 500 hours of community service after the bracelet was removed. I was further ordered to pay $13,492 in restitution, a fine of $3,000.00, a $100.00 special assessment, and costs of approximately $100.00 a month for electronic monitoring. Last, I was given five years of supervised probation and surrender of my passport.

Even though I had anticipated what would occur, hearing the actual sentence was like having a tidal wave break over me.

I would have to report to a probation officer in Chicago on January 23, 2007, to be fitted with an electronic bracelet and begin serving a year of confinement. I would begin serving five years of probation and restrictions that prevented me from traveling outside the Northern District of Illinois.

I found myself struggling to breathe.

A week later, I saw the written pronouncement of my Conviction: Aiding and Abetting the Embezzlement of Education Funds; 20 USC 1097 (a). It was a continuation of a bizarre nightmare. The Associated Press (AP) printed a story of my having embezzled millions of dollars and accusations followed that alone was responsible for the demise of Morris Brown College. The spin was accepted by reporters throughout the country. For the U. S. Attorney in the Northern District of Georgia it was never about fairness. It was about winning. For the media it was about sensationalizing and feeding into the profound grief of the Morris Brown College community in the aftermath of the loss of their accreditation and my indictment. The long-term fallout for Morris Brown College, its alums, students, black leadership did not matter.

Part IV

Chapter 15

"But I have an appointment. I was told to be here at 10:00 a.m. I have an appointment. Will you check again?" exclaimed a thin white male in suit and tie, who quickly surveyed the waiting room which, with the exception of a few vacant chairs, was occupied by blacks and Hispanics of various ages. He went on insisting he had an appointment. He was anxious and appealing to the young woman behind the Plexiglas screen that he "had an appointment."

My eyes met those of a young black woman, who had been pensively filing her nails; knowingly, we smiled and suppressed a grin. We were both aware that this was the first time for this puzzled, tense, young white man.

It had to be his first visit to the United States Probation Office, Northern District of Illinois, for he was the sole white person and he was insisting he "had an appointment." He couldn't fathom the fact that we had all been told to show up at 10 a.m. and he was just one more person waiting. White or black made no difference. We were inside the criminal justice system, and whether it was color blind, I couldn't say. But what I could see was that its wheels turned very, very slowly.

The eye-contact exchanged with the young woman helped me relax. It was my second meeting with my probation officer (PO). I was there to be fitted with an electronic ankle bracelet. I'd heard about the monitoring device when reading accounts of Martha Stewart's sentencing. I read how she strove to create a view of normalcy despite her electronic ankle bracelet and public ridicule. Yet I had questions that I wished I could have raised with those who were waiting with me. I recalled that one rule of my status as "felon'" was that I could not associate with other felons. This stipulation may have accounted for the quiet in the room.

I continued to think about the young man and observed his movements in the empty space, his fidgeting and anxiety.

I almost missed my name being called. "Ms. Cross? Ms. Cross?"

"Yes?"

"Ms. Cross, it's time for you to go to the 'drop room."

This was the first stop before meeting with my P.O., Ms. England. I was to sign up and be accompanied by a female while I provided a urine specimen in a cup. She looked away while I complied. The experience was clinical and impersonal.

After I went into her office, my probation officer informed me that I was the first person with an electronic ankle bracelet assigned to her. She would work with me in developing a schedule that provided time for me to walk my dog twice a day, and to allow me to leave my house for an additional four hours a week for shopping, laundry, and errands. I could, with approval, leave to go to appointments with my dentist, physician and psychotherapist. The times away from my house would be transmitted to an agency monitoring my whereabouts. I would be required to pay $100 a month to a government contractor. Thoughts of Halliburton came to mind and how contracts were developed and folks profited from the prison system.

We went down the hall to get help from a technician in fitting the electronic ankle bracelet. The man explained how the device worked and provided me with a "watch patrol" monitor that I had to install in my home. The monitor had to be plugged into an outlet then into my phone. I would have to purchase a special phone for exclusive use in monitoring. The phone couldn't be equipped with caller ID or call-forwarding. I paid close attention as he demonstrated how the phone functioned. Next came the bracelet. It looked like a pedometer. It was black, water-resistant, and lightweight. Mr. Rose assured me it couldn't be moved past my heel without setting off an alarm. I knew not to tamper with it.

Ms. England placed it around my ankle and allowed a finger's space between the band and my ankle. She looked up as if fitting me for a shoe. "How does that feel?"

"Okay," I muttered.

The electronic monitoring device was meant to provide continuous supervision. It was a tool for monitoring my conforming to "house arrest".

The small transmitter fitted around my ankle periodically sent a signal to a monitoring unit – a small device connected to a power supply and telephone socket outlet. If I moved out of range of my apartment, the violation was reported to a monitoring center as "Left Home." When I returned a report would be transmitted as "Returned Home."

What a fall I've taken, I thought — the loss of dignity and sense of shame. Where is my life now? Disappeared inside an electronic bracelet. I thought: I want it back!

Driving back to my apartment, I recalled the young man and his insistence on having an appointment. I understood his dismay at his predicament and felt compassion for him. I was now in a different space in my awareness of others. Before, I had not given much thought to the criminal justice system and those who fell into its grips. Now I wondered about the young woman with whom I'd exchanged a glance. How did one become accustomed to the periodic visits to the probation office and having to make routine "drops?" How did one maintain distance from other felons? How did you know when you are in the company of one? The rules said you must not be in the company of felons; did I need to identify myself to others? I was in a different social sphere. Wearing an electronic ankle bracelet would be a constant reminder.

My thoughts centered on my "just wanting it to be over." As someone who had spent almost the past 40 years of her life in academia, I knew that it was more than the experiencing of wearing an electronic ankle bracelet that would challenge my reality. The greater challenge for me would be using my confinement to continue to share in the experience of education. I swore not to let my home confinement seal me off from the world.

Still, I dreaded the idea of an "electronic ankle bracelet." I saw it as a shackle to remind me of the cruel indignities of slavery. As with slaves, my movements would be restricted and whereabouts checked. Electronic monitoring was seen as a compassionate alternative to incarceration. It was less costly and communicated the status of a "felon" or "criminal." The bracelet was meant to remind the wearer of having transgressed and the ensuing punishment. The bracelet was meant to give me another reality and another identity.

"I know who I am," I told myself. "I am a black woman. I know where I am. I got caught in the grip of mean times."

At home after stopping to purchase the special phone, I got the monitoring device hooked up and tested to show it was working. Looking down at the black box I asked myself, how did I let my life dissolve into the darkness inside? I felt like an insect trapped in a wedge of amber.

A month after being fitted with the electronic bracelet, I had a 10 a.m. meeting with Ms. England and knew to arrive early. The waiting room in the probation office was likely to be filled with fellow felons who were also there for the DNA sample required by the criminal justice system. My probation officer signaled for me to join those lined up. "This shouldn't take long. It moves quickly," she said. I felt the tension as I waited. This would be no ordinary experience in providing a blood sample. My DNA would be recorded forever.

I crunched my shoulders up to my ears, took conscious breaths and let my thoughts move elsewhere. Ms. England kept reassuring me as we followed the routine. She was doing her job and conscious of my presence. Within minutes my probation officer and I were inside a small room and I was seated facing a technician. The technician had the forms ready and needed only to prick my finger and get a drop of blood to smear on a small piece of glass. The glass would be placed in an envelope with my personal and criminal record.

I held out my hand as the technician pricked my finger. I watched in awe as the blood from my finger shot in the air, making an arc before hitting the floor. The technician checked her clothing for any drop that might have fallen on her. "This has never happened before," she muttered.

"That makes two of us," I wanted to say, but kept my eyes on my blood on the floor.

As I left the building, I thought of the irony of being fitted with an electronic bracelet and having my DNA recorded in a month that celebrated both Black History and Women's History. Two records at once, I told myself, willing to find any humor that I could in my situation.

I wanted to vent and put in a call to my friend Hal Edwards. "Can you still take your dog out to pee," he asked, knowing that laughter was the best cure when everything else was grim.

Yet the humor melted. When I climbed into bed that night, I knew in an instant that my mind was racing too fast for sleep to overtake it. For hours, I tossed and turned, seeing black and white snippets of the documentary of the life and times of Dr. Dolores E. Cross, former educator, former marathon runner, former enabler, former everything, and now prisoner of one electronic bracelet.

My Movie

Suddenly, I was sucked into a whirlpool of memories and voices, all the way back to my childhood. Like Dorothy inside the tornado in *The Wizard of Oz*, I saw my Aunt Jean swirl past, followed by my father, chuckling to himself. Then mom appeared, not saying anything, not having to. Her look was enough — all eyes, peering into me.

I cried out, "I'm sorry."

Sitting up, I leaned over the bed, staring down a swirling chimney of faces and places; and down I went.

On weekends my mother sent my sister and me off to spend time with our grandparents. We were instructed to listen and understand that our grandparents' parents had once been slaves and were strong people.

Grandma Tucker kept us in her kitchen, fretted over untangling our hair and included us on her Saturday trips downtown to Bamberger's Department Store. She would purchase sticky cinnamon buns from their bakery and occasionally buy a gift for her sister and family who lived in New Rochelle. She made much of how she had to manage on the ten dollars a week Pa provided for the household. On Fridays, Uncle Sam came by to give Grandma special meats for her to prepare for Friday night dinners Pa would host for his 'boys'. As you see in many black families, whose mothers suffered and endured 'white male assault and privilege' during slavery, my father's brothers were every shade of brown and his sister Carolyn, the fairest, had blue eyes. Aunt Carolyn's gender precluded her from being invited to the patriarch's Friday feast. When his boys were seated, Pa began his long prayer. After 5 minutes had passed, when my father blurted "Pa, you worry God to death." Grandma's large bosom shook as she suppressed a laugh and hung on to the plate of steaks she was about to set on the table.

My father and his brothers Sam, Frank, Matthew, Roger, and Carlton and sister Carolyn were a close knit family. They were all hard working and respected for their generosity and community service. Four of the brothers owned the Tucker Brothers Insurance Agency. My Aunt Carolyn, the youngest, became a teacher and established a business making and selling artificial flowers. My father and uncle Matthew became tailors and dry cleaners. What I heard most often from the Tuckers was, "get a good education and give back to the community."

As with Grandma Tucker, our time with Grandma Johnson was spent largely in her kitchen. With a voice so soft that we had to strain to hear her, my sister and I heard stories of lynchings, my grandfather's travels as a stone mason, and how her older children raised the younger ones. Grandma's face tightened as she spoke of Haywood's being part Cherokee. She kept snuff tucked under her lip and spat out the tobacco's syrup as she went on, "Cherokees in North Carolina had slaves just like white people and felt better than us. Slaves were close to Haywood's family," she said, adding her husband's Cherokee father had married a Negro. Grandma left it at that and concluded her sparse sharing by giving us a look at a photo of Haywood. There stood a tall, well-built man dressed in black waistcoat and the attire of a Southern gentleman. His cheekbones were pronounced, and his skin was brown, like mine, with black wavy hair. To me, he resembled a bronze Andrew Jackson.

Grandma Johnson's words of caution to me were always the same: "Don't you think about having babies too young!"

When I turned nine, I really began to worry about Grandma Johnson's cautions with having babies too young. I had started my period and knew it had something to do about babies. Nothing more had been said. I'd told my mother about having seen blood on my underpants. She explained, "It's your period, your sister started hers last year." I was given rags to wear and wash. I could expect the bleeding to happen every month, and I could, if I wanted, get an excuse from gym classes. At nine, the last thing I wanted to announce was the fact that I had my period. I heard the connection of having babies and the "period" from some older girls who confided, "She got her period… been playing around with boys and later had a baby."

I took to running and competing in races in elementary school. My Daddy had spurred me on with stories of the black track star, Jesse Owens. Daddy would watch me run instead of walk and urge me on. With visions of Jesse Owens' gold medals, I pushed ahead hard. The school's track coach encouraged my speed, advised me to pump my arms more and to relax my shoulders. I competed in the Newark Track Relay and beamed as our relay team won first place in 1950 and second place the following year.

While Ma had been proud of the strides men were making in athletics, she faced being on welfare when jobs in the war plants and elsewhere disappeared for many urban blacks. Our experience waiting for government food handouts with my mother was not without adventure. As we stood in line for cheese and powdered milk, Ma would loudly decry the impact of dairy products on the diets of blacks. I would hunch my shoulders in an effort to be less visible. There was no accounting for what Ma might blurt out.

At 18, I'm announcing to a college admissions officer that, "I'm here and I want to matriculate in undergraduate education and become a teacher."

The admissions officer tells me that I had not been advised in high school to take courses required for matriculation into college. How could this be possible? I'd been an excellent student and been graduation speaker at Central High School, Newark, New Jersey.

Ma, Tom Sr. and Tom Jr. had worn their Sunday best to see me receive my undergraduate degree from Seton Hall University. I had seen Tommy Jr. receive his undergraduate degree in sandals and wearing his black robe over a T-shirt and shorts in the warm Sonoma State University sun. I stood and clapped as Jane received one academic award after another at the University of California and scanned the crowd for me. "Mom, where are you?" I could always tell them where I was and what I was doing. I was trying to give them comfort with my achievements and milestones. I'm doing that with myself now in the Kafkaesque nightmare of confinement, of loss of hope not to mention sleep, not knowing where the movie ends and the reality of life begins.

Movie Over

But at that moment, sitting on the edge of my bed in the darkened apartment, with the electronic bloodhound fastened to my ankle, I didn't know where I was.

One thing was for certain: I was not in a place I had ever been before. I am lost inside the system and feel I won't be found for a while.

Maybe my apartment was better than a prison cell, but it was still a prison. I couldn't see the bars, but I could sure feel them.

I dropped back on the bed, thinking of all the opportunities I wasted to spend more time with Tommy and Jane, and didn't. There was always something I had to do for "us," to move us on.

Move on! Move where?

"Dolores, where you moving now?" I heard my Daddy call.

"Nowhere, Daddy."

"Damn right, baby girl. And stop feeling you brought it all on yourself. You didn't see it coming but it is here and you can't run from it. Well, don't let it drag you down, girl, you got spirit."

I feel seasick, from being tossed around on a sea of memories.

"Stop it, Dolores," I told myself. "Stop feeling sorry for yourself."

I'm not; I'm not feeling sorry for myself. I'm feeling much worse than that.

All those times, when I missed seeing Jane as she competed in high school sports, or failed to make one of my son Tommy's music concerts or was delayed on a scheduled flight home--all snuffed out, gone forever.

And all my excuses as to "where I was" and why I couldn't be there with my family because I had to be somewhere else, somewhere more important....all of it crumbled before my eyes.

I got up and started pacing in the hallway.

I would not permit these cruel events to suck the life force out of me. I would outlive the imposed sentence and remain free to continue my journey.

I would not give in, I told myself. Then I looked down and saw that dark snake coiled around my ankle. "That's part of me now," I thought, "I take that off once and I go to prison. I fail to answer the phone once, I will be arrested. That bracelet is you, Dolores. Deal with it."

I walked back to my desk and removed the journal. Opening it, I took my fountain pen and wrote:

"This is my time capsule for the future, for those who might want to know what it was like inside the life of Dolores E. Cross."

Here I have no photographs of the major events, no newspaper headlines, no scientific discoveries to tuck away for the future. No, I have nothing inside my time capsule except these words, words I realize no one but I might ever read. Yet they are the only things that console me to get through the long night of time inside the electronic bracelet.

Putting down the pen, I gazed down at the small device that was more like a wall eclipsing all the sunlight of my life; and I was forced to stay inside, waiting for its dark coil to be unwound from where it held me its prisoner.

Would I have been smarter to have fought for my innocence and lost, seeing myself sentenced to prison with other women? At least there I would have been able to share my solitude with the solitude of my sisters.

Here, alone, under house arrest, I found time anemic and slowing down. A day was a week, an hour a day, a minute an hour, and worst of all were these timeless periods inside the horrible blank called now, in which I wandered for hours and wondered if I would ever reach the end. Then, just when I thought I was at my most alone, the phone rang and a man's cold, harsh voice asked the most absurdly obvious question: "Are you Dolores Cross?"

I felt like saying, I was until you intruded into my life, but instead, I meekly complied. "Yes, I am Dolores Cross."

Without even the most perfunctory goodbye, the voice fell silent, followed by the click on the phone at the other end of the line.

Night after night, I found myself standing in my apartment, wondering if this was what people meant when they said they were losing their minds. Did they mean the slow erosion of their confidence, the gnawing away at what they thought they had known and believed about themselves, yet behind it all, the weight of something foreign, not them, was pressing forward, taking over their lives?

Periodically, the same man always called, always with the same question first, "Are you Dolores Cross?" then every other day, as though to add a little variety, a second question: "Where were you fifteen minutes ago?"

"Here," I answered each and every time.

For a moment, I felt like picking up the phone and calling back House Arrest and asking, "Who are you? Does it bring you pleasure to wait until people are at their most vulnerable to call and ask them the most obvious things? Don't you see that you, too, are under house arrest?" But of course, there was no number to call out, only my number to call in.

Was it because I was older that I endured these long nights so poorly? I never knew I could experience such solitude as the one I experienced inside the electronic bracelet. The solitude felt vast and empty, like unused time. Maybe this was part of the punishment, knowing that for someone like me, used to doing, doing, doing, doing nothing ached.

I read, I wrote, I tried to think, but my thoughts kept circling back, asking the same questions again and again: "Where did I go wrong? What moment could I undo to change everything? Is it too late to emerge from this cave?"

Then the questions stopped and I would simply lie motionless in bed, staring at the ceiling and seeing the windows of my past drift pass saying to myself, "There goes my mother to work. There sits my father laughing while telling a story; and there's my sister walking beside me to school; and Tom Sr., reaching out for our first dance."

A gallery of my family garlands in the dark.

Even when I sat up to free myself of all the memories, I knew they would be waiting for me when I lay back down.

I never wanted to be so intensely introspective. I never wanted to see my past over and over again, like a loop of film I can't stop. I only wanted to do what I did best: teach, educate, enable. Now, like a machine that did one thing well, I had stopped, and I was coming apart.

It was all a dream, wasn't it, what I accomplished? What did all the good that one did matter if one lost one's reputation? It was what people remember last that they remember always.

I heard a woman's reedy voice grow louder. "Dolores E. Cross...oh yes, wasn't she the black college president who was convicted of a crime. Whatever happened to her?"

"She ended up here," I whispered.

Chapter 16

Checking my e-mail the next morning, I found a message from Caroline:

> Dear Dolores,
>
> Well, the news is not good. Ev will have had her colon tumor taken out by now…and then has to wait for a while before they do her liver. I had wanted to tell you earlier and needed her permission to do so. She didn't want to add to your stress.
>
> Caroline

I thought, "My stress? Ev may be dying, and I can't be with her." I understood Ev does not want to give her physical situation life by sharing the reality of her circumstance. I thought of the lines from a television commercial: "Who does depression hurt? It hurts everybody." I could substitute the word 'stress' with 'depression'. Stress hurts everybody. I thought of the impact of my stress on my dear friend Ev. I recalled my friend James confiding how the stress of my situation weighed on his tending to challenge of dealing with cancer. My bizarre nightmare impacted family and friends. I felt useless and of no help when they needed me most.

An e-mail from Ev followed:

> I apologize, Diva D, for not sharing my info with you sooner. I didn't want to add to your worries. The situation is that I am headed for somewhat radical surgery tomorrow.

There is a malignant tumor in my colon and another tumor in my liver. I've been back to the hospital every day. You're in my thoughts often, I marvel at our resilience. We're tough ol' broads. Thank goodness.

I thought about our shared tendency to socialize and make friends with strong men and women. As friends who meet in Rio Caliente, we have shared our history, and with humor reacted to the myths of aging. Ev and I had hoped to be in Rio to celebrate Caroline's birthday. She always let us know how much she hated birthdays and we agreed not to celebrate hers or mine. Caroline embraced the notion of the endlessness of prime time and focused on non-traditional means to extend the quality of her life and that of others.

In her letter, Ev stated that she felt bad that the press and the court had carried on about my age....demanding they show "more respect por favor." Ev concluded that while John McCain could run for President of the United States, a 70- year-old-woman couldn't even get a temp job.

Our Internet chatter affirmed our coming to grips with the reality Ev was facing. Then when I reached the end of the e-mail, I found the empty apartment waiting.

In Extremis

Some days I wondered if I was healing or was I simply burying the pain. I would be moving about the apartment, getting things done, there'd be a hue of normalcy as if everything was like it always was. Then I would feel it down there, attached not only to my ankle, but clutching the very roots of my life, that thing.

But I kept reminding myself that it was a beautiful day and I was alive, no matter what. So I was doing both, I guessed, healing yet burying the pain.

At night, it seemed what I tried to bury through the day erupted for me to feel twice as intensely as before. I replayed being at Morris Brown, from the first time I walked onto the campus to the last time I left it.

I slowed everything down to try and see inside the flow of everyday events the things I should have caught. It was agonizing to go through it again and again, like uncovering a wreck, a catastrophe, the sinking, all of it was lost in a flux of people doing their jobs, of unheard words passing among colleagues. There was no mystery waiting to be resolved. There was only the fabric of my life rolled out before me, and I spent hours moving back and forth, trying to find the flaw in the pattern that had undermined it all.

This enforced hibernation was no spot I was passing through on a marathon. This room, this hand holding a pen, these eyes staring down at written words on a page were the start and finish line merged into one.

This middle of nowhere was my life.

Night after night, I would wake in the middle of the night, called by a woman's voice, one that fell silent as soon as I woke.

Who was she? I wondered. What was she saying? As though all was a pretext to waking me, a swarm of thoughts would engulf me. I'd get out of bed, ordering myself to stop thinking, "Or I'll what, I'll go off the tracks?" I asked myself, only to think, "And you don't think this is derailment here, woman?"

I had to stop trying to find "It." There was no moment beyond which I was innocent and after which I was guilty. There was only the progression of my life and the fall from grace. It was not like a fire whose origin could be traced to a match and the hand that struck it, or a theft that started with a figure skulking through the dark. No, my crime was dissolved inside a process, like a captain who goes below on watch on a clear sea, only to wake with water everywhere, I realized I failed. No matter who was on duty, what happened occurred on my watch. It all led back to the captain of the sunken vessel.

What would have happened had I remained on at Morris Brown College? Would I have discovered what was wrong in time to change course and avoid the disaster? "Who knows?" I thought, wandering through my darkened apartment as though it were a closed museum. In my living room there was no time machine to go back to the past, no laboratory to analyze everything that had been written down in the documents in my attorney's office. No, maybe at most, my apartment was a clearing where I had nowhere to turn. Maybe this was what it looked like: the place where the buck stopped, where everything that wasn't essential fell away, and I was left counting up the sum total of my life.

And if it added up to zero, then what?

But I wouldn't kneel to such thinking. I wasn't raised on the porridge of self-pity. I eschewed the taste of it. Self-pity was poison masking as honey....and I would starve to death before I swallowed it to comfort myself.

"What did my uncle say he was told to say if captured in war?" I recalled. "Name, rank, and serial number."

And mine? "My name is Dolores E. Cross. I am a Black woman. I am an educator. That is what I will take out of this world with me and no one else, judge, jury, rumor monger or outright foe will take it from me. It belongs to too many of my ancestors for it to be taken away. I worked hard to earn it. I won't undo it now."

I put my head down on the journal, listening to another voice, not the strident, willful one, but the softer, more understanding voice that seemed to know at what moment to speak in a voice hardly louder than a whisper. "Yes, yes, Dolores, I know…there are more civil actions to face, there are people saying that you took millions from Morris Brown, who would like nothing better than to see you lose everything and end up out on the street, so they could say, 'See that gray-haired lady over there? That's Dr. Dolores Cross, big shot college president. Look at her now. Yep, uh huh, she fell all the way.' Are you going to give them that satisfaction, Dolores?"

"No way," I said, sitting up. "They won't see me broken."

I got up, made coffee and scrubbed the kitchen floor for the third time that week.

What was causing this swirl of moods? I wondered. What was making me replay my life as though I was nothing but a container for a bunch of old home movies?

"Hey, girl," I told myself, "it's not over. My life is not any movie, and if it is, this isn't the third act. I don't care what they say or write about me. I am not 'history' or 'toast' or whatever expression they use. I'm still in my marathon. I don't care if they've all gone on ahead. I'm still running."

I looked down at my legs, accepting they might be moving up and down just in one place, but knowing they were still moving.

Why was I now going through in the courtroom in my mind what I didn't go through in the real courtroom when I was there? Was this what they meant by delayed-stress syndrome? Everything in my life seemed stamped A.S., After Sentencing.

There was no escaping the electronic bracelet and the thoughts it evoked every day and night. There were days when the bravado was suspended. I plunged down with feelings of unbearable despair. Was I was being seen as having criminal intent just because of my Newark roots? And days when I internalized the view of the oppressor: she is unworthy, bad, guilty and a discredit to her race. How had slaves felt when shackled to prevent a flight risk? What did they do when the pain of the loss of their past was too great? How would I live with this cloud? Where could I go from here?

The turmoil and mood swings circled in the journey inside the electronic bracelet.

Was there a potion I could take to forget everything? If there was, would I take it and lose all the lessons I have learned?

Maybe it was my ego, I thought. Dr. Dolores E. Cross was doing all the fretting. Maybe without the title, the name, the reputation, there would simply be a woman alone in her apartment, trying to figure out how to keep on going. It was bound to overflow, all the damming up of my fear, anxiety, without a way of running it out the way I used to, and suddenly I realized I didn't have to take it anymore. I could just end it; unplug everything in my life, leave.

Suicide.

For the second time since it first flashed through my mind at court suicide didn't seem like the coward's way out. Even though I never liked to second-guess the motives for people who had killed themselves, I always felt they had lacked something: a bit of fortitude, an extra bit of energy to get them through the darkness where they were stuck– and chose to stay.

But I was wrong. Maybe they were simply worn out, frayed, tired of trying to keep at bay what wouldn't stop forcing itself into their lives.

All I'd need to do is to put on my coat and slippers and take the elevator down to the lobby and cross South Shore Drive and walk right into the lake and keep going.

I'd be gone.

I faced the irony of my refusing to drop out of a marathon and now looking at dropping out forever. I was shaken by the thought of Jane and Tom Jr. standing somewhere motionless as if frozen in place by terrible pain. And I saw my friends shaking their heads in disbelief and turning away. How could I have done it? With all that I had endured in life, where was my fight?

I turned on the table lamp and glanced back at the window.

Glancing down, at that strange instrument that had become part of my life, I heard myself saying, "So you're thinking about telling your story, too, huh? Tell you what, it's not worth it. Too many good people are gonna be sad, and too many bad ones are gonna be happy."

Turning, I started back to my bedroom and stopped when I approached the wall of photographs, my ancestors lined up. I felt ashamed, as though they had heard me thinking about giving it up.

I felt more alone than I had ever been. I wasn't meant for being embedded in prolonged solitude. I was meant to be outside, seeing people, not packed in here, night after night.

This marathon was different from any marathon I had run before, because it went nowhere. "Light's coming," I told myself. "Keep a steady pace till morning."

The phone rang as it had before.

"Is this Dolores E. Cross?" asked the familiar voice of the stranger.

"Yes, this is Dolores E. Cross," I said.

"Where were you fifteen minutes ago?"

"Right where I am now, in my living room."

A click on the other end of the line.

I stared at the bracelet and then tossed and turned for hours.

Finally, I saw the glow over the horizon and knew my night of nights was ending. I could sleep.

Part V

Chapter 17

The silence along the lake was slowly replaced by cars and the punctuation of horns and an occasional siren. Day was safely in place.

Leaning across the bed, I patted my companion, this woman's best friend: Cassie. She lifted her head, staring at me with those eyes that never questioned or judged me. They simply saw me as I am. Not once in this entire ordeal had Cassie failed to be beside me. The great German poet Rilke wrote that without animals, life would be unendurable. He was so right. Even though I had the love of my two children and the support of friends, it is Cassie who shared the darkness and long nights.

Sitting up in bed, I stared down at the bracelet, grateful it was only a tracking device. "Imagine if it had an electronic eye," I thought, "that could follow me everywhere I went." Shuddering, I cast off the image and got up to go feed Cassie.

The day waiting before me was broken into grids of time. And inside those grids were rules and restrictions concerning how long I could be outside, shopping, seeing my doctor and therapist, or even going to church.

As for space, it was no longer endless. I had invisible walls beyond the window, places I couldn't go to without permission of my probation officer: who, in doing her job had consistently refused to deviate from "the book," and let me visit a sick cousin, or attend a conference of educators. Being marooned was part of the punishment, and for me, the hardest to deal with. Unable to give back, I felt as useless as a spoon with a hole in it. After Cassie was fed, I did my morning stretches, knowing they were poor compensation for the exercises I used to do along the lake. As for the twenty minutes jogging I did on the treadmill, it was almost a parody of the five-mile runs I did daily.

"But, hey," I told myself, "this is what home confinement comes down to: compromises with freedom."

Sensing that I might already be slipping back into a "blue spell," Cassie came over, tugging my jogging pants. She wanted out, needing to make her little inspection of the bushes and trees in the park across the street.

An hour to exercise and walk for my dog: yes, it was allowed. But should I stay ten minutes longer watching the waves wash ashore off the lake, I would have an alarm going off when I got back; and within minutes of returning home, Big Brother would be calling me about my violation.

If it happened too many times or if I was gone too long, I could have my home confinement revoked and be sent to prison. And there, no Cassie. And there, no view of the lake. And there the endless days would be dangerous, yet just as endless.

I never knew a day could be a trek round the clock. For all my years as an educator, mother, marathon runner, time belonged to me: I used it. Now, maybe for punishment, it had slowed down and made me feel every tiny increment: instant, second, minute, hour…leading to night and the cave where I could escape time by falling asleep…until the infernal caller would find me and bring me back.

The days were structured the same: checking my e-mail, a morning call to my daughter then one to my son. Late in the morning, there would be a call to my attorneys to see if there was any chance to begin court-ordered community service. My appeals in the past had been refused.

Then I would start down the list of former students who have asked for recommendations, who wanted to talk about teaching as a career, or simply wanted to get an older woman's advice on trying to raise a family while writing a dissertation. I shared what I knew, sad that I couldn't be in a classroom or on a campus somewhere, but I knew there were all sorts of shackles; the worst were the ones that limited one's ability to share one's talent and experience.

At 3:30 I was dressed to leave my apartment for an hour and a half of exercise and another dog walk. I checked my watch and looked down to ensure that the electronic bracelet couldn't be seen from the hem of the leg of my pants. We were ready for the outside world.

Cassie bounded out of the building and scurried over to two other dogs from the building whose owners were usually walking them at the same time each day. I stopped to chat with them, not the leisurely way I did before the sentencing, for time now no longer belonged to me.

Walking to a wooded area, I paused to salute the stately maple tree I called Ma, for I could see her from my window, and over the years, I had watched her take on snow storms, rain, and heat waves without ever yielding. She was the distant cousin of that tree of my childhood that still stood proudly in Baxter Terrace. And if I really wanted to feel good, I would close my eyes and imagine the roots from this tree beside the lake going way underground and stretching across the land, to link up and entwine with my "family tree" in Newark.

I spent the allotted time outside with Cassie, alternating walking and running, and disciplining my mind to take in the trees, my surroundings. One morning, as we sat on the rocks watching the waves of Lake Michigan cascade to the beach, my thoughts drifted to a recent monthly visit to the probation office. I arrived in full business attire, St. John black pants suit, carrying a brief and wearing my tiny pearl earrings. As I stepped off the elevator on the fifteenth floor, a young woman approached me with an earnest expression and asked, "Are you an attorney, I need help?" I smiled and responded "No, I'm here like you, to see my P.O." Her response was quick "Oh, Shit!" I laughed and read her saying "It's come to this, grey haired, professional blacks here, too." She joined me in the waiting room and saw my status confirmed as I was requested to 'make a urine drop.'

I lost track of the time as I gazed across the lake and considered the irony of voiding in a cup while 'dressed for success.' When I glanced at my watch, I found I had four minutes to cover in what I estimated to be a ten minute walk back to make it back to my apartment in the scheduled time to be out with Cassie. I began running at a marathon finishing line pace. Cassie sensed the urgency as we made our dash home. What if I failed to make it? Would the electronic bracelet sound off? Would a signal be sent to the police? Would there be a call from House-Arrest on my return? Would a violation be cited on my record? My heart was pounding and Cassie was panting as we made it in the building and to the service elevator by 9:30 and upstairs into the apartment by 9:31. I stroked Cassie, gave her extra treats and listened for the phone to ring. I was relieved when there was no call from House-Arrest for my being tardy by one minute.

I settled in and thought about the distress my confinement had caused Cassie on a night when I couldn't take her out. At 3 a.m. one morning she communicated her discomfort as she tried to control the need to relieve her bowels. She jumped up my bed and tugged at me. Her eyes pleaded 'time to go out'. I spoke as if she could comprehend "Cassie, mommy can't take you outside now." I considered the risk of defying the bracelet and stepping out the door and decided against it. Instead, I lined the kitchen floor with paper and enclosed her in the space. I sat outside the door and listened to her whine, moan. I heard her relieve herself and cry. A short time later, I opened the door and viewed the mess and smell from her sickness. I saw her concern and managed to soothe her as I cleaned her and took her to her familiar bed and gave her medicine I had on hand from her having a previous bout of diarrhea. I cleaned the floor and felt good in our having made it through the night.

Late afternoon now. A new set of rooms waiting in my head.

"Keep busy, Dee," a voice said.

I did, I did, and I did, until I felt like one of the brooms in Fantasia, cleaning the refrigerator, vacuuming the rugs, washing the laundry, then dusting off the book shelves.

Only two hours consumed.

The rest of the day seemed to be mocking me, saying, "We'll still be with you till it gets dark."

"It's already dark," I felt like shouting, but the day wouldn't understand.

On most nights, I refused to turn on the television and fall into the vat of distraction.

No, I had the radio for music. I sat down and wrote in long hand to all those special friends for whom I wanted to take the time to send a letter by surface mail, letting them see the shape of my words on the page, and hear me thinking slower than when I was at the keyboard, multi-tasking, thinking of half-a-dozen things at once.

Maybe time was being kind, letting it pass without my watching it go.

After dinner, I prepared Cassie for our last walk as permitted on the schedule. We had from 7:00 to 7:30 p.m. to walk.

Then when the wind started gusting off Lake Michigan, I'd called for Cassie and we'd head back.

Seconds after I closed my apartment door, the phone rings. It was Tommy, calling to cheer me up with news of the music classes he was teaching, and then passing the phone over to my grandson who told me about his second-grade class.

I was grateful for the love I heard in my ear, for to be truthful; I could not have lasted out the sentence if there weren't people who loved me moving parallel to where I was serving it now.

Almost a ritual, every night I sat on the sofa watching the light fade across the now steel-gray waters of the lake. As though carrying the day away itself, a barge moved into the wall of black moving ashore.

"Night," I said aloud, causing Cassie to turn, thinking I was calling her.

Turning on the lights, I went to make dinner. While I was doing the dishes, Jane called to see how I was and to tell me about a new class she was teaching in legal writing skills.

That phone, enemy and friend both. I hated it when the home confinement monitor called. But I craved it for being one of my bridges to the world beyond the bracelet.

Starting back to the living room, I spotted a spider scurrying across the tile. I remembered one sleepless night when I found myself down on my hands and knees with a jar in my hand, trying to scoop spiders into the jar. As soon as I had caught three, I stared into the jar, seeing them trapped inside the prison I had put them in. I let them loose on the back porch. Even spiders deserved their freedom.

After watching the news on television, I took a bath and got ready for bed. As I went to turn off the lamp, I stopped at the roll-top table in the living room. I could see myself that night, writing that ultimate note to my children.

I couldn't help it. I sat down, depleted of energy, feeling the cold flow of sadness of that night just out of reach, but so close. I shifted my gaze to photos on the wall: Nelson Mandela standing beside me when I went to South Africa for a conference of educators. And there I was with Hillary Clinton, standing proud to be with such an extraordinary woman. Next was a photo of Muhammad Ali and me. My eyes moved from photograph to photograph… a memory bank from which I kept withdrawing deposits of confidence. "There I was," I told myself, at the top of the world, "and now, here I am, at the bottom."

When they sentence people to home confinement, they should warn them to be ready to live their life a second time.

I felt like a projectionist inside a movie theater with one seat, the one I was sitting inside, facing the screen in my mind watching my ancestors pass, sometimes stopping and moving toward me. That's when I would step through the screen.

Strange, I told myself, how many things I now saw that I didn't see then, when I was living the moment….like the rock beside the lake, and the way my blouses would stir on the clothesline behind my apartment building, raising their arms in the wind like they were dancing.

Before I was running too fast to see anything but the road ahead. But the running had come to a stop. Now I could sit for hours, staring at every little facet and niche without ever coming to the end of them.

I put in a call to my friend, Hal Edwards. Hal was the former Director of City Quest. I had been on the board of City Quest and observed his leadership in responding to communities and individuals in distress. He and his wife Betsy have been close friends since I arrived in Chicago in 1990. I was accustomed to meeting periodically with our 'network' group of a dozen friends. The network's times together were informal as we each took time to 'check in'. We listened to each other and responded with advice, encouragement and prayer. On this day, I was calling Hal to check in. I told him of the worries I was having and the endless replaying of everything that had happened to me.

Hal urged me to pay particular attention to any repetitive patterns, those old audiotapes that have been playing in your head for many years.

"Listen to the voices in your head, be there as the witnessing presence. When you listen to that voice, listen to it impartially. That is to say, not to judge. Do not judge or condemn what you hear, for doing so would mean that the same voice has come in again through the back door. You'll soon realize: there is the voice, and here I am listening to it, watching it. This I AM realization, this sense of your own presence, is NOT a thought. It arises from beyond the mind." He said the words were from Eckhart Tolle, in his book Practicing the Power of Now.

I concentrated on what Hal shared from Tolle…to listen to the voice within. It was not easy to do and stay calm. I was trying to recover the gift of finding myself and the voice inside was the one I had always trusted, always followed.

Whatever I experience due to this journey in an electronic bracelet will serve my highest good. I know this in my heart as I listen to the tick-tick of the seconds of my life and how it fits into the heart of so many women and men, black and white, living and dead, who struggled.

Sylvia had volunteered to call me every Monday from her office in Oakland, California. I took notes during our 2 p.m. to 3 p.m. meetings. With her, I questioned if I had been 'hooked' to struggling against the odds. Had I been, "Dolores, the little girl", stuck on trying to please voices that called on me to 'give back to the community'. Or had I, in wearing the 'robe' of the President of the college, lost touch with my weaknesses. She guided me through the DVD, the Secret. The DVD provided the testimonies of scientists, authors, philosophers and ordinary people whose lives had been changed through an understanding of the' laws of attraction' and how by visualizing the outcome you wanted you could attract the very best. As recommended in the DVD, the Secret, I set up a bulletin board and applied notes on what I envisioned for now and the future: early termination of probation, completion of my memoir, dismissal of civil action suits, travel to Rio Caliente, completion of a half-marathon, and accreditation for Morris Brown College, I also added a gratitude list: good health, a loving family, enduring friendships, a pet companion, a forgiving spirit and so much more.

From the time the electronic bracelet had been placed on my ankle, Sylvia encouraged me to write this memoir. I would use the stillness of my circumstance to respond to her coaching, answer questions of whether the lessons of my life and those of my ancestors would permit the strength to grow beyond the crucible of my life. By honoring the marathons of my life and living in the present I found a path beyond the wall of the electronic bracelet. She urged me to re-read my autobiography and study photos taken in earlier times to connect with my resilience. Writing, she offered, would help me move out of my cocoon and "transform to a butterfly".

As scheduled by my probation officer, on Fridays from 10:30 to 11:30, I met with Dr. Martha Elder, a therapist recommended by my friend, Janet Morrow. Her office on Michigan Avenue was five blocks north of the U.S. Probation Office on Monroe Street near Michigan. Dr. Elder was a black female who I estimated to be in her mid-sixties. Traveling to her office on Michigan Avenue provided time in downtown Chicago. I'd leave the apartment at ten and had to be home by 12:30. Martha wasn't inclined to raise typical therapist questions, such as: Are you feeling angry? What makes you upset? Are you more comfortable? My meetings with her provided face-to-face meetings with a colleague, one with whom I could converse and reduce the feeling of isolation. I was reminded of meeting with friends at educational conferences when we would talk about the impact of challenges in higher education on us and how, no matter how small we were, we fitted into the big picture. With Martha, I could freely associate my experience with the pattern of the development of social and educational policies that did not address underlying problems in our minority community: the absence of jobs and the lack of a level playing field.

She listened as I spoke of the trials of being monitored by the bracelet. I confessed how on some nights I was awakened by a terrorized voice— mine—and that I kept having flashes of nightmares. Was I getting rid of stuff? Was I experiencing a loss of hope as well as sleep, not knowing where the nightmare ended and the reality of life began? I didn't know.

One Friday, Martha asked to see the bracelet and I lifted the cuff of my pants to show her the device.

"Not too cumbersome?" she asked.

"A lot lighter than a ball and chain, but it does the job," I exclaimed.

"You feel like a prisoner then?"

"Wouldn't you?"

Leaning back, she stared at me for a moment. "I suppose I would."

I told Martha how I had to cope with a malfunction in the electronic bracelet. "For the past few nights, I have been receiving several calls from House Arrest, where usually there are only two. I finally told the man he had already called five times in the same night."

"What'd he say?"

"Nothing. It was like he hadn't heard me. I felt I was talking to a computer, not a human being."

"That's pretty bizarre," said Martha. "How can you relax if the phone is ringing all hours of the night?"

"I can't. I keep anticipating the next call. I try to read books that take my mind off of where I am. No detective stories, nothing heavy, just light, escapist reading that makes me forget for a while where I am, until the phone rings again and my checker is back." I suddenly fell silent, staring down at the swirling pattern on the carpet.

"What's wrong?" asked Martha. "You look so serious."

"Oh, I was just wondering if they are deliberately harassing me. God, I would never survive being one of the prisoners in Guantanamo, being awakened at odd times. I quickly realized how my experience paled to theirs and to that of others confined behind prison walls. I smiled at Martha. "At least my bracelet comes off one day."

She nodded. "And your bracelet <u>will</u> come off."

On the Tuesday following my session with Martha, I went to meet with my probation officer. I was hoping to get the problem with the device rectified. She agreed to visit to do a signal check throughout the apartment and suggested that coils in the mattress may have caused a problem.

The next day she came to my apartment. First, she checked the watch-patrol device and swept the apartment to make sure their signals were being picked up throughout the apartment. She concluded there was a problem with the bracelet. The bracelet had to be changed and the watch-patrol recalibrated.

The process took over an hour. I grew tired as my P.O. checked receiving a signal in every area of my living quarters. She was efficient and precise in doing her job. I hadn't let her see my discomfort at having someone checking my apartment to make certain a piece of surveillance equipment worked. It was just plain demeaning, but I couldn't tell her. It was one more thing I had to work through.

I continued to reach out to Sylvia. She listened as I spoke of the daily climb back up the deep pit where I found myself. "The hurt is always with me," I said. "Sometime I'm stuck, and I don't have the strength to keep climbing out. I want to let go and fall back into the darkness."

"But you don't," she replied. "You kept forcing yourself back."

"Yes, but when I do, I find myself trapped in the apartment. I'm not used to not having a hundred things to do, outside, with people."

Her response was always strong, clear, unwavering: "Dolores, continue to work on your memoir like the book you did on marathons."

"It's not the same," I told her.

"It's your book," she replied. "Put whatever you want in it."

It was up to me, I realized. It would be good to write down what had happened even if it wasn't over.

Strange, within a few days of beginning the memoir, I found my mind liberated of the mundane. I didn't have to plan anything. My bracelet was my calendar and clock.

Then I looked down at the lines of black ink moving down the white fields of pages. "Who would I write for?" I asked.

"Them," I replied.

"Who's them?"

"All those I want to reach with my words, to show them."

"Show them what?" the voice demanded.

"Show that I wasn't broken by my sentence."

"Not good enough," the voice said.

"What is?" I asked.

"Go figure," came the reply.

For a few weeks, I stopped writing, letting the sessions with my therapist absorb the questions I had been asking in my memoir.

With Martha, I enjoyed being relaxed and candid. At one Friday's appointment, she was wearing jeans and a black vest over a long-sleeve blouse, just like my outfit, except my vest was red. The mirroring resemblance gave us a laugh. I found my usual spot across from her and settled in as we engaged in small talk about our children and news of the day. She turned to the topic of my home confinement. "When will the electronic bracelet be removed?" she asked.

Without even thinking, I recited the date I know by heart. "July 22."

"Then what, Dolores?"

"For the remaining six months of my sentence I will maintain the same time restrictions and be monitored by phone calls and periodic home visits from my probation officer." At the end of the year of house arrest, I would still be on probation with monthly reports and visits to the probation office and restrictions that precluded my traveling outside the Northern District of Illinois until June 23, 2012.

"How are you handling all this stuff?"

"Okay," I answered, then realized she really wanted to know.

"Fine, thank you," I responded, watching her reaction and not seeing one, then sensing she wanted a more specific answer to how I really felt. "Can you tell?"

"Tell what?" she asked.

"That I'm still grieving for what happened? I'm not home free yet." I paused, counting off weeks and months in my head. "The house arrest portion of my sentence goes on until January 23, 2008. I'm halfway through 13 of a 26.2-mile marathon. In my heart, I know you can't take a trek like this alone. I'm finding my way and it hasn't been easy. I keep myself going with the knowledge that I am a product of a family that gave me courage to get through some difficult times. I'm learning more about what's in me. I'm troubled sometimes just dealing with the truth of my getting older and wanting to do something meaningful."

"What makes you think that? You're here, aren't you?"

"You know what I mean. I'm not off running a…"

"A what?"

I paused, trying to find the answer. "A marathon, I guess. I know it's gonna sound stupid, but I miss <u>meeting</u> people. I long for the world outside of my confinement."

I stared at the long lines of books on her shelves. Then I dropped my head, rubbing the corner of my eye to warn that first tear to turn back, and to tell the others, too. They weren't allowed to make an appearance.

I looked back at Martha. "I'm worried how people are going to treat me when this thing is over. I don't want to be caught up in labels. I don't want to be defined by my circumstance, by what I did once. I mean, I know my life is more than the sub-total of whatever crime, if it was a crime, I pleaded guilty to. If I hadn't, I might be sitting in some women's prison now, talking to myself."

"Dolores, look at me. You're not alone in your apartment. I'm here. What are you worried about? They can't take away your honors, or your diplomas, or all your teaching experience."

"No, but they can, and have, taken my reputation."

"If they do, you take it back."

"How?" I said a bit too sharply.

"With your actions in staying strong and the words in the memoir you're writing. They'll know who you really are."

"You don't understand. I don't want to spend all my time apologizing for the one major mistake I made in forty years of being an educator. I want to encourage others to achieve all they are capable of achieving. I want to make a difference again. I want to be back in the flow again."

She smiled. "That's quite a list of wants."

"I've been saving up."

Nodding, she leaned back and took an open book off her shelf and handed it to me. "Look what I've been reading," she said.

I stared down at the open pages.

"Why not read it aloud?" she asked.

"What?"

"The passage that starts with, 'In the calm.'"

I glanced at the page and read:

"In the calm of self-surrender you can free yourself from the bondage of virtue and vice during this very life. Devote yourself, therefore, to reaching union with Brahman. To unite the heart with Brahman, Go. That is the secret of non-attached work. In the calm of self surrender, the seers renounce the fruits of their actions, and so reach enlightenment. Then they are free from the bondage of rebirth, and pass to that state which is beyond all evil.

I turned the cover over and read the title, The Bhagavad-Gita."

"I've seen students reading this."

"I think we all should, over and over again, until we understand how simple its truth is."

"You mean, self-surrendering?"

"Yes, but surrendering doesn't mean giving up. Dolores, you are a runner. You know, when a faster runner overtakes you, you're still in the race. You are just at a different place in it."

"You mind my asking something?"

"Please."

"Why did you think of me and this passage?"

"Not just you, Dolores. All of us. I was reading it last night and I thought, 'I must show this to Dolores. She'll understand.'"

All the way home, I kept thinking about what Martha said. "Dolores will understand."

"Understand what?"

Even though I was risking being late for my monitor's call, I parked for a few minutes by the lake and gazed out at the horizon where the sky and the water seemed to become one.

"Understand. Stand under," I thought. "Stand under what?" I knew the answer lay in the ability I had to stand in my truth: The race was not over, and, while not the fastest I was still in it.

Chapter 18

Tommy and I continued talking by phone daily. Ironically, my being under house arrest gave him greater access to me. My tending to matters of consequence in the past had limited my accessibility to him and his sister. They were doing their own loving by checking on me now and, at the same time, making it clear that I was not to use all the free time on my hands "to butt into" their lives. They knew me too well.

In case of illness in any member of my family outside Chicago, the court order did not permit me to travel outside of the Northern District of Illinois. I contacted my attorney and asked him to petition the judge to amend the court order to permit me to visit with Tommy, who had been in constant back pain after injuring a disc in his lower back.

After a few days, I telephoned my probation officer to see if she had heard anything from the court. After she advised me that the court order had not come through, I reluctantly put in a call to Tommy to say I couldn't come, and then heard the disappointment in his voice. Even more, he could tell how much I wanted to see him and find out how he was doing.

At five the next morning, I was awakened by a phone call. "Now, they're going to start making random calls," I thought, going to answer it. Instead of my monitor, it was my son. "Mom, get ready for company. I have Jackson in the car. I left St. Paul, Minnesota at 11 p.m. We've been driving all night and I'm on Lakeshore Drive, about 45 minutes from your apartment."

I quickly started scrambling to get myself together. Within minutes, I was dressed, had made coffee and was preparing the guest room for Tommy and my grandson Jackson. Minutes later, Tommy appeared, wearing a back brace and the broadest grin I've ever seen. Jackson leaped up and gave me a big hug. "Hi Nana, do you want to see my new snail?"

I was elated to see my grandson and ran my fingers through his curly blond hair as I appraised his new height.

The reconnection was easy.

Between yawns, Tommy asked me to prepare a list of things that needed to be fixed in the apartment. I had mentioned a leaky faucet and he had bought tools to repair it. There would be no putting him off and I added items for his to-do list: a wobbly table top, a showerhead replacement, and an oil change for the car.

While Tommy took care of things for me, I watched cartoons with Jackson, prepared oatmeal, and had him join Cassie and me for a walk outside.

Later, I observed Tommy sleeping and thought how few stories are written about strong black men who love and care for their families and manage as Tommy did, to endure pain and discomfort, and to do what it took to help and be present for their families.

Walking provided relief for Tommy's pain. He required a brace for his back and special seating in his SUV. He made the trip by stopping to walk and stretch every hour. I was relieved to see how he was handling the situation. His humor had not been dampened.

I observed his gregariousness as he talked with a Chicago policeman preparing to write Tommy's car a parking ticket. In seconds, both of them were laughing. "No one remains a stranger to Tommy," I thought.

This was the big weekend. We would be celebrating the electronic bracelet being removed. Tommy had planned to stay in Chicago until Jane arrived Friday night. We were disappointed when Jane missed her flight and would have to wait a day. Tommy couldn't wait for her arrival. He had to get back for a scheduled weekend with house guests in Minnesota.

Jane arrived late Saturday night, July 21st. This was Jane's fourth visit since my sentencing in January, but I had not wanted her ever to see the electronic bracelet on my ankle. Each time she visited I made sure to wear pants to cover the contraption. And when she once asked to see it, I said it was bad enough that I had to see it. I didn't want my daughter, or my son for that matter, to see my high-tech shackle. I did not want her to bear the situation with me. She understood and did not ask again.

On the morning of July 22nd, I felt like a child on Christmas morning.

I knew what a special day it was. I sat at my dining room table with a cup of coffee and began writing down all the gifts I had received from my children, most of all their strength and loving presence in my life. I added the names of every family member I could recall and all of the friends I had, as though I were compiling an invitation list for the biggest party of my life.

In a sense it was My Freedom Day Party.

No sooner had I finished one list than I started writing down all the important dates in my life, from my marriage to my divorce, dates of marathons I had run. My electronic bracelet was coming off, and I was grateful for my health and being able to soon say farewell to the electronic bracelet and not be emotionally shackled.

After an hour, I went to the computer and ran through my address book to address a note of gratitude to friends listed. I explained the ritual of gratitude, announced the removal of the bracelet, and shared plans to enjoy the flowers sent by Caroline. I was feeling light and forgiving. While I had no illusion of moving ahead with an absence of pain, I was grateful for the moment.

The next morning, July 23, 2007, I joined others at the bus stop to wait for the No. 6 Express to take to Monroe and Michigan for my 10:30 appointment with my probation officer. Passing the Lakefront minutes later, I couldn't help but smile at seeing the path where I had been running a couple of hours earlier. The Lakefront had now been taken by a contingent of runners from the University of Chicago. Their pace was much faster, but I had been out there running before most of them were born.

The bus route took me past the Field Museum. I had watched the museum campus expand since my days on the board of the Field Museum. It hardly seemed likely then that one day I would find myself passing enroute to visit my probation officer.

I disembarked at Michigan and Monroe. The United States Probation Office was on the 15th floor, almost diagonal to the University Club of Chicago. I was no longer bothered by the irony of having once fretted about being a few minutes late for a meeting with a colleague or potential donor at the University Club when I now felt pressed for an appointment at the United States Probation Office.

I was there to return the bracelet and say goodbye to the watch-patrol device. I couldn't say I had ever gotten used to the bracelet. How could one anyone get used to it? It was like having a snake coiled around your ankle, and not a tattooed one, either, but one made of rubber and metal. Tired of hiding it underneath trousers for months, I wore a long dress for the occasion. I wanted to walk out of the probation officer's office with my leg free of the impediment tracking me the past six months of my life.

At the federal building, a camera signaled my presence and the door was released for me to enter and move to the receptionist to announce, "I'm here to see Ms. England." The process in the office was business-like without the bureaucratic hassle that one might have expected in an appointment with a probation officer. The receptionist recognized my name and called the officer to whom I had to report. Motioned to take a seat, I found a table in the back of the room and pulled out my journal to record the time of my visit and make notes for my meeting with Ms. England.

A young black man was pacing back and forth, skipping and moving in what looked like a prance. He was mumbling, "I gotta pee, gotta pee, gotta pee." He was pacing in front of the occupied "drop room" and I could almost feel his full bladder and sense of urgency as he continued to pace and say, "gotta pee, gotta pee."

He appeared to be no more than 20-years-old as he pressed his legs together and moaned. He had to be there to meet with his P.O. and was required to make a "drop" first. The waiting room was filled and the receptionist didn't have a key to the restroom in the waiting room. I could only watch him and hope that the door would soon open. I couldn't intervene, even though I could sense his discomfort and resignation as he waited his turn.

As I tried not to notice the young man's discomfort, my name was called and Ms. England appeared to escort me to her office. On the walls of her office were photos of Denzel Washington, and I'd grown comfortable in discussing movies with her. She began our discussion with the usual questions on how I was doing and if anything new had happened in my life, such as a change of address, a new job, or anything unusual.

She didn't make any speeches or seem to think there was anything important about the occasion. She had instructed me on how to remove the device and was now carefully cleaning it before placing it in a box.

My ankle was my own again.

Ms. England must have wanted to dampen my elation, for she quickly explained that while the electronic monitoring was over, for the next six months I would continue to be subject to house arrest. The electronic bracelet had been a reminder of the devastation that slaves had felt wearing leg irons, so I was now free of that restriction and free to visualize more clearly the end of my confinement.

Ms. England also informed me that it would take a month or so before I could begin serving my 500 hours of community service. I would be monitored by a second probation officer, Ms. Roundtree. She would visit volunteer job sites to interview potential supervisors, advise them of my criminal offense and inform them of the requirements of the U.S. Probation Office in recording my assignment and time. In completing community service hours, I would be subject to the rules and regulations of an employee and monitored within the government guidelines through April, 2008.

When I returned home, I described to Jane the meeting I had with my probation officer on my request to commence community service now that the bracelet has been removed.

Over dinner, we toasted with a glass of red wine. "Me and Martha Stewart," I said laughing. That night, for the first time in six months, I took a bath without the electronic bracelet dangling above me as I kept my ankle out of the water. No, this time, I sank lazily down in the water, staring at the pale line where the bracelet had rubbed against my skin. A scar? Yes, but a faint one and it would disappear in time.

I felt more than pounds lighter. I felt relieved of an unjust weight, which, no larger or heavier than a bracelet, still weighed me down with a gravity not my own. At two a.m., I woke waiting for my nightly caller from House Arrest to telephone and check up on me. But the phone didn't ring. I was off their list. I had my ankle back.

The journey inside the electronic bracelet had enabled me to connect with my history and choices. Step by step I imprecisely moved ahead, regaining my energy, pride and humor and, in the process, dealing with an ordeal meant to humiliate me.

Along the way, I came to realize the thread of resilience that had held my complex life together and made it possible for me to endure from tough times to better times and would hold me together through the more dismal of times.

Just when the news was nothing but good, a kill-joy showed up. A registered letter arrived to inform me that I had been stripped of my rights to secure employment in education.

I can't believe it, I thought. Educating is what I do best. It's not fair. That's how I live and breathe and give best. It didn't matter to the letter.

219

The Notice of Proposed Government-Wide Debarment from Federal Procurement and Non-Procurement Transactions stated:

> On or about December 27, 2001, in your capacity as President at Morris Brown College, you, aided and abetted by another, knowingly and willfully embezzled, stole and obtained by fraud, false statement and forgery, funds and property insured by the Department, that is, loans for ineligible students totaling about $25,000. As a direct consequence of your actions, the Department has suffered and continues to suffer substantial loss. As a consequence of debarment you would not be eligible to receive funds from any federal agency under procurement and non-procurement programs and activities.

I dropped my head on the kitchen table and for the first time in weeks, I cried.

Was there another bracelet, an invisible one that I would never get off but which would follow me till the end of my days? Was this letter one of the links of how it would feel?

The Department of Education willfully went beyond the language of the plea I entered in court in which I acknowledged responsibility. The punishment included my being fined, making restitution, and serving home confinement and probation. I couldn't believe I was now being prohibited from seeking or obtaining employment in any agency that received federal funds. As an educator, I was distraught at the thought of being barred from the opportunity to find employment in the field where I had worked most of my life. The blow had sent me sobbing and to my knees. It was up to me to get up and not be silenced or intimidated.

I immediately consulted Randy Gepp, my attorney, to contest the proposed debarment. In contesting the debarment he pointed out that the DOE explicitly and implicitly accused me of various criminal offenses that had not been substantiated in court. For example, the DOE contended that "the factual basis for the plea evidences a far greater pattern of abuse" and that "the acceptance of a plea to a single charge did not mean that the government did not believe that massive misconduct took place." While the DOE states that MBC had liability in the millions of dollars, the government accepted that Dr. Cross was criminally responsible for the College in applying $25,000 in the fall of 2001 to the operating expenses of the college but did not personally benefit. Moreover the offenses of the plea occurred between October and December 2001, and Dr. Cross' tenure ended in February 2002. And, the DOE ignored the fact that Dr. Cross was neither convicted nor pled guilty to any offense prior to September, 2001.

The DOE made the unsupported statement that efforts by Dr. Cross to improve MBC's financial aid operations took place long after the transgressions were uncovered. Randy pointed out that I invited and provided full access to MBC staff to DOE officials, MBC's auditors, as well as an external auditor recommended by DOE to assist with procedures. Within a month of my December 1998 appointment as president of MBC I arranged to meet with DOE officials to establish a cooperative approach to address long standing problems in MBC's Office of Student Financial Aid.

A month or so later I would learn from Randy that the DOE ultimately imposed a debarment of one year. He felt that it could have been worse. While I continued to seethe, I knew I had to be patient.

Everything looked up when a week later Jane called to tell me she would be visiting for a few days. We wouldn't be constrained by restrictions posed by the continuing home confinement and could have some fun. We planned an in-house vacation with outdoor scheduled events. When my schedule permitted me to leave the apartment, Jane said she wanted to accelerate her exercise routine and had brought ski poles to use on her walks with me. Heads turned as we proceeded down the bike trail. She trudged ahead, knowing that she couldn't get as much accomplished as in the heat of Florida. We spent time checking our e-mails and reading.

I cooked for us, preparing our table and taking time for leisurely meals. There was no struggle in our communication. In her conversation I sensed the balance in her life. Her health and relationship with her brother, his family, and me were her priorities. She was present for her friends and she had a firm grip on what it would take to survive, indeed flourish, as a single black woman.

The 10 days with Jane passed quickly. In our time together I had gotten to know my daughter again in familiar ways and also glimpsed new facets of her character. It was the best time together I could recall. Daughter, friend, Jane was my living bridge to the past and the future.

The home confinement schedule continued another six months without electronic monitoring. Ms. England called me on my designated phone to check my adherence to the schedule and continued to visit my home unannounced. Still, I was relieved and saw relief from daily dullness and routine coming from court-ordered community service. Ms. England reminded me again and again that the process took time.

I waited out the summer with running and walking along the lakefront with Cassie. To keep me going, I envisioned racing to a banner across the finish line of a race. My Sunday schedule reflected time to visit the First Unitarian Church in Chicago. At church, I experienced an unspoken awareness of my predicament and imagined assumptions they might have of my circumstance. Some friends at the church had views shaped by what they had read in the newspapers or rumors. And in reaching out didn't seek to learn more from me. I held back, sometimes aloof and caught in the notion that as in every forum, I had lost my credibility. Sermons and discussions on "injustice" would hit a nerve. Did the notion of justice include me or others in the congregation? Injustice was "out there." I used the time in church to continue the process of maintaining consciousness of freedoms we take for granted. I carried a pad to write out things I want to accomplish in the coming week. I tried but found it difficult to think about life outside my confinement. I focused on getting home before my allotted time ran out. I obeyed the rules and felt safe in the cell that was home. "Is this how incarcerated individuals experience their days?" I wondered. I was just counting the days for the year's sentence of home confinement to end.

In September 2007, I began my 500 hours of community service at Midwest Workers Association (MWA) located in one of the poorest areas in Chicago. Drive-by shootings have occurred less than five blocks from the office. The drive from my apartment on the coast of Lake Michigan took less than twenty minutes. But the distance was far greater than the time suggests. The route took me past the expanse and plush, largely white-student-body of the University of Chicago, and then continued through established Hyde Park and, presto! -- a few blocks beyond the Dan Ryan Expressway, I was in another Chicago. In the time it took me to get there, I passed 11 churches of different denominations, fast food restaurants with different smells, boarded homes (some of which were grand in earlier days), barred liquor stores, and an elementary school with police patrols.

As I turned into the block there was a familiar woman in oversized clothes with a Bible in one hand and bullhorn in the other, singing, quoting scripture, and imploring those within ears' reach to stop the killing.

Inside the agency office, I signed in at 9:45 a.m. and signed out at 3 p.m. I alternated between typing, filing, washing dishes, delivering food baskets, and driving errands, as well as interviewing new members. The staff was all-volunteer. With the help of donated labor, the building operated 24 hours a day, seven days a week. I understood the mission of the agency was to become a voice for the unrecognized and the lowest-paid workers through systematic organizing. The bulletin boards on the walls contained articles that described government policies that impacted access to health care, low cost electricity and conditions of workers. Volunteer professionals provided dental, medical, and eye exams as well as legal services to members. Here, I was Dolores E. Cross, working alongside student volunteers from local universities, residents of the Englewood Community, volunteers from all walks of life; and after the six months alone, it felt great!

The days were busy and time was needed to review the purposes of the organization and the needs that had to be addressed: people had more and more difficulty keeping their lights on, getting medical services and having food on the table. Emergency food and clothing were distributed. I gladly donated clothes and food from my home to serve the members. I recalled having to accept food and clothing when, at 13, we were homeless and I lived in the Salvation Army.

It was not unusual for members to request support in getting help from a public agency. People would come in for assistance. Their phones had been disconnected or they had been frustrated by the "bureaucratic run around." I met members who had left shelters to volunteer with only a few hours experience, to veteran organizers from all walks who assist daily and on special events.

The pre-Thanksgiving event was special for all of us. I chose the chore of boxing and delivering holiday food baskets. The day began early in space donated at the University of Chicago. MWA had a system that permits things to flow smoothly and I awaited instructions on filling the boxes for families of one up to eight.

On Thanksgiving, I was given the job of driving, as Bernice and I delivered baskets to six homes in the Englewood area. Bernice lived in Englewood and had become one of my best friends at the agency. She was street savvy, funny, and took no foolishness. I learned that she took care of an ailing parent, children, and was unemployed herself. When taking a position on where things were going in Chicago, she often apologized, saying, "I'm not educated like you, Dolores." Her common sense and wisdom though were indisputable. I laughed and told her, "Bernice, you're just trying to con me."

We had two baskets to deliver to homes on Garfield Boulevard. I made a call from my cell phone and residents came to the door. If the box was not too heavy or the person was elderly, Bernice would deliver it to the door. She looked around and told me to stay focused. We didn't get far away before a man reeking of alcohol confronted us, demanding, "Where is my basket? I ordered a basket." He draped over the car and declared he wasn't leaving until he got his basket. Bernice checked the list and assured him it would come along in another delivery. He lingered. Bernice turned to me. "Be prepared to move, Dolores. Then she reached into one of the bags and planted an apple in the man's hand. "Drive on, Dolores," she said, quick to add, "You may be from Newark, Dolores, but I know these people and you're too nice. You need me with you."

She was right, I may have been from Newark, but this was Chicago and I was learning about urban life today and needed her wisdom.

What I was doing as a volunteer made a difference. The lives of the people I encountered were more complex than those I experienced in Newark. I was engaged with what I was doing and had no time or inclination to stay stuck in self-absorption and the nightmare I was passing through.

By averaging 25 hours five and six days a week, I had hoped to have the 500 hours of community service completed by January 23, 2008, the end of my home confinement sentence. While it didn't work out that way, it felt good when Ms. England advised me that I would no longer be restricted to the confinement schedule. I would continue to have to request permission to travel outside of northern Illinois, submit monthly reports, and be available for unannounced visits by my probation officer.

On January 23, 2008, I completed the year of home confinement. Supervision by my P.O. and restricted travel within northern Illinois would continue until the end of probation in January 2012. And it would be mid-March 2008 before I had completed 500 hours of court ordered community service. There would be no turning back to the way I lived prior to the year of confinement. Everything had changed. How? I wasn't sure, but I could feel everything about the way I lived my life was different. Maybe it was like how someone surviving a plane crash feels about time. Each instant taken for granted was now precious.

One day organizing my papers, I came across an e-mail which Hal Edwards had written in October 2004. He writes:

"I observe from my little porthole that your familiar pattern is to come and bite and nibble and then pull back and disappear again. Does that really serve your deepest needs? I am only interested in that which genuinely serves your True Self, that woman inside you who transcends whatever outer challenges may dictate. She's back in there; I have seen her and she is some awesome, unique, unrepeatable miracle of the Divine wrapped in human flesh. She is more than a persona with degrees who gained national awards and positions. She is more than a survivor from the projects placed into power positions. She is more than and different from what most people perceive her as being. In fact, most people only play to a persona, not to the Real Dolores. And yet that wonderful woman remains hidden behind that beautiful persona. And she "wants to flee.""

I no longer wanted to flee. I am grateful to be where I am now in mind, body and spirit and in the here and now. The wall could have been fatal and could have existed all the way out to the end of my life. I recall the Chinese word for CRISIS is: danger and opportunity. They come from the same place. My inner wisdom, my hunger to know and seek the truth whatever it reveals has been a fruitful course to take. It has caused me to stand alone and enjoy interacting with greater authenticity. I'm grateful for the new lessons learned. Without these lessons, I could have, in the truest sense, remained hidden emotionally and spiritually. I have made it through invisible finish lines. The scars I carry are eclipsed by rainbows. I have greater clarity and understand that both are part of the race.

A JULY 2008 REUNION

My probation officer approved my travel request to attend a family gathering in Nevis, Minnesota. It didn't matter that I just had a ten day pass and would have to report to my P.O. when I returned to Chicago. I was in the 'moment', feeling giddy, joyous and indescribably alive at the prospect of fun and fellowship at Lake Belle Taine. I packed my car and with Cassie on the back seat set off on the eleven hour drive to our cottage on the lake. Tommy had decided this year we would be celebrating Jackson's 8th birthday on July 29th, as well as the end of my year of home confinement with a reunion. His wife, Patricia and her sisters, made their nearby lakeside cabins available for our family and friends.

I was given the task of e-mailing and phoning family to get reservations and commitments for the week of June 27, 2008. Jane would have the job of transporting folks to and from the airport. Getting the family together would not be easy. My sister, Jean, and her children of necessity, had to come together in round the clock support for my brother-in-law, Jake. His health was failing and the trip to Nevis would be too arduous. They would not be able to join us at Nevis. My cousin Lillian worked with me in encouraging others in the family to join us in Nevis.

I had no trouble getting Alis Howard Murphy, my ex-husband's first cousin, aboard. Our families had maintained ties of friendship over the years. Alis had traveled from Cape May, New Jersey to visit during my year of home confinement. She was tuned in to celebrating and her children were committed to ensuring that she got there with her daughter Jeanne and grandson Julius. Julius and Jackson were cousins and had never met. Alis' son, Pat Murphy was employed at Frontier airlines and made arrangements for them to 'fly standby' into Fargo, North Dakota.

I extended the invitation to friends. Sylvia Warren understood my need for fellowship and connection. We joked about my recreating the Rio Caliente experience. She affirmed her presence. My dear friends, Marva Jolly, Frances Parks, James Willis, and Renee Williams Jefferson and her husband TJ were quick to keep a rousing amen. They were prepared to make the 11-12 hour drive from Chicago. Renee made it extra special by bringing their dog, Maxwell, as a playmate for Cassie. Eunice Holder made plans to travel from Tarrytown, New York with her grandson, Justin. Justin was a year older than Jackson. I arranged for James Willis to pick up our friend, Rasheeda Israel, to provide massages and enjoy the excursion.

Alis' energy set a tone. She liked everything about the lakefront. "Dee, this is wonderful," she said. "I could live here forever." With the aid of a cane, she moved along, exploring the wild flowers, pebbles on the beach and full trees on the property. In no time she was making a list of food for a tea party and giving Jane shopping orders. Late one night we gathered in the kitchen of the cabin Marva, Frances and Sylvia shared, and listened intently as Alis slowly turned the pages of a book in which she had sewn and stitched on fabric the family tree and history.

The joyful mood at the gathering was infectious. Frances spent hours drawing the view across the lake, Marva prepared the evening meals, Sylvia toured the paths by bike, and Renee took endless photos. I couldn't remember a time in recent years when I had been quite this happy. We didn't have to spell out celebration to give a rousing amen. It just unfolded.

I had let friends and relatives into my life and was Dolores with them. The nights were cool and we sat around the fire every night, dancing, drinking wine and watching night set in over the lake.

Nothing eclipsed Jackson's birthday celebration at the lake. We settled in a nearby gazebo. The table was set with a birthday cake and loads of presents. Jackson stood facing the table and festive party goers with his violin at his side. His curly, long, light brown hair framed his angelic face. I felt a lump in my throat as he pushed his glasses up, lifted the violin to his chin, assumed a virtuoso posture, and effortlessly played three classical scores. He bowed to the applause, placed his instrument in the case and joined Patricia in opening his presents. I'm feeling "This is my grandson; through him I have made a different contribution to the world."

Cassie and I at finish of the Half Marathon 9/06

My dear friend, CD,
who runs the Rio Caliente Spa in Mexico

Alis Murphy at Lake place in Nevis, Minnesota, June 29, 2008

Sylvia Warren, friend and Executive Coach

Former advisee and doctoral student David Fishman and his wife Cynthia

left to right: Renee Williams Jefferson, Marva Jolly and Frances Parks.

Jackson, age 7 – playing the violin

Edward Lindsey enjoying his avocation, fishing on Lake Michigan

Jane and Dolores at Rio Caliente Spa, November 2009

Tom Cross Jr., March 2010

Cassie, December 2009

Chapter 19

Today, August 29, 2008, is my birthday. Jane calls to remind me that presidential hopeful John McCain and I share the same birth date. I see the day as the anniversary of Hurricane Katrina. I don't have to turn on the television to recall the devastation, displacement and anguish that prevailed when the levees broke in New Orleans. The images of people on tops of roofs, bodies floating in the flood-waters and victims crowded in the Convention Center. My birthday will always be a reminder of the tragedy and the dispassionate manner in which it was initially addressed. My journey tells me that residents and former residents of the 9th Ward in New Orleans will be expected to move on and get on with their lives as if it never happened. America has forgotten. Their loss is in the category of "shit happens". Feet will shuffle and eyes will shift as survivors of Katrina continue to recall the cascade of water filling their homes and hours spent fearing the unknown.

The ordeal of Katrina has been explored in the media, rationalized by the government and placed in the archives. I'm looking out at Lake Michigan and envisioning the speech I would be making on the analogy between the neglect of New Orleans and the fragile state of struggling Historically Black Colleges and Universities. In the case of Katrina, government oversight agencies had known for years that the walls of the levees would not hold. The pre-existing holes in the levee were allowed to persist and put largely black people at risk. The levees collapsed despite the so-called 'vigilance' in monitoring and reporting of government agencies. In following the news I would not have been surprised if the Mayor of

New Orleans were indicted and held responsible for the demise of the 9th Ward of New Orleans. The ordeal of the journey experienced by residents of the 9th Ward does not go away nor does our need for the inspiration of its survivors.

I'm grateful that I haven't mellowed. I know all about me there are people who suffer in silence through ill health, poverty, injustice, and ironically, through their own callousness. I know as well that through adversity the purpose of my life can continue to unfold.

I watched from the lakefront as runners were being drenched in a downpour as they ran in the September 9th, 2008, 13.1 miles Chicago Half-Marathon. As I watched, I recalled moving through a thunderstorm while running the New York City Marathon in 1997. Gail Vanderheide was running beside me and urged me to stop. She and I completed several marathons together and she wasn't surprised when I answered, "I don't know how." We were running in rain-soaked clothes and shoes to the finish line. I saw the same look on the faces of the runners on Lake Shore Drive. Cassie and I were dripping water as I applauded and cheered the runners on. From them I had learned to endure good and bad weather and to affirm the gifts of endurance and resilience.

My sister Jean had been with me from the starting line. Not a day went past when I didn't feel her presence and regard. She experienced the impact of the changes in my life and had to balance them with her own challenges. Her home in Plainfield was a haven for her children and extended family. While Jean ran the show, my brother-in-law, Clinton (Jake) McRae was the one we turned to for the last word. I had grown accustomed to Jean advising me to "Ask Jake" for a response she felt would be better received from Jake. Together they had stayed on course and used me as a model of going the distance.

In October 2008, Jake died. Not only had I lost a brother-in-law, I had lost the energy of a friend who had endured and given a personal best. I could not be at my sister's side without approval of my probation officer, who required evidence of Jake's passing. In a flurry of calls, I contacted my niece Karen for a newspaper print of the obituary for forwarding to Ms. England. She made me aware of the short notice and made the customary call to affirm where I would be staying when out of the Northern District of Illinois. I dreaded the thought of my sister being reminded of my status and having to receive a call from a probation officer charged with my supervision. Jean's responsibilities in working full-time and caring for Jake had precluded her from being present since the indictment. I saw the phone call as drawing her into the realities of my fall from grace.

I was wrong in expecting us not to be able to bridge the distance created by circumstance. The day prior to Jake's funeral Jean and I walked around the high school track close to her home. I listened as she shared her own confinement in caring for Jake and my mother. She had been through a great deal and didn't want to be reminded of what I had endured. It was just "too much". I longed to communicate the personal transformation I had experienced. While a part of me had died, another part had blossomed and absorbed the darkness. I was with her to celebrate our lives as well as Jake's. A door had closed and another had opened for Jean and me.

In My Stride

While I hadn't planned to run a half-marathon, I continued to train. One morning I called my running to a halt as I received a call on my cell phone from Vicky, a young black woman. She had been referred to me by my attorney, Drew Findling. As she spoke, I recalled meeting her and visualized a younger black woman with a confident smile. She told me that she was being investigated and feared the possibility of an indictment. Her call to me was for her to get insight on getting through the horrendous experience. After she explained her background, contributions, and relationship to her children, I shared what I had learned in my ordeal. I advised her to stay strong physically, mentally, emotionally, and spiritually, to seek support from her children, to engage Drew Findling as her attorney and to stick with him.

In subsequent conversations with her, I spoke about what I had learned from my ordeal and from the current political environment. Without qualification, I made myself available for her to reach out to me.

I had opened an emotional door and soon other calls came in. I heard from Qiyahama, a black woman who knew of my experience in South Africa. She asked me to advise her on developing a proposal to undertake research on implementing a curriculum on gender studies at Historically Black Universities in South Africa. I had met her in Atlanta and provided encouragement as she pursued her doctorate at Clark Atlanta University in Atlanta. She had moved to Chicago, sought me out, and asked for help.

While the one year debarment denies me the opportunity to teach in a traditional classroom, I have discovered that there is no limit to the number of places where one can give and educate. The world truly is a schoolhouse where all of us are teaching and being taught. Strangely, having taught within a conventional campus for so long, I had lost sight of the immediate contact of learning available to people in dialogue outside of the classroom.

After all the isolation, it was as though my past were trying to find me again. I began to connect with former students from Claremont Graduate School where my ideas about education and multicultural education had been shaped in the 1970s.

I received an unexpected package from Dennis Cabral. He had been a doctoral student in my class at Claremont Graduate School. I had in my files a paper he'd written that referred to his Portuguese heritage and his family's life on sugar plantations in Hawaii. As a white male, he had experienced both class discrimination and the promise of education. In his paper, Dennis integrated his history with his social science research on counseling as well as with his perspective and model for helping students. I had convinced Dennis to join my administrative team at the City University of New York, the New York State Higher Education Services Corporation, and the University of Minnesota. I missed him and had longed to hear from him. Then came the package containing sculptures of two seated women and a note from Dennis in which he reminded me of the network formed with my students and encouraged me to speak to the women. How wonderful…I named them avatars and placed them on my desk where I could see them projecting their strength outward.

I had also taken time to reread letters from students. Among my letters and papers I have correspondence from a former doctoral advisee, David Fishman, whose friendship spans 30 years. David was injured in a fall as an undergraduate at Pomona College and has since then had to learn to walk with the aid of braces and crutches. He enrolled in my class on Multicultural Education and contributed views on the challenges and obstacles faced by people with physical challenges. I was honored to chair his doctoral committee. David is a marathoner in the truest sense of the word. Walking can be a laborious exercise for him. In one communication, he writes of having completed eight tenths of a mile over an uneven, unimproved, up down path. He adds his views on education, "I firmly believe that a school or college is only as good as how well it treats its students and other constituents, and that we need a diversity of institutions to serve the diverse needs of the country as a whole." As his former teacher, I have read his presentations with great pride. His passion for life and helping others has made it possible for him to overcome obstacles, achieve success as a distinguished administrator at the University of California, Santa Barbara and encourage his wife, Cynthia's work as an artist.

The Board of Trustees of Kalamazoo College unanimously elected Dr. Wilson-Oylelan the 17th president and first woman and first African-American president of Kalamazoo College. I beamed when I received the Magazine of Kalamazoo College. The cover featured another former doctoral advisee from Claremont Graduate School, Dr. Eileen Wilson-Oyelaran, showing her smiling and walking hand in hand with her husband, Olasope. Eileen had been a black student leader at Pomona College of the Claremont Colleges. And her talents made her a star at Claremont Graduate School. Her experience includes teaching in Nigeria and rising to the position of Vice President and Dean of the College for Salem Academy. I had encouraged her to become a college president and I could hardly contain myself as I read her words drawn from the inspiration of Martin Luther King: "You can't live the dream if you don't know it." "Education should be the means...." She let me know that the lessons learned in teacher education at Claremont Graduate School are reflected in her students who themselves are tutoring youngsters in the middle grades.

Marcia Cross, my former Vice President of College Relations at Morris Brown College had remained in touch through phone calls and inspirational e-mails. I was elated when she called to announce the publication of her first novel, *Survival in a Sea of White*. Her novel is based on "the real life experiences of an African American woman's spiritual, racial and professional journey at a white college." I saw indelible traces of what I and generations of black women and men before and after have endured when engulfed in an environment that marginalizes their presence, contributions and feelings. Through her novel Marcia has made the choice and taken the risks of presenting her challenges and what it took to persevere. She and her husband Barry live outside Atlanta and remained big supporters when people tried to threaten or coerce them to go against me. I had seen her encounter difficult situations at the college and knew they were barking up the wrong tree. Even more, I have seen her tenacity in others of her generation. They are talented, tested and tough and all too often invisible in efforts to recruit and retain black faculty and professionals in higher education. I view her novel and my memoir as part of an intergenerational thrust to teach and communicate that despite setbacks the steps gained by education are worth it.

I was pleased when Cindy, a former Morris Brown College student, relocated to Chicago to begin her graduate work at DePaul University and called on me to resume my role as her mentor. She had transferred to Spelman College to complete her degree and communicated periodically with updates of her progress. As an undergraduate at Morris Brown, Cindy had succeeded in securing an internship at CNN, completed an intensive study abroad experience in China and represented the college on the Atlanta University Center Library Council and qualified for the position of Resident Advisor at Spelman. Our time together in Chicago focused on the guidance she needed to balance her time while working part-time, attending graduate school full time and adjusting to a new city. I learned from Cindy that the Morris Brown College student president who had given me my initial tour of the campus was now running for public office and that another student leader was completing his graduate work at the University of Chicago. She remained uplifted and inspired by the knowledge we shared of the leadership of HBCUs in producing PhD's, engineers, medical doctors and educators. And now, she was joining the ranks of thousands who credited their experiences at HBCU's as the building block for future successes.

I know who I am. I know my life matters. I know I can still make an impact. And as I reflect on my life up to now, I know what I would tell students to help keep their perspective:

"Remember, as you read the newspaper or listen to the news, that education is the means to improving the economy, breaking the cycle of poverty, strengthening families, heightening sensitivity to the impact of globalization, climate change, and enhancing physical, emotional, intellectual and spiritual health."

"Remember, as you listen to politicians, educators and government types, that cost of attendance continues to be a barrier to going to college and completing an undergraduate degree."

"Remember, as you travel in this country and throughout the world, that people continue to be judged by the color of their skin, by accents of their speech and by their gender."

"Remember, as you rise through your careers, that despite the risk it is important to serve, give back, and exercise humility and--even more--stay in touch with who you are."

"Remember, as you decide to engage in figurative and literal marathons, to check the course, remain conscious of your inadequacies, appreciate the journey, and be the architect of your own recovery."

"Remember, as you think about quitting, that true resilience and endurance is measured by an inner strength that takes you beyond artificial boundaries and finish lines."

"Remember, the world is full of deception, so proceed with caution, discernment, and discretion."

"Remember, as you decide to let your light shine, someone is watching and choosing to stand on your shoulders."

My children were the first to read these thoughts that I would present to students. Jane was first to say it sounded like a lot to remember, but she soon referred to it as "Mom's Mantra".

Chapter 20

For the Ancestors

I took the five-mile walk along the lakefront from my Chicago Hyde Park apartment to Grant Park early on Election Day 2008. As I drew near, I could see people approaching from every direction and feel the energy in their converging movement. Reaching the park entrance, I paused on Roosevelt Road to view the fenced-off area and envision the crowd that would amass that night to celebrate Barack Obama's election as President of the United States.

Watching people of all ages and races move past into the park, I recalled some years ago first noticing Barack Obama, then an Illinois State Senator, running along the same path I was.

As he came up beside me, we spoke briefly of the joys of running and of his upcoming visit to the predominantly black university on the Southside of Chicago where I was then president. As a marathon runner I was taken by Senator Obama's running discipline; and as a black woman educator I was intrigued by the young senator's interest in learning the steps to ensure the success of Chicago State University.

In his forbearance with me and the elders when we met at Chicago State University, I sensed his understanding of "foot soldiers" from whom he might gain new energy and insights.

In deciding not to remain in Grant Park that evening, I knew I wanted to go home and experience the events of election night in the seclusion of my apartment. It would be a time to reflect on what got us to this point in history of seeing a young African-American son of a mother from Kansas and a father from Kenya be (here, I prayed with all the words I had to pray with) elected President.

As I watched the first election results trickle in, the image of Barack Obama running along the lakefront came to mind. In 1996, I had been visualizing competing in the Boston Marathon that year. Could Barack have been visualizing his run for President in 2008 as well?

All evening I watched the process of voting results coming in from across the nation. Finally, victory was declared, and I soon experienced the moment I had been waiting for: first, seeing Barack Obama and his family appear. Then his words, the words I am hearing now, I find myself whispering, "Yes, yes, yes." Unable to contain my emotions, I begin pacing the room, tears flowing from my eyes.

I'm saying Yes! for those of my generation who grew up when segregation was the law of the land, when people died fighting for voting rights for blacks; and when attendance at a Historically Black College or University was one of the few options open to blacks who could afford to go on to college. I'm saying Yes! for the future while remembering a time in my own past when even imagining such a moment as this would have been unthinkable.

Making it for us meant defying the odds, talking and standing tough and being willing to give voice against policies that failed to address poverty, inadequacies in education, housing, and health care for unemployed and working poor blacks, Hispanics and whites.

I come from a generation of blacks who made their way through discrimination, racism, and poverty, and yet reached their goal, one now shared by millions.

I looked up and saw in the reflection that my hands were thrusting up in front of the television. I shivered, imagining all the homes across the nation, where countless black Americans like me were now weeping with joy at the undeniable truth before our eyes.

Truly, I thought, beyond the private experience of giving birth to my daughter and son, this is the greatest moment of my life; it is even greater because I know it is being shared with so many others who lived through the Civil Rights Movement of the 60s.

We inherited courage from sacrifices of earlier generations; and if we faltered or stumbled we could be denounced for having dropped the torch I now see blazing inside each face shown in Grant Park.

Listening to Barack Obama's victory speech, I hear the words of a black man not constrained by fear, who understands that though he did not create the race problem, as our new leader he recognizes he will have to move through the fear and at the same time remain aware of the close connection between racial myths, and confront generations of racism -- not as most blacks experienced it, from the bottom, in daily act of ordinary lives, but from the top down, as President of this nation.

He will have to guide us all, black and white.

Listening to Obama's wisdom and humility, I feel the resurgence of what hundreds of millions of people around the world have yearned for so long ago: hope for all. Obama is the beneficiary of those in the community who preceded me, those who viewed education as a necessity and who believed as well that higher education made a difference and went on to create new opportunities for the individual, the family, and society as a whole. He is a product of a family who gave him the courage to confront the harsh realities of life, and then go on to encourage others to achieve their own potential beyond what government assistance alone can provide.

In my heart, I have always believed that one can encourage others to experience all they are capable of achieving. Now I see it manifested before my eyes.

True, I know there are enormous social constraints and attitudes embedded in the United States that will require a collective effort to surmount. Yet, when I look back in time only 43 years since the Freedom March in Selma, Alabama, a time when blacks in the South weren't allowed to sit anywhere but at the back of buses and then look back at the radiant face before me on the television screen, I know hope has returned.

Change has indeed come.

Through the ages, countless men and women have given their lives for us, we the living, to experience this moment of freedom and recognition. Yet they are not gone, for I see them returned, resurrected in the faces of the youth standing in the crowd, crying, smiling, shouting their joy. Yes, the ancestors have returned as the children of hope.

Sitting here, feeling enthralled, even mesmerized by Barack Obama's victory speech, I am honored to be poised at the pinnacle of such dreams and change.

I open the bottom drawer of my desk and lift up the memoir I had struggled with for so long before putting it aside. Although I have never dropped out of a run, I felt close to giving up writing the story of my journey, prevented by not knowing how it would end. Now, watching the radiant faces in Grant Park on the television screen, I know, and I pick up my pen to write again:

For all of us in the race, my finishing lines join those in a new beginning.

A few days after the election, I join the crowd at Valois, Obama's favorite restaurant in Hyde Park. Valois is a non-pretentious setting where elbows touch and where there is a mix of people from every walk of life and from a variety of ethnic and linguistic backgrounds. The sight of the long line doesn't deter me. It is a challenge finding a place to sit after I have my tray.

I join a black male whom I judge to be about my age. There's no hesitation as he makes room for me. Our introductions flow, as does our conversation. His name is Ed. We soon discover we are both divorced, are grandparents and have enjoyed successful careers. We talk, pausing only to take bites of food. Two hours pass and he asks for my phone number. I'd been emboldened to the point where I had relaxed, joined a stranger, and moved out of my cocoon.

I felt I couldn't let him leave without telling him more about me. I didn't want him to tell his buddies that he'd met this interesting woman, Dolores Cross, only to hear the stories that had been spun about me. I realized I had to tell him of my indictment, sentencing, probation, and status as a felon.

During our two-hour talk, he said he had heard of the problems at Morris Brown College, but I sensed he had not connected them to me.

I provided a thumbnail sketch of the indictment, trial, and sentencing. Sadness and tension gripped me as I waited for him to respond critically then find an excuse to leave. I paused, thinking of the risk I had taken in relating my predicament and even more what might be the reactions of others who would read my memoir.

He said he knew nothing of what had transpired, but then placed his hand on mine. "You need to have some fun, Dolores, and I enjoy your company. I have opera tickets for Porgy, and would like you to join me with some friends. What do you say?"

I say yes.

Epilogue

Beyond The Wall

On September 13, 2009, I ran the 13th Annual Chicago Half Marathon. Bib number 3158, indicated I would be running in the 70-75 age group. My running resume of having run 20 (26.2 mile) marathons, close to fifty races beamed the hope that my body would remember and take me to the finish line. Over 19,000 runners from 34 different countries would be competing. I took my place among runners expecting to complete the distance in two and a half hours. Thousands of runners were ahead of us and it would take 17 minutes to cross the start line. I was calm and feeling the power of being back in the race. I owned the steps I would take to the finish line. I have experienced hitting the wall, recovering and moving beyond the wall to see what is on the other side. I am pumped and ready to 'get it on.'

I'm listening to my body as I cross the start line and move toward Lake Shore Drive. The drive has been closed off to traffic and I feel the positive energy of being in a sea of runners who like me have the goal of seeing the finish line. I look around for runners with a pace in line with mine and stay with them or alternatively fall back or move ahead. This race is not about time. It is about resilience and endurance. I'm in it and not caring if anyone is watching. I own this race.

I proceed ahead checking the race clocks along the way for a steady 12 -minute mile. The morning is warm and I mix water and Gatorade at every stop. In previous races I have used images and events to get me through and in the process relax my body. Today is different. I am monitoring the steps I'm taking and staying motivated by the running bodies ahead of me. I am gentle with myself as I pump my arms and maintain a cadence.

At mile 12, I look up to see my apartment window...for a brief moment I slow. The body remembers the anguish of being confined within an electronic bracelet and looking out to the drive and Lake Michigan with incredible sadness. I shift my thoughts to the distance I must go to the finish line. I check my watch and realize that the distraction of the glance to my window has slowed my pace and caused me to lose time. In continuing to move ahead I am saluting my transformation, rebirth and marathon recovery.

A smile crosses my face as I get a glimpse of the finish line. The crowds are there to cheer us on and I join the runners in picking up speed....as I sprint to the finish line and collect my finisher's medal. I had gone the distance in 2 hours and 47 minutes with a third of the runners in the field coming in after me.

On September 17, 2009 I received a call from Drew Findling advising me Judge Carnes had accepted and signed the early termination of probation recommendation submitted by Ms. England, my probation officer in the Northern District of Illinois to the U.S. Probation Officer in the Northern District of Georgia. Drew forwarded an electronic copy of The Order to Terminate Probation that bore the signature of Judge Carnes and the U.S. Probation Officer in the Northern District of Georgia dated, September 13, 2009.

Within a week I applied for a new passport. I received a call from the United States Passport Officer in New York City. Communication on the termination of my probation had not reached her office. After receiving information from Drew she agreed to expedite my passport so that I might keep travel plans for a trip to Mexico. In issuing my passport, the passport official has informed me that there are some countries that will not accept "felons." Mexico is not one of those countries. I know, as well, that there are some States in America where, as a "felon", I can no longer vote. I can vote in Illinois, but should I move to either Minnesota or Florida where my children live, as a "felon" I cannot vote.

As guest of Caroline, Jane and I could now plan to spend Thanksgiving, 2009, at Rio Caliente, Guadalajara, Mexico. It had been almost five years since I had been there. I focused on the moment and possibilities afforded by my health and spirit. I did not know what to expect. Would I encounter problems when I presented my passport? Would I experience the Spa as I had before the ordeal of the past years? I set aside the feeling of dread, focused on counting my breaths and became absorbed in the fun of sorting through clothes for the proper attire. I had received the blessing of the early termination of my probation and I gave myself room to receive it. I sensed how much I had changed and been transformed by the journey beyond the wall. I was learning to concentrate on the present with gratitude.

I arrived at a wonderful time at Rio Caliente. As Caroline had promised, Jane and I would be joined by some talented and fun guests. I met the published writer, Lesley Hazelton and participated in workshops she led on writing. She gave me pointers and urged me to persist. I encountered an educator, June Noronhe, whom I had attended meetings with in Minnesota and Deborah Jacobs, a Librarian who encouraged me to share the journey that prompted me to write my memoir. The collage of people present for the Thanksgiving week were among the most spirited and interesting that I had encountered on my many visits to the Spa.

On the morning of my first hike, our guide approached me and said "Señora, Dolores, how are you doing, it has been almost 5 years, no?" It was easy to feel home again. There was no let up in the enjoyment of being there. Caroline had arranged a feast for Thanksgiving with dancing and wine. I was on my feet and moving with the music. My mind, body and spirit were free.

The lesson I have learned from completing my memoir, Beyond the Wall, is that the only instant I can really affect is the present. As in a marathon, I have had to relax, release and relate. Every word written provided greater clarity of the past and what I might expect as I moved on. Ruminating over the past was a means not an end. It became a means to uncover the depth of my resilience and endless opportunities for forgiveness, grace, love and peace beyond the electronic bracelet. Like running, writing became a form of meditation. Each word and every change written provided space for opportunities to connect more with people, nature and my power.

Acknowledgements

My cousin, Alis Howard Murphy, had a special knack for remembering birthdays, anniversaries and special moments in the lives of others. Her cards and letters were an expression of gratitude toward the individuals who gave her energy, love and hope. I had seen how in her address book she added pages to keep up with my different addresses and never lost touch. Were she alive today, she would say "Dee go through your photo album and address book and mention in your acknowledgements all the people who have helped you along the way." As in a marathon there are many people to cheer you on along the way, the list of family, friends and collegial relationships on which this memoir was realized exceeds what is presented here.

I am indebted to my parents, Ozie Olean Tucker and Charles T. Tucker who believed in education as a tradition in the black community and never doubted that I would succeed.

My gratitude has no bounds.

I could not have embarked on the journey of writing my personal account of how I experienced the past few years without the love and support of my children, Jane and Tom Jr. With humor, purpose and wisdom they kept me grounded. I am very proud of them and honored to be their "Mom."

My grandson, Jackson Tucker Cross hugs for his "Nana." beams me up.

The love of my family was always there: my wonderful sister Jean Dale, and her late husband Clinton (Jake) McRae for letting me be myself and their children, Karen, Steven, Leslie and Tina for keeping me in their hearts; for my cousins: Lillian Tucker Thomas for never letting me forget how much family matters; for Francine and Ronnie Diggs for keeping me in their prayers; and thanks to Carl Gregory, Gerald Roper, Ronald Parm for caring and for the late Alis Murphy and her children Karann, Pat, Jean, and Allie for a loving connection that was never lost.

I am profoundly grateful for the patience and dedication of my friend, Dr. Stewart Lindh, English Professor, writer. His belief in me provided inspiration throughout the course of my writing my memoir. Stewart was the "runner beside me." He was always there to encourage my personal best and coach me through the finish line. When times got tough, Stewart's insight and talent guided me onward.

And thanks to Dr. Dean Y. Deng, an exceptional acupuncturist for not giving up on me and for providing non-traditional and lasting approaches to strengthen my mind, body and spirit.

And my special gratitude as well to the professionalism of Dr. Fred Daniels who has for years been my primary physician, friend and been on the forefront of providing services from his office in Chicago's southside.

Sylvia Warren, executive coach and friend who resides in Oakland, California called weekly and urged me on. She helped me to clarify events, feelings and to achieve the balance I needed to move forward.

A special salute to my dear friend and lil' Sis, Caroline. Her wisdom, sense of humor and caring are a constant. During the many days and nights I worked on the memoir, Caroline offered editing support and remained in communication. Caroline and Evelyn Oliver provided words of encouragement and financial resources as part of a 'Diva Defense Team of three" A very special salute to our friend Ev who passed in 2007.

At various points in writing my memoir, I turned to friends to read and edit, as well as review thoughts on drafts presented to them. Their invaluable help and support helped to get me to the production stage. My thanks to Eva Thorn, Marilyn Sango-Jordan, Marcia Cross, Renee William Jefferson, Jim Smith, Joyce Ann Joyce, David Fishman, Tom Montiero Grant Venerable, James Willis, Gwendolyn Mitchell, Kathleen Spivack, Drew Findling, Randy Gepp, Joe Pagani, Tom Huyck, Hal Edwards, Debra Thomas, Elvira Pellitteri and Edward Lindsey. And thanks to Jane who maintains a file of dozens of drafts and who urged me onward with my memoir.

Without the professionalism and commitment to the project by Westbow Press this memoir would not have oved forward as it has.

And my unending gratitude to a long list of Sister Presidents including: Johnnetta Cole, Gloria Scott, Eileen Wilson-Oyelaran, Dianne Boardley Suber, Delores Spikes, Barbara Hatton, Julianne Malveaux, Yolanda Moses, Carol Wallace and Niara Sudarkasa.

I am especially grateful for the love and support I share with a circle of Chicago Divas: Marva Jolly, Renee Williams Jefferson and Frances Parks. Our good fun, good times and memorable times sharing good food and great wine are a source of much joy.

I have deeply appreciated the inspiration of my dear friend Susan Lourenco. She has been a close colleague through the years. In writing my memoir, I kept in mind her strides as an activist in the promoting and leading humanitarian efforts in disadvantaged communities in the U.S. and in Israel.

My gratitude as well to the host of friends and colleagues where I have run figurative marathons in New Jersey, New York, Michigan, Illinois, Minnesota and Georgia. And thanks to the thousands of runners who have shared 20 marathons and over 50 races throughout the country.

There are no words to express my gratitude and love for my dog, Cassie. She has been a loyal, sweet, patient and constant companion.

And a very special thanks to Edward Lindsey, a dear friend, who with love and caring encouraged me to break my silence and move across the finishing lines of my memoir.

Author's Note

In BEYOND THE WALL: A Memoir I explore events that remain lodged in memory. The memoir tracks my memories, thoughts, events and how I experienced my life. I have allowed my feelings to flow freely from my mind and heart. In the process of writing I brought suppressed nemeses to the surface. Memories are important to me and became a treasured journey for me to forgive and for others to learn from.

In writing the memoir, I have changed the names of my therapist and probation officer and referred to associates at Morris Brown College by the titles they held during my tenure as president. I refer to others by the names they are known by in the wider world.

About the Author

Born in Newark, New Jersey, Dolores E. Cross completed her undergraduate degree at Seton Hall University, her master's degree at Hofstra University, and her PhD at the University of Michigan. In a career that has spanned more than thirty years, Dr. Cross has been an educator and administrator at several prestigious institutions. She is the author of *Breaking Through the Wall: A Marathoner's Story* and has contributed to many publications about the quality and accessibility of education, and is the recipient of numerous awards and honorary degrees. In her free time, she enjoys training for marathons. She ran her first marathon at age fifty, and has completed twenty since.